D0122619

The Soul
OF THE
New Consumer

The Soul
OF THE
New Consumer

The Attitudes, Behaviors, and
Preferences of E-Customers

LAURIE WINDHAM
with KEN ORTON

ALLWORTH PRESS
NEW YORK

05   04   03   02   01   00   5   4   3   2   1

Published by Allworth Press
An imprint of Allworth Communications
10 East 23rd Street, New York, NY 10010

Cover design by Douglas Design Associates, New York, NY

Page composition/typography by SR Desktop Services, Ridge, NY

ISBN: 1-58115-066-0

Library of Congress Cataloging-in-Publication Data
Windham, Laurie.
    The soul of the new consumer : the attitudes, behaviors,
and preferences of E-customers / Laurie Windham with Ken Orton.
        p.   cm.
    Includes bibliographical references and index.
    ISBN 1-58115-066-0
    1. Electronic commerce.   2. Consumer behavior.   3. Brand choice.
I. Orton, Ken.   II. Title.
HF5548.32.W56   2000
658.8'34—dc21   00-040611

Printed in Canada

Contents

List of Figures

Chapter Five

Chapter Six

Chapter Seven

Chapter Eight

Chapter Nine

Acknowledgments

The inspiration for this book came from the thousands of e-customers we have talked with over the past few years in our client work and in our Pulse of the Customer℠ research series. Reflecting upon the perspectives of these "souls," we realize that the Web has been an empowering tool for all types of consumers, opening up new worlds of information, opportunities, and opinions to millions of mainstream people. The Web applies to all different aspects of our lives. It appeals to the intellectual, the voyeuristic, and the aesthetic parts of our personalities. It serves a commercial, an educational, and a communications role. How we as consumers respond to the Web has multiple dimensions. We have attitudes and preferences about what we want from our online experiences and we exhibit behaviors unique to our online pursuits. Consumers' relationships with the Web are personal, complex, and alive—thus the soul metaphor throughout this book. Thanks to all those consumers who have been willing to bare their souls for our research.

I thank Ken Orton, my collaborating author and partner and chief e-business strategist at Cognitiative. Ken spent many hours working with me on key concepts, poring over drafts, and watching focus groups, as well as keeping Cognitiative, Inc. running while I concentrated on writing. His in-depth experience in leading and advising dot coms brought a critical real-world business perspective to our data analysis.

Thanks to Janet Raupp, who was my right-hand person, diligently assisting with a full range of work—from online research, to editing every version of the manuscript, to overseeing production. Her resourcefulness in secondary research contributed substantially to the supporting content in this project. Her even-keeled nature and positive outlook helped keep me and the project on the right track. We couldn't have completed this book on time without her.

Thanks to Tara Brown for her graphics and production support. Always able to keep a cool head under pressure, Tara is a real asset in any setting. My appreciation goes to Kathy Kleinhans for her eagle-eye editing of the manuscript. And to Cognitiative's clients, I appreciate your patience in allowing me the necessary space and time to write this book.

Thanks to the many people who helped us with quick-turnaround, informal research while developing some of our hypotheses for the book. This includes Leslie Windham who has relentlessly pursued answers among her Web-user and non-user friends—hopefully they are still speaking to her. Also, thanks to the friends and family of Cognitiative's staff who have responded to our continual probing for their Web opinions.

I want to thank Tad Crawford, publisher at Allworth Press, who encouraged me to write this book. It has been a pleasure to work with him and his company throughout this process. We wouldn't have attempted this project without his strong support.

Finally, thanks to my parents, Betty and Malcolm Windham, who taught me from a very early age about the proper care and feeding of the soul.

1

What Is a Soul, Who Are These Consumers, and What Makes Them New?

Being a child of the Bible Belt, I have had many encounters with the word "soul." The well-worn noun packed an intimidating, if not awesome, punch that was the by-product of my weekly experience with fire-and-brimstone sermons at the Southern Baptist church. I remember in those days of my childhood being preoccupied with the word "soul," wondering what it really meant and where it was actually located. Was a soul a vital organ, like your heart, your brain, or your pancreas? Was your soul what ascended from your body when you died? What do souls look like? How can you be sure you have one? How do you know if you have a good or a bad soul? These are the types of questions that soul-saving practitioners evoked in a curious child.

The term "soul," in the context of this book, isn't nearly as puzzling or arcane as it was for me back then, although it does share some common properties. In this frame of reference, soul means the essence of an individual; what makes him or her act; the emotional and motivational parts of a person that cause him or her to be unique. The soul is the animating principle—the bundle of feelings, thoughts, and actions that drive all human beings.

What is a new consumer? According to Webster's dictionary,[1] a consumer is a person or an organization that consumes—spends, absorbs, devours—commodities and services. The act of consuming is as old as time itself. There have been

The new consumer is in an unprecedented position of control

consumers on this planet for thousands of years. What is new about "the new consumer?" The new consumer uses the Internet to facilitate the consumption process: identifying needs, searching for solutions, buying products and services, answering questions, and resolving problems. Many "old" consumers have become new consumers and, in doing so, have transformed into more powerful beings. The new consumer has easy access to countless information sources, innumerable products and services, and greatly extended communities. This has put the new consumer in an unprecedented position of control. The new consumer knows more, has more choices, and can act with fewer logistical constraints than ever before.

So, what makes new consumers "new" is that they are empowered by the Internet. While they live among other seemingly similar consumers who crowd the busy highways, stand in lines at theaters, and push around grocery carts in supermarkets, when they are on the Internet, they are different from their unwired peers. They have been transformed. They have different attitudes. They behave differently. And they have a set of preferences that has been shaped by the empowering qualities of the Internet.

There is an additional dimension to the definition of consumer. For the purposes of this book, our consulting firm, Cognitiative, Inc., defines the new consumer as a *shopper* who is acting on behalf of his or her *personal*, rather than professional, needs. While we present our perspectives on business e-customers in chapter 7, the primary focus of Cognitiative's research and analysis for this book is the online consumer—the average citizen, the next-door neighbor, the person on the street. And we focus on her as a shopper—as a spender of money.

In this book we explore the souls of the new consumers; we study the attitudes, behaviors, and preferences of these brave new souls. We analyze the psychodynamics of the buyer and seller relationship. We get into their heads. We listen to their voices. We learn what attracts them, what repels them and what makes them loyal. We discover what makes them tick.

Acceptance of the Internet

It is interesting to contemplate how quickly the United States population has adopted the Internet. The rapidity of Web acceptance has truly been remarkable. Historically, the United States has been a country in which new technologies are assimilated fairly rapidly, given the prevailing economic constraints and manufacturing realities of the time. For example, by 1954, a mere seven years after the introduction of television, 55 percent of American households had a television set.[2] This was considered very rapid acceptance, especially because of the relatively high prices of TVs at that time and the nascent quality of broadcast program content. However, the Internet and the Web are breaking those records. The Internet reached as many Americans in the first six years as the telephone did in its first four decades.[3] Every day, Web access is becoming available to a growing percentage of the United States population.

RESPONSE TO CHANGE

Despite the rapid embrace of new technologies by Americans, there continue to be anxieties stimulated by change. For example, there were many concerns among human behavior theorists during the early years of television about the potential negative effects of the media. And similar anxieties were voiced about earlier modes of communications as well. In their article "Historical Trends in Research on Children and the Media: 1900–1960,"[4] Ellen Wartella and Byron Reeves document the apprehensions raised with each introduction of new media throughout the twentieth century. They point out that predictably, there were alarms sounded soon after the advent of every new media concept—reaching as far back as dime novels, and spanning the introduction of movies, radio, comics, and television. They observe that "whenever there is a new social invention, there is a feeling of strangeness and a distrust of the new until it becomes familiar."

True to form, today's researchers and social critics are debating whether the Internet is improving or

Despite the rapid embrace of new technologies, there have always been anxieties stimulated by change

harming participation in community life and social relationships. It is a subject of extensive academic research.
As stated in the article "Internet Paradox" by Robert
Kraut and Vicki Lundmark,[5] "Some scholars argue that
the Internet is causing people to become socially isolated
and cut off from genuine social relationships, as they
hunker alone over their terminals or communicate with
anonymous strangers through a socially impoverished
medium. Others argue that the Internet leads to more and
better social relationships by freeing people from the constraints of geography or isolation brought on by stigma, ill-
ness, or schedule."

A recent study by Stanford University's Institute for
the Quantitative Study of Society provides further validation for concerns about technology-driven isolation in our
society. They found that as Internet use grows, Americans
spend less time with friends and family and more time
working for their employers at home. In fact, the study
observes that "the more hours people use the Internet, the
less time they spend with real human beings," thus continuing the trend of isolation due to technology.[6]

Other editorialists have entered the fray with concerns
about Internet security, consumer privacy, and objectionable content distributed via the Internet. The security
breaches that blasted onto the e-business scene in early
2000 contributed significant fuel to an already healthy bon-
fire of paranoia. Awareness was raised among businesses
and consumers that online security must be shored up to
avoid potential system-wide disaster. In addition, the ongoing debate about online privacy has stimulated many consumers and activist groups to advocate better business
practices and potential government intervention to ensure
consumers' rights to privacy. At the same time, government, businesses, and consumers struggle to find solutions
for filtering Web-delivered content to protect the innocent
without violating the right to freedom of speech.

Indeed, the Internet has wrought great change and the
ripple effects are significant. The argument about its
impact will continue for many years to come and there
will never be a conclusive answer. The population is too
diverse and the Internet is too versatile to reduce the rela-

tionship between humans and the Web to a rhetorical argument of good versus evil.

The Internet has wrought great change and the ripple effects are significant

So it is to be expected that we have heard from alarmists as well as from enthusiasts regarding the Internet. Human reaction to change hasn't evolved much over the past one hundred years. Despite anxieties that some people may have about the Internet and the multiple ways it may be used and abused, the American public has positive attitudes about it. According to research published in *Understanding*,[7] consumers give high scores to the value of e-mail and the Internet in improving the quality of life in America: 71 percent indicated that e-mail had made the quality of life better, and 69 percent said that the Internet had made the quality of life better—a very high level of endorsement for such a fledgling innovation.

THE WEB EFFECT

A notable attitudinal tendency that we have observed in our research with new consumers is something we call the Web Effect: Once consumers gain access to the Web, they quickly adapt to it and, in very rapid order, perceive the Web as familiar ground. This is a concept we introduced in our first book, *Dead Ahead: The Web Dilemma and the New Rules of Business*.

As shown in figure 1.1, the Web Effect unfolds in the following sequence. Access leads to preference. Preferences become demands. Demands guide selection criteria. Selection criteria first include minimum requirements. Once the minimum requirements are met, then the most important criteria become the characteristics that differentiate the chosen solution from the rest. Businesses who target new consumers must recognize the rapid pace at which the Web Effect materializes. Not offering an online alternative as a way of conducting relationships with new consumers will result in being dismissed from consideration. But, offering a Web alternative is not a differentiator among these consumers. It's simply a price of entry. As more consumers integrate the Web into their daily lives, the Web Effect becomes a critically important force for businesses to reckon with because ultimately, the only set of alternatives consumers will consider in their consumption decisions will be Web-based.

FIGURE 1.1: THE WEB EFFECT

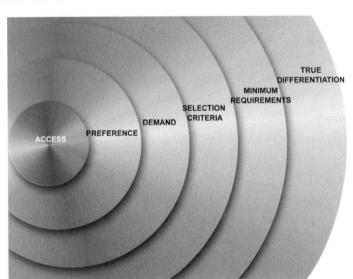

Necessary Precursors to the Acceptance of the Web

The Web Effect didn't just happen overnight. There were necessary behavioral shifts that served as precursors, preparing society in the late twentieth century for the Internet. Of course there were myriad technical developments that were prerequisites to the existence of the Internet and the Web as well. But here we are discussing the behavioral shifts in the consumer population that paved the way for the acceptance of the Web.

THE DE-PERSONALIZATION OF RETAILING

One of the key factors that facilitated the acceptance of the Web was the de-personalization of retailing, a gradual process that took years to unfold. Many economic and cultural factors caused these waves of change to occur. Retailing, as an industry, evolved in the second half of the twentieth century from primarily small, independently owned businesses to an industry dominated by much bigger corporations. This shift from "mom and pop" merchants to larger enterprises created a different shopping environment for consum-

In the spirit of progress, there has been a steady march toward the alienation of customers

ers. Small specialty stores where merchants knew their customers by name were replaced by department stores that offered a wider array of products but less personal services. Suburban malls replaced downtown shopping communities as cities geographically expanded. Department stores were threatened by discount department stores that offered less service and little ambiance, but lower prices.

Parallel to these developments was the growth of the direct-mail catalog industry. The first catalogs were introduced in the late 1800s[8] to provide consumers in remote locations with access to goods and services. The catalog industry experienced a significant spurt in the late 1900s as catalogs multiplied and the range of products offered through these vehicles expanded. Catalogs were the essence of impersonal shopping. In the early days, orders were placed and fulfilled through the U.S. mail. No direct human contact was made at all. While catalog shopping became somewhat more personal when telephone call centers began to be used for order taking, the person on the retailer end of the telephone connection was still a faceless stranger.

All told, many of the evolutionary changes in retail were for the better, in terms of consumers having more convenient access to better and cheaper goods and services. Because of this evolutionary process, however, the retailing experience has become less personal. Merchants no longer recognize their customers. Consumers aren't even sure who owns the stores they patronize. But it doesn't seem to matter—at least not enough to regress to the way things used to be. In the spirit of progress, there has been a steady march toward the alienation of customers in the retail channel and consumers have come to accept it. In

De-personalizing the consumer shopping experience in retail outlets was a necessary precursor to the acceptance of the Web

fact, consumers' demands for more choice, lower prices, and greater convenience have been the catalysts for these changes.

Of course, real humans staff today's retail storefronts, and, in some cases, these retail personnel offer customer service. But more typically, the human serves the primary purpose of operating the retail machinery—the cash register, the bar code reader, and the credit card verification device. The value-add of humans in the retail environment is negligible, and so we consumers have become accustomed to not expecting or needing other humans to assist us in the purchase process, at least for many types of products. Once consumers make that transition to being more autonomous shoppers, the move to shopping online is a small leap.

Some people might consider this de-personalization of retail to be a bad thing; others may think it's a good thing. We are not here to cast judgment or to mourn the good old days. Our key point is that the steady move toward de-personalizing the consumer shopping experience in retail outlets was a necessary precursor to the acceptance of the Web as a consumer commerce vehicle. Consumers had to reach a point where they were comfortable with relying on themselves and technology to successfully locate and purchase the goods they needed.

A CONSUMER SPEAKS

"The personal touch in commerce, at one time, was very important. You could go down to the hardware store and Joe greeted you when you walked in the door. But that went away with the 'big box' stores. Because they're so large, there are some places where I have literally spent thousands of dollars, and when I walk in the door, they don't know who the hell I am. The people I see in there today aren't the people I saw in there three months ago because of the constant turnover. As a consequence, I don't find dealing on the Internet to be any different than going into retail stores."

TIME DEPRIVATION OF CONSUMERS

Another key prevailing condition that has made the consumer market ready for the Internet is the ever-increasing time demands in our lives. On a daily basis, consumers face a set of responsibilities and tasks that are often too multitudinous to accomplish during waking hours. This trend toward overcommitment began in the last three decades of the twentieth century, and was stimulated by both economic and cultural changes.

From an economic perspective, many households transformed from single- to dual-income homes because of the increased cost of living. Families needed the paychecks of multiple wage earners to get by financially. This resulted in more household income, but it also created a time deprivation dilemma that had not existed previously. Households no longer had the luxury of full-time home-makers managing daily-life routines, as these individuals were pressed into the workforce. Time for conducting the more mundane aspects of life, such as grocery shopping, clothing care, and home improvements evaporated. Time deprivation impacted everyone in the household, as life-maintenance tasks were spread among all members of the family. The result—everyone had less time.

Today, the situation has continued to become more intense. Commonly accepted workplace practices pressure workers to put in more hours. More dense urban and suburban populations create more highway and transit-system traffic, which makes for longer commute times. We as consumers are literally running out of time.

Another cultural shift has contributed to the time deprivation situation. The trend of women joining the workforce was not only economically driven, it was psychologically driven as well. The women's liberation movement of the 1960s and '70s created a cultural environment where women were challenged to develop careers. Many young women began to consider staying at home or taking up mundane nine-to-five–type jobs unacceptable. Therefore, women were

Consumers face a set of responsibilities and tasks that are often too multitudinous to accomplish during waking hours

Widespread time deprivation among consumers has been an important precursor to the acceptance of the Web

going into the workforce not only for economic reasons, but for personal-development reasons as well. Women became more career oriented rather than job oriented, which resulted in longer working hours, more business travel, and more arduous intellectual challenges for professional women. All of these factors resulted in women having less time to manage their lives and the households for which they were responsible.

This megachange has many sociological implications for our lifestyles. From a consumer behavior perspective, the changing landscape has created a significant need for the activities of daily living to be more efficiently performed. Consumers need systems, services, products, and modes of living that save time and provide convenience. This environment of widespread time starvation among consumers has been a very important precursor to the acceptance of the Web.

THE ACCEPTANCE OF CREDIT CARDS

Pragmatically, one of the reasons for the rapid success of e-commerce in the United States is that we have a currency—a method of financial exchange—that works very well in an online environment: the credit card. Without the widespread consumer adoption of credit cards, the Web as a shopping vehicle would not have gotten traction in consumer markets. Fortunately for e-merchants (and for credit card companies!), credit cards provided an easily adapted method of payment for products and services online. EFT (electronic funds transfer) infrastructures were in place, approval processes were established, and consumers' wallets were bulging with plastic. The conditions were ripe for e-commerce.

Putting credit cards in the context of economic history, these plastic rectangles are fairly new avatars of money. Franklin National Bank in New York launched the first real credit card in 1951,[9] but the industry did not experience dramatic growth until the last three decades of the twentieth century. Prior to that time, shoppers had to pay for their purchases solely with cash or checks. Clearly, cash or checks are not an acceptable means of purchasing online due to the logistical problems that those currencies would represent in an electronic transaction.

The acceptance of credit cards has been an important prerequisite for e-commerce

To be sure, the use of credit cards for online commerce has encountered stumbling blocks. Attempts by felonious hackers to steal credit card numbers and use them fraudulently have, from time to time, set off panic among financial institutions and consumers. But consumers are becoming increasingly confident. Despite some concerns about credit card security, consumers are willingly using their credit cards for all types of online purchases. Therefore, the advent and acceptance of credit cards, and the comfort level in using them as a means of spending, has been an important prerequisite for e-commerce.

THE FAMILIARITY WITH PERSONAL COMPUTERS

A fourth important contributing factor to the market's readiness for e-commerce is the adoption of personal computers in businesses, homes, and schools. Personal computers were the sole access vehicle for the Web when it first became available to the mass population. Developing a comfort level with PCs was an important hurdle that consumers had already cleared. This made it much easier for the Internet to get rapid traction in the market.

By the mid- to late 1980s, PCs had become a common productivity tool in offices. In fact, it was in the work environment of the 1990s where many consumers first began to comprehend the powers of electronic communications and online information retrieval. Schools had been using PCs as educational tools from kindergarten to twelfth grade, and many universities required students to have PCs in order to be accepted into college programs. Millions of households owned PCs as well. And across the population, more people outside of clerical professions learned a vital skill: the ability to type.

Prior to the advent of the Internet, PCs were solidly entrenched in many aspects of consumers' lives. In fact, when asked which technologies had a positive impact on consumers' lives in the twentieth century, home computers were named by 87 percent of consumers polled, ranking just below automobiles (91 percent) and above television (73 percent).[10]

If PCs had not already successfully penetrated the market, the adoption of the Web as a commerce device would have been much slower. Consumers would have had multiple obstacles to overcome in learning how to use the gadgets and technologies required to make online contact, not to mention the expense of acquiring the requisite set-up to do it. Certainly, there are still large portions of the population who do not yet have access to PCs or to the Web, but every day more people gain access.

MASS COMMUNICATIONS AND CONSUMER BEHAVIOR

Another consumer behavior shift that made the market ripe for Internet adoption was the widespread acceptance of mass communications, particularly television. Prior to television, consumers were dependent on other modes of communications to stay abreast of important events. They read newspapers, listened to radios, talked to friends, and participated in community events. In addition, people were more outward bound in seeking entertainment. They had to leave the house to take in a movie, see a play, or enjoy a concert. Prior to TV, people were more involved with each other and the environment outside the boundaries of their homes.

Academic research supports our observations. In "Bowling Alone: America's Declining Social Capital,"[11] R.D. Putnam asserts that in the last three decades of the twentieth century, there was a diminished civic engagement and social connectedness among Americans. The decrease in common activities is cited as evidence of his assertions: We vote less, socialize with neighbors less, and trust each other less. In his estimation, one of the causal factors is the technological transformation of leisure. He believes that TV has "privatized" or "individualized" our use of leisure time and that TV has occupied an increasingly large proportion of the ways that Americans pass their days and nights.

The acceptance of TV in the home was a necessary precursor to the success of the Internet in our culture. People were already accustomed to being isolated from other people during their leisure time. The one-way communication of TV created a sense of anonymity—no one outside of the home knew what consumers were watching, what interested them, or what made them laugh and cry. We as consumers became more accustomed to experiencing emotions in isolation. We also became dependent on this one-way communications device to fill our time, educate ourselves, and baby-sit our kids. The TV era made an important contribution in preparing our current generations for the Internet. We became habituated to staring at a screen for entertainment, and, as a result, we became lonely and isolated. Consequently, when the Internet arrived at our PC doorstep, we were comfortable with the singularity of sitting in front of a communications device. We had become social animals who were reliant on a non-social method for filling our leisure time and satisfying our need for information.

The Web offered a benefit that TV lacked: two-way communications. Consumers who were weary of the isolation they were experiencing in the TV era began discovering other people online. The interactivity of the Web provided a solution to some of the social problems created by mass communications. Chat rooms, communities, e-mail—these are all devices created because of consumers' needs to affiliate with other human beings.

While some researchers believe that the Internet will only perpetuate this isolation, there is also some evidence that supports the possibility that the Web will counter concerns of technological transformation of leisure and reverse the trend toward Americans' social disconnectedness. For example, in the election year 2000, the Internet is playing some new roles. Several million military personnel have the ability to cast their presidential ballots via the Internet, which may help to reconnect this

When the Internet arrived at our PC doorstep, we were comfortable with the singularity of sitting in front of a communications device

important part of the U.S. workforce. In addition, presidential candidates for the first time raised campaign contributions via the Internet. Republican presidential primary hopeful John McCain used the Internet to raise campaign funds, and, in doing so, attracted consumers who were not previously big campaign donors. Thirty-nine percent of those who contributed to McCain's campaign had never given to a candidate before, and 70 percent had only contributed once.[12] If these examples are any indication of a trend, the Internet may prove to bring people back to the community and to the political process.

Diffusion of Internet Innovation

Of course, there are still many people who continue to experience a feeling of strangeness and distrust about the Internet. The assimilation of the Web is a process that will continue for several more years—a normal circumstance for any significant innovation when it is initially introduced to the market.

As was originally realized by Everett Rogers in the early 1960s, every innovation goes through a time-phased diffusion process as segments of the market adopt the "new thing."[13] As shown in figure 1.2, the diffusion process begins with innovators and early adopters, who constitute relatively small portions of the total market. The process then moves into the early majority part of the market, as more people adopt the innovation. It is always difficult to know when the cycle has moved from the early adopter phase into the majority phases, because you don't really know the ultimate size of the total market—at least while still in the midst of the diffusion process.

It is our belief that the diffusion of the Internet among U.S. consumers has already moved into the early majority phase of the cycle, based on the characteristics and attitudes of the new consumers we have studied, and the Internet market penetration estimates. The early majority is classically defined as "deliberate: They adopt new ideas before the average person, although they rarely are leaders."[14] Today's new consumers share some common characteristics as a group. At the same time, we believe that the number of Web adopters has reached such a mass that we

FIGURE 1.2: DIFFUSION OF INNOVATIONS

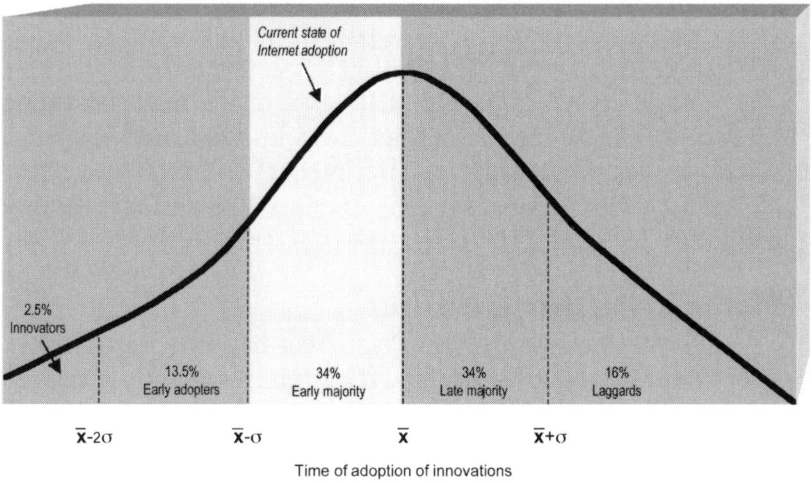

Current state of
Internet adoption

2.5%
Innovators

13.5%
Early adopters

34%
Early majority

34%
Late majority

16%
Laggards

$\bar{x}$-2σ $\bar{x}$-σ $\bar{x}$ $\bar{x}$+σ

Time of adoption of innovations

Source: Redrawn from Everett M. Rodgers, *Diffusion of Innovations* (New York: Free Press, 1962), p.162.

Source: Redrawn from Everett M. Rogers, *Diffusion of Innovations* (New York: Free Press, 1962), p.162.

are seeing distinct market segments emerge, a topic we discuss in chapter 2. These segments are formed based on the primary benefits they derive from Web usage, i.e., some are driven by convenience, some are price sensitive, and so on.

Given the speed at which the Internet is being adopted, we project that we won't be in the early majority phase for long. According to recent research, there are seven new people on the Internet every second.[15] At this pace, we will soon be in the late majority of Internet adoption, where the new consumers will comprise people who typically only adopt an innovation after a majority of people have tried it.

As the Web penetrates the early majority more deeply and subsequently is adopted by late majority consumers, we believe that we will see further crystallization of the customer segments we have already identified. In addition, new segments will likely emerge. And the proportion of the new consumer population that each segment represents will continually change. For example, a larger proportion of the newest adopters are likely to be

The Internet will become a vehicle as intrinsic to our daily existence as TVs and telephones are today

more price-driven, rather than convenience-driven—as compared to earlier Web adopter generations—due to a wider range of demographic profiles becoming part of the new consumer population.

Ultimately, we believe that the size of the new consumer market will be as large as either the television market or the consumer telephone market. The Internet will become a vehicle as intrinsic to our daily existence as TVs and telephones are today.

Profile of the New Consumer

The penetration of the Web has become sufficiently pervasive, to the extent that Web consumers now represent a wide range of demographic attributes. The mix of consumers is constantly changing and becoming more generalized as Internet usage becomes more mainstream. Statistics regularly released by the major market research firms show that the demographic and psychographic profiles of Internet users are increasingly becoming more aligned with our general population and that the "digital divide" is becoming more narrow—a trend expected to continue as usage becomes an early-to-late majority activity.

There are, however, some demographic segments that are being left behind in the move to the Internet. The least educated and the oldest Americans are less likely to have Internet access at this stage in the diffusion process.[16] Even among consumers who have Web access the access is not equal; the digital divide is not just a have- and have-no-access issue. There are increasingly significant differences in the speeds of consumers' Internet connections. Some consumers are dialing into the Internet through antiquated rural phone lines that cannot handle high data speeds.

The profiles of Internet users are increasingly becoming more aligned with our general population

Other more fortunate Web users have access to very high-speed connections at work or at home. And millions of others are getting their connections only occasionally from public facilities, classrooms, and cybercafés.[17] So while the profiles of consumers who have Web access are beginning to approximate the overall United States population, unequal access among these consumers has created an unequal ability to fully comprehend the power of the Web—at least in current market conditions.

EXPERIENCE LEVELS

At any given time, the Web-consumer population comprises people with different levels of Internet experience: those who were early enthusiasts and have been online for several years, those who have recently become very experienced, and those who are Web neophytes.

To illustrate this point, figure 1.3 provides a snapshot of the proportion of Web consumers in early 2000, sorted by the number of years they have been shopping online.

FIGURE 1.3: EXPERIENCE WITH ONLINE SHOPPING

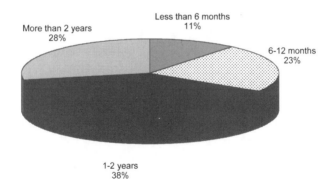

Source: Pulse of the Customer

How experienced a consumer is with the Internet influences how he or she approaches the Web and what sites they frequent. Thus there is a temporal segmentation effect in the Internet diffusion. Consumers new to the Internet tend to use sites that are optimized for ease of use, such as America Online (AOL). Certainly the constant flood of promotional AOL CDs aimed at converting old consumers to new consumers has had an impact on driving people to the Internet. Plus, the easy interface and familiar environment of AOL makes newbies feel more comfortable during their early encounters with the Web. Consumers develop confidence in their ability to use the Web and in the AOL brand, and so they feel they can trust the other brands of content areas represented on AOL. They experiment with chat rooms, online shopping, e-mail, and instant messaging, and quickly develop an understanding of what is possible in the online environment. And they do all of that without having to leave AOL's site.

Once new consumers are more confident, they begin to stick their toes in the Web water. Leaving the AOL cocoon, they venture to other sites and learn how to use search engines. They experiment with creating personalized pages on portal sites. They go to the e-commerce sites their friends have recommended and buy something inexpensive, just to see if it works. If they are successful with these experiments, they continue to go to the recommended sites and buy more. They also start to pay more attention to the dot-com advertisements, because they are confident in their Web abilities and they are interested in sites that will help them reap the newly discovered benefits of the Web.

In contrast, highly experienced new consumers become more habitual in their behavior and more demanding of the Web performance. Certainly, highly experienced new consumers continue to be interested in learning about new sites, but they also establish routines that they know consistently work for them, i.e., how to search for good prices, which sites deliver lots of value time and which sites store their individual profiles and preferences, and how to avoid unwanted promotional e-mail (a.k.a. "spam"). Experienced users also want higher-speed connections. They tend to abandon the familiar environments where they began and switch to Internet service providers (ISPs) that can deliver greater bandwidth and faster performance or upgrade to higher-speed alternatives with their existing ISPs. These consumers are very dependent on the advantages of the Web; they use it for many aspects of their daily lives. Therefore, their demands for more convenience and greater timesavings grow with time.

NEW CONSUMERS' EXPECTATIONS AND HABITS

Regardless of consumers' depth of Web experience, the Web seems to be meeting their expectations. We learned in our 1999 post-holiday studies, conducted in early 2000, that expectations had been met or exceeded among more than 90 percent of the consumers we polled. This represents a big improvement in e-business performance, as compared with previous years. And consumers expect to continue buying more online. In the same survey, 80 percent expected to increase their online shopping in the coming year, as shown in figure 1.4.

FIGURE 1.4: EXPECTED CHANGES IN ONLINE SHOPPING BEHAVIOR

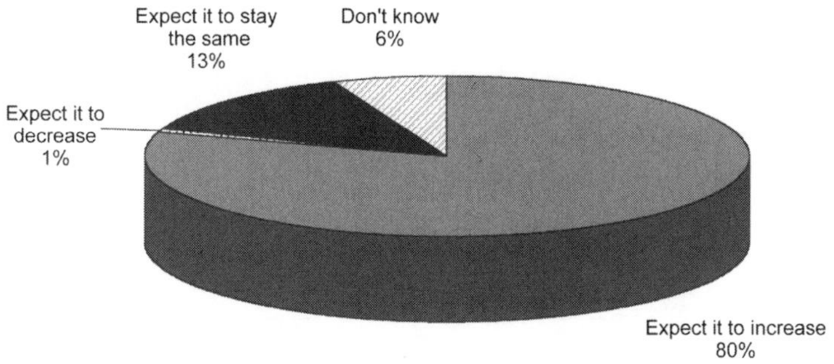

Expect it to stay the same 13%

Don't know 6%

Expect it to decrease 1%

Expect it to increase 80%

Source: Pulse of the Customer

TYPICAL NEW CONSUMER ONLINE BEHAVIORS

There are strong behavioral indicators that the Internet is becoming a fixture in consumers' daily lives. As shown in figure 1.5, consumers regularly frequent a full range of sites—portals, e-retailers, entertainment and community, news, travel, and banking. The majority uses the Web for e-mail, shopping, and searching, as shown in figure 1.6. Shopping in this context can include a wide range of activities: finding products, comparing prices, and making purchases. Many consumers report using the Web to shop, even if they don't conduct the entire purchasing process online.

Despite the commonalities in how people use the Web, at this point in the development of the market there is little consistency in the specific sites at which consumers prefer to shop. As consumers name their favorite sites, there appears to be significant fragmentation in the e-business market. Beyond the large proportion who report themselves as Amazon.com customers (46 percent), the incidence of other e-commerce site brands mentioned falls below 15 percent. Consumers seem to be enjoying the wide variety of Web sites available to them to satiate their shopping needs.

FIGURE 1.5: TYPES OF WEB SITES REGULARLY VISITED

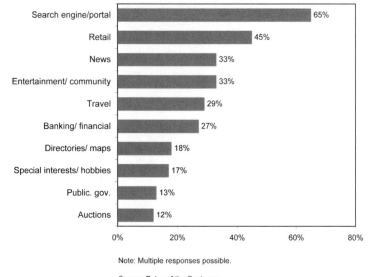

Note: Multiple responses possible.

Source: Pulse of the Customer

FIGURE 1.6 TOP ACTIVITIES PERFORMED AT FREQUENTED SITES

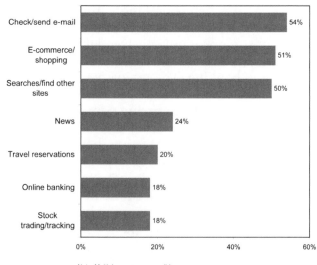

Note: Multiple responses possible.

Source: Pulse of the Customer

Figure 1.7 provides an overview of the types of products e-shoppers actually buy—versus shop for—online. Leading the list are the typical "low-involvement" products we have come to expect consumers to buy online. High involvement products, particularly ones that require a tactile experience prior to purchase, are less popular for online procurement. This consumer purchasing trend is analyzed in chapter 5.

FIGURE 1.7: PRODUCT CATEGORIES PURCHASED ONLINE

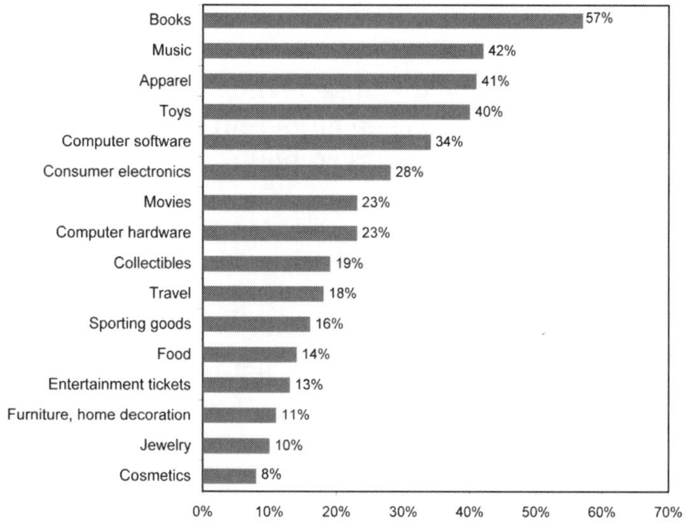

Category	Percent
Books	57%
Music	42%
Apparel	41%
Toys	40%
Computer software	34%
Consumer electronics	28%
Movies	23%
Computer hardware	23%
Collectibles	19%
Travel	18%
Sporting goods	16%
Food	14%
Entertainment tickets	13%
Furniture, home decoration	11%
Jewelry	10%
Cosmetics	8%

Note: Multiple responses possible.

Source: Pulse of the Customer

The Internet Changes Just About Everything

There have been business prognosticators and dot-com advertisement headlines that say, "The Internet changes everything"—that all aspects of our personal, professional, even spiritual lives will be altered by the advent of information technologies. Some say that as consumers our lives will become more enriched, easier to manage, and ultimately dependent on the effective application of technology. We happen to agree with these sentiments.

WHERE WE BEGIN

You don't have to be a believer in the metaphysical powers of the Internet to realize that the Internet has had a powerful influence on our "origin instinct"—a term we have coined for the subconscious drive that naturally directs our behavior to a starting point where we begin an ordinary task. The origin instinct is developed through habitual behavior that consistently results in success. People learn which methods work for beginning a task and repeatedly use those methods until they become second nature and instinctual. We believe that the Internet is changing the instincts that determine how we begin a myriad of daily-life tasks.

Consider the following. Before the Internet, where did we begin the following tasks?

- Finding out how to contact someone
- Learning the answer to an obscure question
- Checking the prices on something we are considering buying
- Gathering information on competitors
- Soliciting investment advice on a company's stock
- Buying that stock
- Catching up on the latest news
- Finding out tomorrow's weather forecast
- Obtaining directions to a new destination
- Getting a job

In the absence of the Internet, getting answers to those questions involves a broad array of information sources. We go to encyclopedias to get answers to obscure questions. We use the telephone book or directory assistance to find someone's phone number. We go to retail stores, catalogs, and advertisements in newspapers to find out price information. We attend trade shows and read trade publications to learn about competitors. We call stockbrokers for investment advice and trading. We read newspapers and watch television to get the news and weather. We use a street map to get directions. We read the classified ads for employment opportunities.

The Internet serves as a center of gravity, the place where we instinctively begin our tasks

But the Internet is changing all of that. The Web is becoming the place where people begin all of these tasks. In the minds of new consumers, the Internet is evolving from a potential source of information to the place where they instinctively begin their tasks. The array of those tasks is very broad. The Internet serves as a center of gravity, an organizing principle for how we begin many activities of daily living. The Internet is reshaping our origin instinct. That's a very dramatic change, not only for the new consumers whose activity initiation behaviors have migrated to the Web, but for the businesses that have been serving consumers in the traditional ways of beginning.

Prior to the emergence of the Internet, no single information vehicle so pervasively and effectively served as the point of origin for common, everyday tasks. There is nothing in history with which to compare it, nothing that can help us contextualize it. Therefore, it is difficult to fully comprehend the implications of the change in origin instinct we are experiencing due to the Internet.

CONSUMERS SPEAK ABOUT HOW THE INTERNET HAS CHANGED WHERE THEY BEGIN

"If there is something specific I want to buy, before I pick up my catalog and look for it, I just get on the Internet."

"The Internet has changed the way I shop for used cars. I can quickly scan dealer inventory without having to call all the separate dealers."

"I start my vacation planning on the Internet. We travel for pleasure more now, because we can get better deals."

"I can get directions. I use Mapquest. I give it the address I need and I can actually print directions for how to get there."

"I use Digitalcity.com to find out what movies I want to see instead of looking in the paper or calling the theater."

"I started my job search on the Internet."

COMMON UNDERSTANDING GETS THROWN INTO CHAOS

For many consumers, the Internet phenomenon defies logic. As children of a capitalistic culture, we have learned the way things work. But the Internet seems to break the economic rules that we have come to accept. For instance, we expect companies to make money. As consumers, we don't need college degrees in business to know that without breaking even, businesses cannot survive. Furthermore, companies are expected to be profitable. When we shop at a retail store, we know they make money on our patronage. We understand that manufacturers pay retailers a margin for everything they sell. We realize that there are multiple players in the value chain that starts with raw materials and ends with finished products. We know that if companies don't make money, they can't meet payroll and they lay off people. We've learned these economic truths from our experiences and what we have witnessed in our surroundings.

But in the world of the Internet, things seem to work differently and consumers find it confusing. Companies that don't make profits have high stock valuations. Many e-businesses don't expect to make a profit for years, and yet no one loses their jobs. Investors continue to be upbeat about these stocks, even though the companies lose millions every quarter. Companies go public. Young people with no work experience get rich and become CEOs. Unemployment is at an all-time low. What's going on?

On top of that, Internet companies give stuff away— free shipping, free products, big discounts. Consumers wonder, "How can they afford that?" It boggles consumers' minds. Not that consumers mind getting free stuff and low prices, they just can't figure out how the world works anymore. They don't know what to expect next.

The enthusiasm for dot coms in the capital markets paired with the desperate attempts by dot coms to acquire customers has created a situation that consumers don't fully understand. The internal checks-and-balances system that we maintain in our heads has become confused. The conventional wisdom and economic principles we have accepted our entire lives are suddenly being turned upside down by the Web world. Below are some common economic maxims that no longer seem relevant, at least in the world of e-commerce.

YOU CAN'T GET SOMETHING FOR NOTHING

From the time we were small children, it has been ingrained in our capitalistic minds that nothing is really free. In fact, the title of noted econo-mist Milton Friedman's 1975 book eloquently stated that "There's No Such Thing as a Free Lunch."[18] He, as well as many other economists, postulates the simple economic prin-ciple: You can't get something for nothing.

In the Web world, you can get something for nothing

As consumers, we have learned that often manufac-turers and retailers will offer loss-leader promotions designed to build allegiance to their brands or pull traffic into their stores. And, we realize that these promotions have ulterior motives—that once consumers are hooked by the special deal, they will be enticed to buy more profitable items, thus offsetting the loss from the promotion. While consumers happily take advantage of these promotions, they do not fool us. Because we all know you can't get something for nothing.

But in the Web world, is it really true that you can't get something for nothing? Our experiences as new con-sumers fly in the face of that conventional wisdom. Dot coms are spending massive amounts of dollars in their attempts to acquire customers. These customer acquisi-tion programs are funded by the capital raised in the ven-ture community and in the public stock markets. The theory is that they need to spend heavily to acquire cus-tomers because competition is so intense. So dot coms offer some pretty lucrative deals to consumers: free deliv-eries; free gift boxes; free returns; $10, $25, $100 off first purchases. Consumers take advantage of the offers, ben-efit from the freebie, and then move on to the next site that offers something free. They realize their volume of business with that particular dot com will not offset the dot com's loss from making the promotional offer because they don't necessarily plan to continue shopping there. But they don't care. In the faceless world of online shopping, loyalties are rare and new consumers' senses of accountability are low. Besides, there's an overall assumption that everyone in dot-com companies is a mil-lionaire, so taking advantage of free offers makes new consumers feel like they are evening out the score—on a very small scale.

New consumers expect to get more than they pay for

The upshot is this: In the Web world, you *can* get something for nothing, at least if you are a new consumer who takes advantage of the profuse wild-and-crazy dot-com offers.

YOU GET WHAT YOU PAY FOR

Another dot-com customer-acquisition strategy that can throw conventional wisdom out the window is to offer deeply discounted products. In fact, some dot coms actually sell products below cost, with the goal of attracting high volumes of site traffic so they can charge their advertisers for the consumer "eyeballs." For example, Buy.com's launch strategy was to sell goods at or below cost, just so they could attract consumers' attention and charge high fees for advertisements on their site. On top of that, they offered $10 to every first-time customer as an additional incentive to buy. This business practice can make the old maxim, "You get what you pay for" an empty platitude, because, in fact, consumers can actually get *more* than they pay for.

Of course, many consumers are very enthusiastic about these deals. However, because they don't fully understand why all the old rules are changing, they are either highly suspicious of the offers—which prevents them from buying—or they come to expect such deals to persist. In the latter case, rather than appreciating the special offers extended by a site and becoming loyal to the site as a result, they begin to feel entitled to better deals. And their loyalty will constantly shift to the site that offers the best deal. This is a behavioral trend we discuss more thoroughly in chapter 3.

IT WILL ALL COME OUT IN THE WASH

The practice of loss-leader marketing is familiar to all consumers, as discussed above. Even though we appreciate special bargains, we realize that the losses from one product sale are offset by another product purchase and so we realize that eventually "It all comes out in the wash." The business still makes money and profits are realized. In the grand scheme of things, it all balances out.

But is that true in the world of the Web? Will these seemingly illogical promotional offers made by Web sites ever be offset by other purchases made on those same Web sites? Will the dot coms reap benefits from the efforts to acquire customers? Will all of those unprofitable e-businesses ever become profitable? And if they don't, what happens next? Who gets hurt? Who gets stuck holding the bag? The fundamental belief that everything eventually attains equilibrium is truly threatened in the e-commerce world.

HONESTY IS THE BEST POLICY

Hopefully, the Web won't cause people to abandon the fundamental virtue of honesty. But the cyberspace environment is one that tests the veracity of both businesses and consumers. The opportunities to defraud businesses and consumers are ever-present on the Web, making both buyers and sellers somewhat wary of transaction processes, and giving rise to many security mechanisms to ensure honest business practices.

In addition, some e-businesses have been less than open, and a few even dishonest, about how they use personal information collected from their e-customers. As a result, consumers feel violated when they realize the infraction. Some consumers retaliate by providing bogus information so that e-businesses can't send them unwanted communications.

Another aspect of less-than-truthful online behavior is in interpersonal communication. In the protected world of chat rooms, consumers can take on any identity they choose. To make chat room experiences more entertaining, or to protect their true identities, consumers learn to take on online pseudonyms and act out their fantasies without the accountability normally attached to their real-world identities.

The Web also seems to alter some people's perception of what is legal and what isn't. For example, a controversy was stimulated by Napster, an online service that acts like a music search engine and makes it easy for consumers to find and copy a wide variety of music. The Recording Industry Association of America (RIAA) filed suit against Napster alleging that the company was operating for music piracy on the Internet and charging Napster

The cyberspace environment is one that tests the veracity of both businesses and consumers

with copyright infringement. According to a press release issued by RIAA, Napster provides users with a hub of central computer servers to which they connect a continuously updated database of "links" to millions of pirated recordings. Its software allows fast, efficient identification, copying, and distribution of the pirated recordings, which enable and encourage users to download millions of pirated songs as well as make their own music available for others to copy.[19] As pointed out in a story in the *New York Times*, through Napster, "Every day, about a million otherwise law-abiding adult citizens are demonstrating no compunction about using the service to get free what they would have to pay for in a record store." Carey Sherman of the RIAA is quoted as saying, "There's an incredible disconnection out there between what is normal behavior in the physical world versus the online world. There are people who think nothing of downloading entire CD collections on Napster who wouldn't dream of shoplifting from Tower Records."[20]

Is our ability to distinguish between right and wrong being clouded by what has become technically possible on the Internet? Does the implicit anonymity of the Internet give consumers and vendors permission to act dishonestly? Does the old argument of "Everybody is doing it" justify wrongful acts? If there is no threat of being caught, is it acceptable to misbehave? These are tough questions for any society to face and the issues have become more pressing due to the advent of the Internet.

Whatever the rationale or extenuating circumstances for these deceptive actions, in the world of the Web, the conclusion is sometimes this: Honesty must not always be the best policy, because so many normally honest businesses and people are behaving dishonestly.

YOU CAN'T ALWAYS GET WHAT YOU WANT

The conventional wisdom chronicled by the Rolling Stones, "You can't always get what you want,"[21] is also subject to extinction in the world of the new consumer. Before the Web, we consumers had to face the reality of supply. We could only purchase products that were available to buy within our physical reach. Our reach was typically only as far as our geographic mobility could take us. For most consumers, if the products and services were not available from our local retailers or catalogs that arrived in the mail, we simply couldn't buy them. On the Internet, the range of products and services is so vast and so astounding that you can—almost literally—always get what you want. We are no longer limited to what's available in our town, on the retailers' shelves, or considered attractive by the local retailers' buyers. We can go to sites and buy just about anything. We consumers are indeed learning that we can always get what we want—assuming, that is, we haven't reached our credit card limits and the desired products are in stock!

So, the playbook that consumers have learned since birth is being rewritten for many aspects of consumption. As the Web becomes more entrenched in our daily existence, we will continually be presented with new ideas, new business practices, and new offers that will cause us to re-examine what we believe are fundamental truths about how things work. And, as a result, we will evolve our expectations and demands as consumers.

Rules of Empowered Consumers

In *Dead Ahead: The Web Dilemma and the New Rules of Business*, we termed the current era as "the age of the empowered customer." Our thesis is that the Web has created a new dynamic between buyers and sellers. The net result is the emergence of the empowered customer, as discussed earlier in this chapter.

The Internet is an empowerment tool, providing customers with myriad options they never had before—countless brands to choose from, searchable databases, unique personalization features, numerous shopping options, built-to-order merchandise, instant access/downloads of electronic content, close-out items, items up for auction . . . The list goes on.

Consumers are indeed smarter and more powerful than ever before. The Web is a tool that strengthens their shopping intelligence. Throughout the process of deciding what and when to buy, e-customers have

Consumers are indeed smarter and more powerful than ever before

access to a wealth of information from many companies; and they have lots of choices. Therefore, control of the purchase transaction has shifted from the merchant to the consumer. We believe that this balance of control has permanently and irretrievably shifted toward the consumer because of the properties of the Web.

Through the empowerment process, online consumers have developed preferences of how they wish to be treated by companies with whom they interact. We call these preferences the Rules of the Empowered Consumer. Regardless of the value proposition an e-business brings to customers—whether they are consumers or businesses—the following rules apply.

- *Don't waste my time.* The primary reason consumers use the Web is to save time. In this rushed world, the Internet has become a means of conveniently conducting activities of daily living. Gone are the days when consumers aimlessly surfed the Internet out of curiosity. The power users of the Internet are busy. E-businesses should evaluate their propositions to ensure that they are fulfilling the primary need of timesaving.
- *Give me what I want when I want it.* Empowered consumers want to easily find the content and functionality they seek and then move on—regardless of where they are in the consumption cycle (shopping, buying, tracking, taking delivery, or getting customer service). E-businesses should anticipate the needs of their target customers and provide the tools and information they require to successfully make decisions to buy and buy again. Web sites should be designed to guide people through the consumption cycle.
- *Give me meaningful content, not fluff.* Increasingly, empowered consumers are becoming jaded and resistant to content they perceive as meaningless. E-customers scorn material if they perceive it to be too "salesy" or self-serving to the business.
- *Don't exploit me.* The more Web-experienced consumers become, the more suspicious they are of time-

wasting, i.e., intrusive actions initiated by e-business-es. Unfortunately, the amount of unwanted e-mail goes up exponentially the more consumers shop online because of the Web business practice of send-ing promotional e-mail to customers. Consumers are increasingly wary of these tactics and are beginning to alter their shopping behavior as a result. Simply put, Web consumers do not want to be taken advantage of. That violates their sense of control.

- *Don't disappoint me.* E-customers can be an unfor-giving bunch. This is a result of their empowerment. New consumers know that they have many choices. If one Web site disappoints them, they have myriad online alternatives to satisfy their needs.

Analyzing the Soul of the New Consumer

In examining the soul of the new consumer, we look closely at many critical issues relating to e-customers, and advise businesses on how to successfully sustain online relationships with this increasingly important segment of the market.

In chapter 2, we discuss the challenge of building and sustaining customer loyalty in the Web context. We present analysis of consumers' reactions to tactics designed to build brand loyalty. We present a new market segmentation model, identifying and profiling distinct and addressable clusters of e-customers.

The challenge of driving traffic, closing sales, and retaining online customers is the subject of chapter 3. In this chapter, we present a new model for understanding the e-customers' purchase decision cycle. In that context, we evaluate the effectiveness of advertising and promotions in the Web world, from the consumer's point of view. We explore the rapidly developing set of services, perks, and freebies that consumers are coming to expect.

In chapter 4, we discuss consumers' sentiments about privacy: What are acceptable and unacceptable business practices and uses of information. We delve into concerns about credit card security, the use of personalization tech-nology, and the growing practice of using e-mail for unso-licited promotional offers.

Consumers are vocal about the areas in which e-businesses need to do a better job. Those opinions are voiced in chapter 5. Here we discuss issues such as customer service, site performance, and other glitches that interfere with consumers' successful e-commerce experiences. We also analyze what products sell well online, what products don't, and why.

The new consumer is not only a new consumer, but a traditional consumer as well. In chapter 6 we explore other aspects of consumer shopping behavior and how the Internet has changed the way we do things. Specifically, we evaluate consumers' opinions on the relative merits of shopping in retail stores, via catalogs, and online. And we look at how the Web has changed consumers' preferences for news media, leisure activities, and interpersonal communications.

While consumers are the topic of most of this book, in chapter 7 we focus on business e-customers. We analyze their attitudes, behaviors, and preferences for e-business relationships. And we identify the obstacles to greater adoption of online business practices among small businesses, procurement professionals, and IT departments.

In chapter 8, we take a fresh look at the e-business road map, originally presented in *Dead Ahead*. We discuss how to factor consumer demands into the process of planning, creating, and launching a Web presence, suggesting when and how to collect customer feedback, and advising how to interpret and operationalize customer input. In addition, we discuss key issues that companies encounter in creating successful e-business strategies.

In chapter 9, we discuss the next frontier—where consumer expectations are heading and what strategies e-businesses must take to sustain customer loyalty. And we look at the next phases of market development—what it will take to get the late majority and laggards involved with the Web.

METHODOLOGY

The Soul of the New Consumer is based on three continuous years of qualitative and quantitative research conducted by our firm, Cognitiative, Inc. Through our Pulse of the Customer℠ research series, we have talked to thousands of e-customers, in both consumer and business contexts, about their attitudes, behaviors, and preferences regarding the Internet. Our methodologies, which we explain in more detail in the Appendix, include many nationwide focus groups, telephone interviews, and e-mail panel surveys. While we do not design our research methodologies to be "statistically" representative, we are confident that our research findings truly capture the psychodynamics of the new consumer. Our confidence is corroborated by statistical research conducted by the leading commercial and academic market research organizations; our research data, presented in graphic formats throughout this book, reflect very similar patterns and trendlines of other industry studies.

PREVIEW OF WHAT'S AHEAD

What does our glimpse into the soul of the new consumer tell us? As you will learn in this book, the soul of the new consumer is a labyrinth of emotions, preferences, behaviors, anxieties, and loyalties. The new consumer is confused but awed, trusting while still suspicious, afraid yet adventuresome, busy but curious, anonymous but uniquely individual. And while many forces are at play in the soul of the new consumer, one quality is absolute: The new consumer is empowered.

2

Customer Loyalty and the Emerging E-Customer Segments

L istening to consumers talk about what they do on the Web is a fascinating experience. It's so new and yet so familiar. You hear how a busy single mother and her sixteen-year-old son "virtually" tried on new hubcaps for his Mustang. You hear a secretary talk about buying medicine and supplies for her dogs online. You hear a father of three gloat about no longer having to load his kids into the car and go to the local discount store to buy shampoo and diapers because he is now buying staple products online. You hear a machinist talk about how he plays online poker with his pals overseas. These people are not the prototypical "lunatic fringe" or even "early adopters," who were the initial Web enthusiasts. They are mainstreet folks—the ones that so many companies are hoping to reach via the Web.

The notable trend is that the Web is increasingly integrated into consumers' normal daily activities. Activities the average e-consumer performs on the Web are expanding, in both depth and range. As the Web becomes more mainstream and increasingly larger proportions of the population become Web users, the more complex the challenge of establishing and maintaining customer loyalty becomes—because the target market is rapidly growing more diverse and the competition is fierce. Consumers are complex animals and the competitive landscape is maddeningly dynamic. People behave in different ways at different times. What works to capture site traffic for

Creating customer loyalty requires listening to customers and truly comprehending what they are telling us

one set of consumers may not work for another. Incentives to maintain loyalty in one product category may be meaningless in another. Effective loyalty programs one month may be countered with more popular competitive offers the next month. Despite the difficulty of navigating through this wildly chaotic and bewildering environment, e-businesses realize that they must strive to understand what makes online consumers loyal. Conventional business wisdom tells us that acquiring new customers is much more expensive than maintaining customers, once you have captured them. That axiom is strongly believed by many e-businesses—although some of that wisdom may be outdated, as discussed in chapter 3.

It is a fundamental business principle: Creating customer loyalty is essential to building market share and long-term staying power. Understanding how to create customer loyalty requires listening to customers and truly comprehending what they are telling us.

To gain insight into online customer loyalty, we begin by profiling new consumers' online preferences. Why do people like using the Web? What are the key benefits? What are the drawbacks? Then, we relate these preferences to loyalty, evaluating the relevance of loyalty to the new consumer. How does the delivery of expected benefits correlate to customer loyalty? How do you create customer loyalty? How do you win back lost loyalties? Finally, we explore the emerging market segments in the new consumer population and identify clusters of people who share attitudes, behaviors, and preferences in their online experiences.

Benefits of the Web to Consumers

When we ask consumers why they like the Web—in general, for any type of activity—their answers have common threads: the Web gives them access to more people, more things, more information. It gives them more freedom to speak, to be heard and to choose. For many consumers, the Web also makes life easier, more fun, and more entertaining. Consumers who use the Web are quite enthusiastic about the benefits. Even people who are just starting to use it are enthralled. And, the more they use it, the more zealous they become in their perceptions of its general benefits. Consistent in all attitudes expressed is the resounding theme: The Web gives them more power to control many aspects of their lives—their time, their money, their decisions, their gratification, their knowledge, and their communication.

WHY CONSUMERS LIKE THE WEB

MODERATOR: What are the main benefits you derive from the Web?

CONSUMER: It's a lot faster than doing things the old way. More convenience, more variety, endless options.

CONSUMER: I stay in touch with people more frequently. It's cheaper than making a long-distance phone call and I can access more information.

CONSUMER: The access to information is nearly instantaneous instead of waiting on the phone or waiting for someone to get back to you.

CONSUMER: It keeps me up-to-date with what's happening.

CONSUMER: It's entertaining.

The Web is much more than a commerce vehicle. As seen in chapter 1, people like doing all sorts of activities on the Web—searching, buying, and chatting. But typically when we think about "customer loyalty," we view the consumer as a person with money to spend, a person we want to sell something to. And so, our discussion about loyalty focuses on consumers as customers. We know that the activities related to shopping—product searches, price comparisons, product reviews, and purchases—combined are the most frequently mentioned favorite activities on the Web and an area that most businesses deeply care about.

BENEFITS OF ONLINE SHOPPING

To understand the emerging consumer segments and what constitutes loyalty, we must examine what consumers consider to be the benefits of online shopping. Every time we talk to consumers about the primary benefits of online shopping we hear similar themes. Whether they are shopping for routine items, for holiday gifts, or simply locating products and doing price comparisons, the same advantages are consistently listed time after time.

As shown in figure 2.1, online consumers name convenience and timesavings as the top reasons they prefer shopping online. Buying online is viewed as significantly more convenient than any other mode of shopping—at least for some product categories. This is the primary reason for the success of e-business today. The time-deprived consumer meets the convenience of the Web. It's a powerful combination.

FIGURE 2.1: BENEFITS OF ONLINE SHOPPING

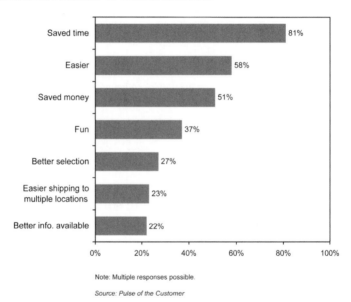

Note: Multiple responses possible.

Source: Pulse of the Customer

A Web site actualizes its potential for convenience and time efficiency when it becomes *familiar*—a word that is used time and again when consumers talk about their preferred Web sites. Human beings are creatures of habit. We get accustomed to our daily routines and—assuming we are satisfied with how things work—we are happy to stick with

The word <u>familiarity</u> is often used when consumers are asked to describe their preferred Web sites

what we know. Online consumers get used to the way a site is designed and how it works. This is an important aspect of convenience and time efficiency. It is convenient to use a familiar site and it takes less time to get around. Once a site has become familiar, a set of consumers settles in as loyal customers.

On the Web, consumers can perform price/ feature comparisons to their heart's content without having to leave their chairs

Other frequently mentioned benefits of shopping online are that it is easier than other modes of shopping and that it saves consumers' money. Online shopping is perceived to be easier because of how simple it is to locate products, through the use of both general and site-specific search engines. There's no hassle of driving and parking the car. And once products are located, price comparisons are easy as well. On the Web, consumers can perform price/feature comparisons to their heart's content without having to leave their chairs.

For many, being able to do extensive price comparisons means that they are saving money. These consumers believe that they can find a better price online and that's exactly why they shop online. Many claim that they have saved money because they found a lower price online than they found in their local stores, even when they include shipping charges. Some consumers point out that the perception that they are getting better prices is just that—a *perception;* in reality, they observe that prices are no better online than in other channels. But it is interesting how many people strongly believe that on the Internet, everything is cheaper.

It is also interesting, however, to note that the "saving money" benefit of online shopping is mentioned with much less frequency than convenience and timesavings. This counters the often mistaken perception that *all* online shoppers are avid price bottom-fishers.

COST SAVING BENEFITS

MODERATOR: Do you think you get better prices on the Web?

CONSUMER: Prices are always cheaper than what you can get at the store. But then, you still have shipping and handling. By the time you add all that up, you could go to the store and buy it.

CONSUMER: The shipping and handling is annoying to me, too. But, I'd rather pay a $5 shipping charge than throw the kids in the car and run down to Target.

CONSUMER: Even with shipping, you still get better prices.

MODERATOR: What if two sites had the same product and slightly different prices? Say you've gone to Amazon to look at a particular book. You're familiar with Amazon, you always shop there, and you know how it works. You hear that the book is $1 cheaper at BarnesandNoble.com, but you've never been there. Do you stick with Amazon because it is familiar, or do you switch to the other because it is cheaper?

CONSUMER: I'd switch.

CONSUMER: I'm lazy. I'd stick with the same one because I have it bookmarked. And so, if I want a book, I go to Amazon. I don't pull up anybody else.

MODERATOR: Are you that way with every product category, or just books?

CONSUMER: I'm different depending on the category. For example, if I want airline tickets, I look at three or four choices. But for books, I stick with Amazon.

CONSUMER: I usually stick with the same site just because it's easier and it takes too much time to look around.

CONSUMER: It gets frustrating to shop around. You point, you click, you point, you click, and you're worn out. You get used to one site. It's easy for you. You can get there real quick. If you switch to another Web site that has the same product, you have to learn all over again.

Other benefits of online shopping are worth noting as well. More than one-third of consumers we poll say that online shopping is fun. This frequently comes from consumers who consider shopping in a retail store or mall as painful as getting a root canal. Shopping online eliminates most of the characteristics that make physical shopping a nightmare for these individuals—the crowds, the parking, the queues, the absence of helpful service people. Instead, shopping-adverse consumers actually enjoy surfing the net, comparing prices, locating deals, and participating in auctions—as long as they can do it in the comfort of their homes or offices.

Many consumers also feel that they have access to a better product selection when shopping online. This relates more to the macro level of the Internet, rather than to the attributes of specific Web sites. Consumers fre-

E-commerce has created new conveniences that consumers may not have expected prior to the advent of the Web

quently comment about the ease of finding obscure products on the Web that they haven't successfully located in nearby retailers or catalogs. Because of the myriad options that consumers literally have at their fingertips, consumers feel that their product selections are almost endless—sometimes overwhelmingly so!

New consumers talk about other benefits of shopping online as well. In fact, e-commerce has created some new conveniences that consumers may not have expected prior to the advent of the Web. Specifically, consumers like the ease of having products shipped to the ultimate destination when shopping online—a service that is hard to come by in a retail store. And they like the fact that online, they can easily ship purchases to multiple locations—a feature that is particularly valued during holiday gift buying seasons.

Consumers indicate that their least favorite sites are those that fail to deliver the advantages of Internet shopping: convenience, timesavings, and good product selection. Typically, these sites have repeatedly had performance problems, delivery glitches, and offer an inadequate inventory of products.

WEB SITE FUNCTION PREFERENCES

E-customers express clear preferences for the specific functions they want to perform and the kind of content they require to shop successfully online. As shown in figure 2.2, when asked to focus on site functionality, consumers indicate the most important online activities they want to perform while shopping: locating their desired product or conducting product searches; being able to comparison shop for features and prices; and having the access to product shipping and tracking information.

FIGURE 2.2: MOST IMPORTANT WEB SITE FUNCTIONS

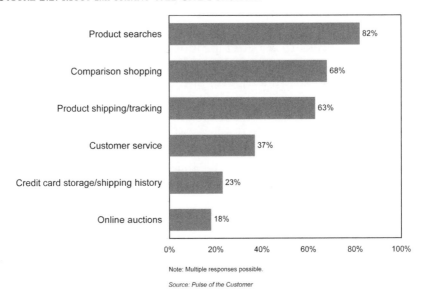

Note: Multiple responses possible.

Source: Pulse of the Customer

These preferred activities are closely linked to what the e-customer perceives as advantages on the Internet—convenience and timesavings. This functionality creates the Web advantages they expect and thus directly correlates to their loyalty.

The Link between Web Benefits and Customer Loyalty

What do consumer attitudes about Web benefits have to do with customer loyalty? Mainstream Web consumers choose to patronize specific Web sites when they have a reasonable expectation that the desired benefits will be delivered. Meeting e-customers' expectations by delivering what they perceive to be the advantages of shopping online is a critical component of creating Web customer loyalty. Web sites that fail to deliver the expected advantages lose consumers to competitive sites.

Knowing which key benefits matter most to your target customers is the first step in building a customer loyalty strategy that fits with your business goals. Consistently delivering those benefits, thus meeting customers' expectations, is required to begin the process of building customer loyalty.

COMPONENTS OF WEB BRAND LOYALTY

The components of Web brand loyalty are very different than those required to build relationships in the analog world. In traditional brand marketing, companies may focus on creating more esoteric or emotional brand attributes, but online, the key issues are: Does the site work?; How fast, how easy is it to use?; and Does it deliver what the user is looking for? Consumers indicate ease-of-use and ease-of-navigation to be their top criteria for Web brand loyalty, along with familiarity and dependability of the site, as shown in figure 2.3. Interestingly, only 15 percent of consumers we polled indicate that competitive pricing creates Web site loyalty, making it a far less important component than those contributing to timesavings and convenience, at least among today's new consumers.

FIGURE 2.3: COMPONENTS OF WEB BRAND LOYALTY

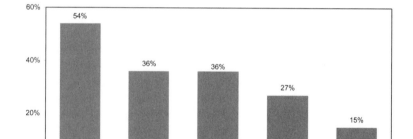

Note: Multiple responses possible.

Source: Pulse of the Customer

So, Web brand loyalty is derived from the customers' experiences when using the site. This is an important realization, especially for brands that existed prior to the advent of the Web. The more the consumer relies on the Web site to transact business with merchants versus other means of conducting buyer/seller relationships, the more the brand image is

The Web site experience is the brand

shaped by the Web site experience. We believe this has pro-
found implications for companies' branding strategies. In
effect, the Web site experience becomes the primary vehicle for building and reinforcing brand identity and preferences. Taking that a step further, the implication is: In the
Internet world, the Web site experience is the brand.

LOYALTY TO WEB SITES

MODERATOR: What makes you loyal to a particular brand?

CONSUMER: Quality of whatever I am buying.

CONSUMER: Customer service, return policy, and the way problems are handled if they arise. Those are the most important things.
Returning something without a lot of hassle if it's not what I
thought it would be.

CONSUMER: Get a good product at a fair price and with good service. You're
going to find bad products every now and then from wherever
you buy, but the thing for me is how the problem is taken care
of.

MODERATOR: Are there any Web sites that you're loyal to?

CONSUMER: Not for me. Not yet, at least.

CONSUMER: I have my favorites.

MODERATOR: What makes you loyal to a Web site?

CONSUMER: I'm familiar with them. I can get in and get out.

CONSUMER: Ease-of-use, the speed at which pages appear, and the number
of pages that I have to go through to get what I want. Those are
the factors that I consider.

CONSUMER: Familiarity, customer service, and follow-through make me loyal
to a site. I will continue to shop around, but if I have experienced good customer service, I will return to the same site.

CONSUMER: The lowest price.

The E-Business Price of Entry

While consistently fulfilling benefit expectations is
required to survive in e-business, unfortunately, simply
delivering to consumers what they have come to expect is
no longer enough to create and maintain customer loyalty.
In the crowded dot-com market, delivering convenience,
timesavings, ease-of-use, and better prices have become the
e-business price of entry. The challenge is keeping pace
with what consumers expect today, because the bar keeps

getting raised by the competition. What was a differentiator one day is a me-too feature the next. More than ever before, customers' expectations are being redefined rapidly—by the day, by the hour, by the minute.

Nothing in our lifetime has had as dramatic an impact on the rapidity of change in consumer's expectations than the Web

Nothing in our lifetime has had as dramatic an impact on the rapidity of change in consumers' expectations than the Web. Certainly, current generations have experienced advancements that impact our consumption behavior. We've witnessed the invention of the suburban mall, the proliferation of direct-mail catalogs, and the introduction of concept stores. But these innovations were created and rolled out into the market over a period of years, not days. The speed at which online commerce alternatives have developed is extraordinarily different. The creativity, free offers, and gimmicks that have proliferated in the dot-com gold rush make consumers expect more, more, more, better, better, better, faster, faster, faster. The Web has created an impatient consumer with a short attention span and a low tolerance for mistakes.

This brings to mind a classic management theory called Herzberg's Hygiene-Motivation Theory[1]—one of those interesting business-school constructs of which the relevance to the real world of business might seem questionable. While the theory was developed to help organizations understand how to motivate employees, we believe the concept is quite helpful in comprehending the complexities of building e-business customer loyalty.

According to Herzberg, there are two categories of factors that influence human behavior: hygiene, or dissatisfiers; and motivators, or satisfiers. In Herzberg's context, hygiene factors are things like salary, working conditions, and job security. Motivators are factors such as recognition, advancement, and growth. He believed that hygiene factors must be present in the environment before motivators can be used to stimulate a person. The lack of hygiene factors creates dissatisfaction, but the presence of these factors is not enough to create satisfaction. Satisfaction is created by motivator factors. And, you cannot use motivators until all hygiene factors are satisfied. Net net: Employees cannot be motivated by recognition, chance for growth, and advancement until their more basic needs for things like salary, benefits, and security are met. By the same token, employees aren't satisfied with simply earning a salary—they want a chance to make their mark, to flourish.

Relating Hygiene-Motivation Theory to the Web world, we believe there are already online benefits that have quickly become so fundamental that they are now hygiene factors. Those e-commerce benefits are convenience, timesavings, information availability, and competitive prices. In the first few years of e-commerce, delivering these benefits could competitively set sites apart from the pack. Companies who consistently delivered these benefits built up loyalty among customers. Today, these benefits are no longer differentiators, and, if delivered stand-alone, will not win the loyalty of the newest batch of e-customers. Convenience, timesavings, rich information availability, and competitive prices have become basic requirements, as shown in figure 2.4.

Consumers expect the fundamental benefits to be delivered in every online experience. Absence of these benefits will create a dissatisfying Web experience and cause a Web site to be immediately eliminated from future consideration. Competitive prices and extensive product information are also expected. If Web sites are not at market parity in terms of convenience, timesavings, price savings, and information availability, they will fail. Potentially, doing a

FIGURE 2.4 E-BUSINESS HYGIENE/MOTIVATOR FACTORS

	Early Waves of New Consumers	Next Wave of New Consumers
HYGIENE/DISSATISFIERS	❑ Offering a Web site ❑ Enabling online transactions	❑ Low prices ❑ Convenience ❑ Easy-to-use ❑ Information rich
MOTIVATORS/SATISFIERS	❑ Low prices ❑ Convenience ❑ Easy-to-use ❑ Information rich	❑ ?????

significantly better job of saving people time and being more convenient can serve as motivators, but the comparative differences must be dramatic.

Other factors will become motivators, or satisfiers, those that cause consumers to be repeat customers and ultimately become loyal. Of course the big question is: What *are* the motivators in the Web world, and what will they be six months or a year from now? Unfortunately, there isn't a one-size-fits-all answer. It depends on the competitive environment, the profile of your target customer, the scarcity of alternatives to your value proposition in the market, and of course, how well you deliver a "better" experience.

The timeline is an important factor as well. What may have been solidly listed in the Web consumer motivator category one day, may be pushed the next day to the hygiene category because of a competitor's actions. The mix, balance, and originality of the motivator and hygiene factors change constantly.

THE IMPACT OF NOT DELIVERING E-BUSINESS HYGIENE FACTORS

MODERATOR: What do you do when a site fails to deliver convenience and timesavings benefits?

CONSUMER: I vote with my dollars. I'll never do business again with a Web site that burned me.

CONSUMER: It's simple. I just click to another site.

CONSUMER: I stop using them. For example, one site I used pretty often suddenly changed their navigation so much that I couldn't find my way around anymore. It was so confusing that I finally gave up. I haven't been back since.

The Impact of Disappointing Web Experiences on Customer Loyalty

As mentioned in chapter 1, most Web shoppers' recent experiences have met their expectations, and so disappointing experiences have not been overly pervasive. To illustrate our point, figure 2.5 shows that in the holiday 1999 shopping season, only 5 percent of shoppers say that their online disappointment was severe enough to keep them off the Internet permanently.

FIGURE 2.5: IMPACT OF BAD EXPERIENCES ON FUTURE ONLINE SHOPPING BEHAVIOR

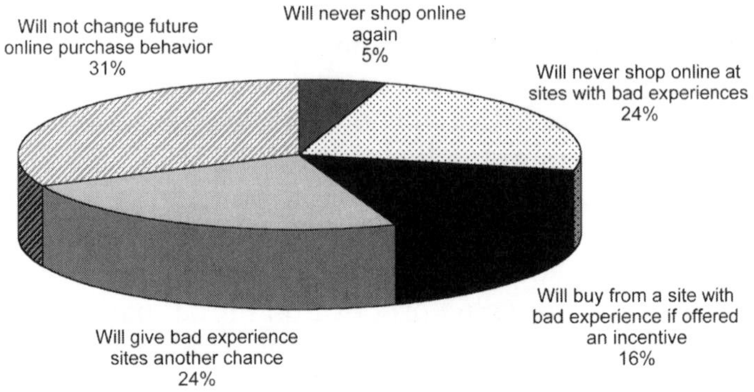

Will not change future online purchase behavior 31%
Will never shop online again 5%
Will never shop online at sites with bad experiences 24%
Will buy from a site with bad experience if offered an incentive 16%
Will give bad experience sites another chance 24%

Source: Pulse of the Customer

Most consumers continue to be committed to the Web as a commerce channel. Nonetheless, consumers have had disappointing experiences and those disappointments are having an impact on their future actions. What happens when Web sites fail to deliver on the basic benefits that consumers have come to expect? Some consumers are willing to give sites another chance, others are unforgiving.

THE UNFORGIVING NEW CONSUMER

Figure 2.5 shows that 24 percent of consumers claim they would never return to a site that disappointed them. This illustrates that customer loyalty was irretrievably lost among a substantial proportion of consumers for the specific sites that disappointed them. When a site lets them down, consumer confidence erodes. So, while consumers aren't giving up on the Web altogether, they boycott sites that have botched their shopping experiences. Moreover, they are very vocal among their colleagues about their bad experiences. So the damage done isn't just one lost customer, it's the negative word of mouth that emanates from the unhappy consumer.

Once a Web shopper is disappointed by a site, it is very difficult and costly to entice them to return

THE AMBIVALENT NEW CONSUMER

Consumers who are willing to extend benevolence toward Web glitches won't do so forever

Sixteen percent of new consumers we polled say they would only give the offending site another try if they were offered a significant incentive to do so, such as free shipping, a valuable coupon, or a free gift. This confirms conventional marketing wisdom that winning back a dissatisfied customer can be expensive. Once a Web shopper is disappointed by a site, it is very difficult and costly to entice them to return.

THE FORGIVING CONSUMER

Another 24 percent of consumers told us that they would give disappointing Web sites another chance, saying they recognized that the technology was new and that some system glitches were understandable. These shoppers also

WHEN EXPERIENCES GO BADLY

MODERATOR: What are some examples of when a Web site stopped being convenient and time efficient?

CONSUMER: If a site takes too long to load, I won't even hang around to see what it might have on it. I have an internal clock that tells me when I've waited too long, then I move on.

CONSUMER: The shopping cart feature was working, but the product screens kept freezing. It seemed like they had the 'buying' part working, but not the 'selling' part.

Consumer: The site was slow, looked funny, they were out of stock on the item I wanted, and then the site ended up crashing.

MODERATOR: Are we expecting too much? After all, shopping online is still pretty new.

CONSUMER: They should get it right. Once they screw up, if a site wants my business back, they should offer me an incentive to return. Whether it's free shipping or a purchase discount, it should be something significant, because they did something to lose my business in the first place.

CONSUMER: I'm not quite so unforgiving. I figure the technology is new and so I'm willing to deal with some of the problems I've encountered. I don't feel like I'll never visit those sites again.

anticipated that glitches would be addressed and resolved in the near future and that their overall Web experiences would improve going forward. This is an important message to all dot coms. Consumers who are willing to extend benevolence toward Web glitches won't do so forever. In fact, we believe that holiday 1999 was probably the last season of forgiveness—there will simply be too many alternative sites who get it right.

Loyalty in the Web Context

A frequently discussed topic among our clients and ourselves is whether loyalty can actually exist in the Web world. The answer to this question is not obvious—there is not a simple yes or no answer. Certainly as humans, new consumers have the capacity to be loyal and have loyalties in other aspects of their lives. But in the empowering environment of the Internet, achieving consumer allegiance to specific site brands is much more challenging. The choices are greater, the competitive sets are larger, and the consumers are adventuresome and experimental.

WEB SITE LOYALTY LOCK-UP

While it might dismay some e-retailers, especially those new to the market, many online shoppers already have established "favorite" Web sites in certain product categories. Not surprisingly, the categories that have the most brand loyalty locked up are those that were among the first on the scene with Web offerings: books, travel, and music. The companies that maneuvered a "first in" strategy online are reaping the rewards of loyal Web customers. Amazon, eBay, and other well-known sites lead the "favorite sites" list. As seen in figure 2.6, over half of our consumers report that they have established allegiance to their chosen Web sites for particular types of products or services. We believe these are the types of shoppers who are most motivated by convenience and timesavings ben-

E-businesses that maneuvered a "first in" strategy online are reaping the rewards of loyal Web customers

efits. They have grown accustomed to how their favorite sites work and there is not a strong enough reason for them to change their habitual behavior. Their loyalty is based on familiarity.

FIGURE 2.6: WEB SITE LOYALTY IS GROWING

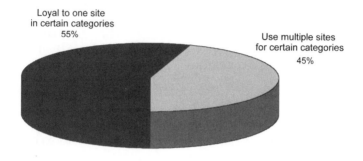

Source: Pulse of the Customer

When loyal consumers talk about what kinds of products they purchase from their favorite sites, i.e., the most popular sites mentioned above, there is a strong tendency to buy from the product categories with which the e-retailer is most traditionally branded. For example, Amazon customers go to Amazon.com more for books than for tools; CDNow.com more for CDs than for videos; and JCPenney.com more for apparel than for consumer electronics. Yahoo.com appears to have a "mall-like" appeal; although, overall, consumers report much lower shopping frequencies at Yahoo.com than at the top branded sites. New consumers tend to keep Web sites in the perceptual pigeonhole where they first began.

WHEN BRAND LOYALTY DOESN'T RESULT IN BRAND EXTENSION

Interestingly, while Amazon.com is a very popular site, some consumers put it on their "least favorite" lists. These consumers complain that Amazon.com had a poorer than expected selection in certain product categories, especially in the newer product categories it had recently added. In

Customer loyalty does not necessarily extend to other categories within one branded site

these cases, consumers report that Amazon.com delivered on expectations in their traditional product categories—books and music—but did not deliver on product depth and competitive prices in new categories, such as toys and electronics. We believe that customers who make these types of observations are motivated by pricing and product selection benefits, rather than by convenience. The ease-of-shopping benefits wrought by site familiarity did not offset the need for better prices and more product choices. (Amazon does report, however, that they are experiencing promising sales in new product categories.)

Based on our research, we believe that customer loyalty does not necessarily generalize and extend to other categories within one branded site for all customer segments. Some consumers resist accepting new product lines once brand experience has been established in one product area, even if, as in the case of Amazon.com, the brand is well established. As we observed above, the primary reason for this reluctance is that price and product selection can be more powerful purchase motivators than loyalty to a Web site brand for some groups of new consumers. If they are the type of customer that is motivated by price and selection benefits, even when they like and trust a brand, such as Amazon.com for books and music, they still comparison shop in other product categories. So, while brand awareness and credibility can help get customers to the site, competitive pricing and rich product selection are what wins sales—at least for some customers. For others, familiarity can make brand extension a winning proposition for e-businesses.

Fundamentally, brand loyalty extension is sabotaged by the empowerment virtues of the Web. When consumers have access to more information and wider price options, and when the barriers to switching are low, loyalty can become an irrelevant notion to the consumer. Therefore, we believe the jury is still out on Web site brand extensions.

PREFERENCES FOR ONLINE MALL VERSUS SPECIALTY SITES

Another reason for why Web site brand extension is being met with somewhat lukewarm acceptance has to do with people's preferences regarding the types of sites they patronize, i.e., electronic mall sites versus specialty sites. When consumers are queried about the type of online store they prefer, we find some fairly polarized views. On one end are people who shop online for convenience and improved productivity. On the other end are consumers who shop online for price and selection benefits.

Shoppers who use the Web for convenience and efficiency strongly prefer a one-stop or "mall-like" store because they feel it saves time and the environment becomes more familiar. They like the idea that they can find everything they want in one efficient shopping session—they can use the same shopping cart, enter the credit card number only once, conduct site-wide searches, and also combine shipping charges. For these shoppers, the electronic malls provide adequate selection and acceptable prices, attributes that are important hygiene factors but not motivators.

Other consumers strongly prefer focused specialty sites, which they perceive to offer a greater depth of product selection within specific categories, more product information, a wider range of price alternatives, and often better prices. If a site specializes in certain types of products, these consumers are more confident that they will find what they want and get all the information they need to make a purchase decision. And they believe that sites that specialize sell more volume of specific products, thus enabling products to be offered at greater discounts.

Some consumers simply don't see the benefits of a branded electronic mall, because on a macro level, the Web functions like a mall. As one consumer said: "To me, the Web is a mall. It's so easy to click from one site to another to find what you want—it's not like having to drive from place to place. If one site doesn't have what you want, go to another."

ENTICING LOYAL CUSTOMERS TO NEW BRANDS

Can loyal customers be lured away from the sites they patronize? The answer is that many customers can be enticed, if the delivery of the primary motivators is significantly better than where they actively shop. Our research indicates that Web companies do have an opportunity to entice customers away from the sites to which they are loyal by offering even *better* convenience, productivity, performance, price, and product selection, as well as other incentives. We believe, however, that consumers who use their favorite sites due to convenience and timesavings are very difficult to sway. Considering new sites takes time. And if they are not experiencing problems with sites they currently use, the incremental value derived from changing is perceived as non-existent. In fact, getting these consumers' attention can be challenging because they are neither actively nor passively considering alternative solutions.

Although some consumers claim that nothing would cause them to switch from a site to which they are loyal, others say that the use of incentives, recommendations from others, better content, a more user-friendly, accessible site, and faster downloading times could persuade them to try a new brand, as shown in figure 2.7. These are typically consumers whose primary e-shopping motivation is price- or deal-driven.

FIGURE 2.7: SWAYING THE WEB BRAND–LOYAL CUSTOMER

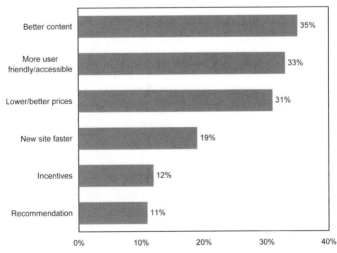

Note: Multiple responses possible.

Source: Pulse of the Customer

Interestingly, although pricing was not highly ranked in terms of creating brand loyalty as mentioned above, better or lower pricing is cited as a reason for potentially reviewing and/or switching Web sites. Lastly, there's always a group of adventuresome consumers who are lured away by the excitement of a discovery or a new experience.

ACTIONS THAT IMPACT LOYALTY

MODERATOR: What would make you switch site loyalty, when you are happy where you are today?

CONSUMER: Nothing. It's not worth the effort.

CONSUMER: I may be lured away by a competitor that had an irresistible incentive.

CONSUMER: If I found another site that provides better information or, in the case of a retail site, offers CONSISTENTLY better prices, I would switch.

CONSUMER: If the content is the same, then better presentation, style, and better search features can motivate me to switch to another site.

Consumers' comments illustrate that loyalties are different for different people. To be competitive, sites will be required to do better—however "better" is defined by the target customer. It also serves as fair warning to those established e-retailers that feel that their current level of performance will be good enough for the future customer. Motivators can quickly be relegated to hygiene factors.

TURNING OFF LOYAL CUSTOMERS

As you would anticipate, Web sites that don't deliver the expected positive user experience are in danger of losing customer loyalty. Consumers claim to abandon their preferred Web brands if the sites consistently fail to deliver the minimum requirements. Figure 2.8 demonstrates that poor performance, whether it is manifested as outdated or stale content, slow response times, technical problems, or difficult navigation, is the leading

Consumers quickly abandon their preferred Web brands if the sites consistently fail to deliver the minimum requirements

reason for Web site defection. These types of problems are directly correlated to expected benefits. If sites perform poorly and the content is too outdated to be useful, then the experience no longer delivers convenience.

FIGURE 2.8: HOW WEB SITES TURN OFF LOYAL CUSTOMERS

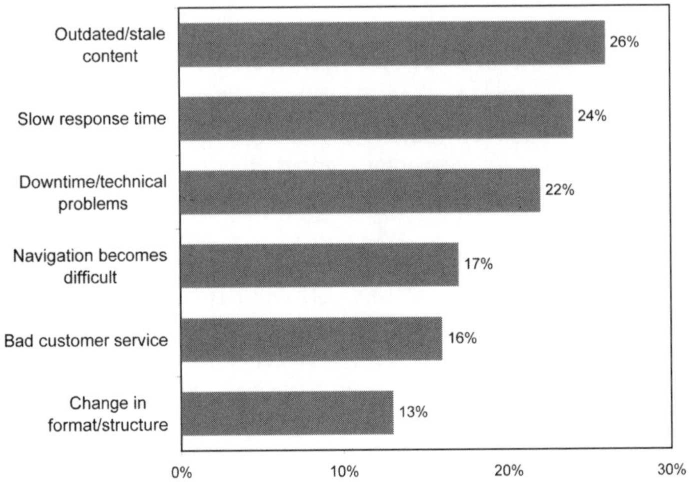

Note: Multiple responses possible.

Source: Pulse of the Customer

WINNING BACK LOST CUSTOMERS

Winning back lost customers can be a difficult, if not impossible, proposition. As shown in figure 2.5, almost 25 percent of the consumers we polled have had experiences so poor that they will never shop again at offending sites. Many say that very little could be done to woo them back. Consumers realize that they have many alternatives. Once disappointed, they see no reason to return when there are hoards of hungry dot coms vying for their patronage.

But, sometimes attempts to win back the disenchanted customer can be fruitful. As seen in figure 2.9, 19 percent of consumers indicate that special offers and incentives could be effective in influencing them to try an abandoned Web site again. In addition, if they hear via referrals from friends or independent reviews or have been assured by the offending company that the site has been changed to meet their needs, they may give it another try. Interestingly, many marketers have learned that the most loyal customers are those you have abused and won back. And often, recommitted customers are very positively vocal about businesses once they have returned to the fold. For this reason, e-businesses should get to know which customers they have lost and strive to win them back. This is not only good for sales, but also for generating positive word of mouth.

FIGURE 2.9: WINNING BACK LOST CUSTOMERS

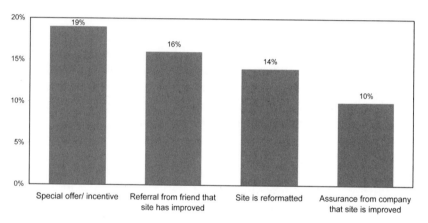

Note: Multiple responses possible.

Source: Pulse of the Customer

WINNING BACK LOST CUSTOMERS

MODERATOR: If a site seriously disappoints you, what can they do to win back your loyalty?

CONSUMER: Nothing!

CONSUMER: There is not much that can make me return. However, if a friend told me that the site improved, I might revisit it.

CONSUMER: An incentive, such as a gift or a personalized letter, stating the site has new management and would like to be given one more try . . . might make me revisit a site.

CONSUMER: An e-mail incentive, such as free shipping for the next order might entice me to return.

As we have seen, loyalty in the Web context is a complex subject: it has to be earned one category and one experience at a time. This will be an interesting phenomenon to track as new consumers become more experienced and as the dot-com market goes through its inevitable consolidation.

Emerging Market Segments

Since the beginning of market analysis, numerous theories have been developed about how to group consumers into addressable segments based on common attributes so that strategies and programs could be developed to effectively market to them. Companies have identified and targeted customers based on common elements, such as age groups, neighborhoods, income brackets, and educational levels. Some believe the market divides into identifiable, addressable segments based on lifestyle. For example, Claritas, a marketing information company that invented a geodemographic clustering system called PRIZM, has identified sixty-two lifestyle clusters in the United States. They believe that these clusters encompass everyone in our population.[2] This clustering technique has been useful to many marketers in the analog world.

Other theorists believe that the market fragments into strictly individualized segments and that the best loyalty building strategy is a one-to-one approach[3]—developing offers through the analysis of customer information that are tailored to customers' unique needs. This theory purports that market segmentation and target market schemes of one-to-many are not effective in satisfying modern consumers' demands.

Applying targeting techniques in the Web environment is essential to creating focused value propositions and, hopefully, new consumer loyalty. In many ways, the same targeting principles of the offline world apply in the online world. After all, new consumers are still people with demographic and lifestyle characteristics, and they buy things that meet their unique requirements. So, developing and emphatically targeting online value propositions to selected segments is the formula for success in e-business, just as it is in the analog world.

Among new consumers, however, there are other dimensions of segmentation that layer on top of the more conventional methods of target marketing. We find that new consumers subdivide based on the key benefits they get from the Web—the perceived primary benefit derived from Web usage. In other words, e-customers form groupings, or clusters, based on why they use the Web. Other cluster criteria, such as demographic and psychographic attributes, are secondary to the primary benefit. And these clusters reconfigure for different types of products and services. So, it isn't enough to know that you are, for example, targeting Generation X—PRIZM's "money and brains" cluster—you also need to know what floats their Web boat, so to speak. Why are they using the Web?

Among new consumers, there are other dimensions of segmentation that layer on top of the more conventional methods of targeting

In addition, new consumers are clustered based on how long and how extensively they have been using the Web. More experienced Web consumers act differently than neophytes. We believe that understanding customers in both of these dimensions is critical to creating and delivering the most meaningful offer to new consumers.

Putting the consumer segmenting constructs in context, we believe the hierarchy is as follows, in this sequence:

1. WHY THEY ARE ON THE WEB. Benefit segmentation tells us what draws new consumers to the Web in the first place and why they use the Web instead of their alternatives.
2. WHERE THEY ARE ON THE LEARNING CURVE. Experience segmentation tells us how anxious, adventuresome, and seasoned the new consumers are as shoppers.
3. WHAT THEY BUY. Traditional methods of clustering, such as demographic, socioeconomic, and psychographic, help target product offerings based on consumer characteristics, as does one-to-one marketing.

Knowing why the new consumer is on the Web is a critical step in understanding how to attract him and build his loyalty. Without appealing to new consumers at the benefit level, you'll never get closer to them and you'll never get the opportunity to sell them anything—regardless of how well your offers fit their profiles.

BENEFIT SEGMENTATION

As the Web becomes more important to a larger proportion of the population, online benefit-oriented segments become more pronounced. Increasingly, we are seeing this mainstream market form into identifiable market segments, based on why and how these consumers buy online. We have also noted that online, people behave differently in different categories of products and services; therefore, they are not the same in every dimension of their online activities. The benefit-oriented segments we have identified include:

- Convenience Shoppers
- Price-Sensitive Shoppers
- Comparison Shoppers
- Brand Loyal Shoppers
- Focused Shoppers
- Storefront-Adverse Shoppers

THE CONVENIENCE SHOPPER

As in the analog world, there are Convenience Shoppers in cyberspace. Convenience Shoppers usually shop at the same sites, for the same product categories because they are familiar with the sites and it saves them time to shop that way. These consumers don't want to fill out a profile on more than one type of site or learn a new navigational interface, even if it means paying more for the same products. These shoppers are time deprived and value their time more than money—at least to some extent. And for many categories of products and services—especially for commodities like books, music, air travel, and stock trading—these customers don't value the incremental benefits or price savings that might be derived by site switching.

Convenience Shoppers are time deprived and often value their time more than money

We believe that many Convenience Shoppers were among the early

Web users. This is why pioneers like Amazon have a first-in advantage among these consumers. They were initially drawn to the Web due to their time deprivation, and because they were more affluent, they were less concerned about price. Many of these early shoppers have never changed their site loyalties since their original shopping forays. Getting these habituated loyalists to change is very difficult. This group is an excellent target for brand-extension strategies in sites they currently favor.

We expect this group to get proportionately smaller as the Web penetrates early and late majority segments of the population because the next wave of new consumers will be motivated by benefits other than convenience.

THE CONVENIENCE SHOPPER—TYPICAL COMMENTS

MODERATOR: When you pick a Web site to patronize, what are the main benefits you seek?

CONSUMER: I just want to have one site where I can shop for what I want. I don't want to bother going to different sites and having to give my billing and shipping information over and over again.

CONSUMER: Returning to one site means saving time. There is no need to get familiar with the navigation or the shopping mechanism. Best of all, the site remembers who I am. I don't waste time entering my personal information.

MODERATOR: Don't you ever look around at other sites, at least out of curiosity?

CONSUMER: To tell the truth, I tend to use one site by force of habit.

CONSUMER: If the site provides what I'm looking for, I will stick with it.

THE PRICE-SENSITIVE SHOPPER

Plainly described, Price-Sensitive Shoppers almost always choose sites based on which offer the lowest prices. Price-Sensitive Shoppers will switch sites they buy from if they learn of a better price on another site. This type of consumer will go to a different book site, for example, if she learns that a book is as little as one dollar cheaper on a different site.

Price-Sensitive Shoppers will switch sites they buy from if they learn of a better price on another site

Price-Sensitive Shoppers are not deterred by the inconvenience of learning how to use a new site functionality or by completing the profile forms on new sites, if a better price is the prize. Online coupons, rebates, and other incentives appeal to this crowd. Because of attention from the media about low-price gimmicks on the Web, the general impression may be that all Web shoppers are price-sensitive. In fact, Price-Sensitive Shoppers do not make up the majority of the market. They are, however, an important market segment to address.

We expect to see this group become a proportionately larger segment of the new consumer population with the next wave of Web adoption. As the Web becomes more mainstream, we anticipate that Price-Sensitive Shoppers will become more numerous.

THE PRICE-SENSITIVE SHOPPER—TYPICAL COMMENTS

MODERATOR: What makes you choose the sites where you shop?

CONSUMER: I always look for the lowest price. Even if it's only a dollar difference, the better price matters to me.

CONSUMER: If you give me a big enough discount, I'll buy anything.

MODERATOR: Are products really cheaper on the Internet?

CONSUMER: Yeah, I would say a lot of times, you get 50 percent off of a lot of stuff.

CONSUMER: I buy a lot of books and gifts on the Internet because it is a lot cheaper.

CONSUMER: It depends on what it is.

MODERATOR: What kinds of products and services do you think you're getting at a better price on the Internet?

CONSUMER: Airline tickets are significantly lower.

CONSUMER: Books. They are amazingly cheap.

CONSUMER: Software, greeting cards, office supplies.

THE COMPARISON SHOPPER

Another customer segment that we see in our research are the Comparison Shoppers—those people who love to shop and get a kick out of finding the best deal. They like to extensively compare product offers before deciding from which site to buy. The deal is defined as the whole product: the price, the selection, the shipping charges, and the special promotional offers. And the best deal, by the way, may not necessarily be the cheapest deal.

Comparison Shoppers are close relations to Price-Sensitive Shoppers, but a little different, because they don't always pick the lowest-price alternatives. Comparison Shoppers enjoy the thrill of the hunt. And the Web is a perfect adventure for them.

Comparison Shoppers enjoy the thrill of the hunt, and the Web is a perfect adventure for them

The power of having information to compare their options is a great turn-on for these consumers, and sites that don't offer enough information to enable comparisons are dismissed from the shortlist.

We expect the Comparison Shopper segment to become a larger proportion of the new consumer population as late majority shoppers come online.

THE COMPARISON SHOPPER—TYPICAL COMMENTS

MODERATOR: Tell me about how you like to shop online.

CONSUMER: Sometimes I'll visit dozens of sites to make sure I've got the product I want at the best price. I always comparison shop, and that's why I like shopping on the Internet. I can comparison shop 'til I drop, and never get out of my chair.

MODERATOR: Is it really worth all that trouble? Do you always get a better deal?

CONSUMER: That's why I like to shop online. I can find products, compare prices, and pick the best deal.

CONSUMER: Sometimes I won't pick the site that offers the lowest price. But getting to see all my options and compare them, that's what I really like. It's the principle more than the price.

THE BRAND LOYAL SHOPPER

Another segment we see in our research is the Brand Loyal segment, a group of consumers who tend to buy from the same brand sites habitually because they trust and like sites. These shoppers become loyal to the brands they trust and are not interested in changing. They would rather "fight than switch" because they are comfortable with the sites where they buy, the value proposition is acceptable, and buying from a lesser-known site is undesir-

Brand Loyal Shoppers become loyal to the brands they trust and are not interested in switching

able. These shoppers select sites based on their familiarity with the brand. They are reticent to buy from sites they don't know.

The Brand Loyal Shopper is closely related to the Convenience Shopper, but more conservative in terms of needing name recognition of brands to feel comfortable. Unwillingness to switch brands is more about comfort than convenience. This group may favor offline brands, which come online with credible offerings. Brand Loyal Shoppers are also excellent targets for brand extension strategies of dot-com companies. We expect this group will increase as more newbie Web consumers begin shopping online, especially among those in the early phases of the Web experience curve.

THE BRAND LOYAL SHOPPER—TYPICAL COMMENTS

MODERATOR: You say you are brand loyal in certain categories. Why?

CONSUMER: I don't want to jump brand loyalties because I don't want to learn about something new. And if you deliver a good product, at a fair price, I'm not going to change because it's too much effort.

CONSUMER: I guess you'd say I'm loyal to Amazon—it was the very first online purchase for me. I haven't had any problems with them. I haven't compared prices anywhere.

MODERATOR: How important is the brand in your choice of Web sites?

CONSUMER: I find that I've started using Web sites of brands I know and trust as catalogs or retail stores—like Lands' End, L.L.Bean, or Neiman's. I know the store, I know their catalog, and I feel confident that the quality is there.

THE FOCUSED SHOPPER

Focused Shoppers are consumers who approach e-shopping with a mission. They are almost clinical about their online shopping excursions. They go to specific Web sites with the intent to buy specific products. They select the product, make a transaction, and move on. These consumers claim to not respond to online offers, ignore banner ads, and tend to be oblivious to other attempts at getting them to stray from their task.

Focused Shoppers go to specific Web sites with the intent to buy specific products

Focused Shoppers are a hybrid of people who shop for convenience and people who dislike shopping in general. They are not curious about deals or offers. They don't take the time to look for the lowest prices. They are very utilitarian in their shopping behavior. We expect the proportion of Focused Shoppers to be roughly the same among the next wave of new consumers.

THE FOCUSED SHOPPER–TYPICAL COMMENTS

MODERATOR: How would you describe your shopping behavior?
CONSUMER: When I shop on the Internet, I have some specific thing that I want to research and buy.
CONSUMER: I'm a pretty directed shopper. I know exactly what I'm looking for with a specific person in mind.
MODERATOR: Why do you like to buy online?
CONSUMER: It's ideal for me. I can go to a specific site and order what I want.
CONSUMER: I know exactly what I want. I go right online and I get it. It's simple.

THE STOREFRONT-ADVERSE SHOPPER

For some consumers, going to a retail store is a dreaded experience, one that is endured only when absolutely necessary. They dislike crowds, find the environment overwhelming, and basically dislike the act of shopping. This is the Storefront-Adverse segment. Storefront-Adverse Shoppers shop online because they hate shopping in retail stores. For these people, the Web provides a welcome relief and, in fact, turns a dreaded experience into an enjoyable one.

We believe that this group will continue in their current proportions among new consumers. They may be

Storefront-Adverse Shoppers dislike the physical act of shopping and the Web provides a welcome relief good targets for Web site brands that are extending their brand to new product categories, as well as for brick-and-mortar companies that are extending their brand online.

THE STOREFRONT-ADVERSE SHOPPER—TYPICAL COMMENTS

MODERATOR: Why don't you like going to retail stores?

CONSUMER: I don't like to shop. It's tiring. It's time consuming. I don't have a car so carrying packages is a hassle. But shopping online is different. I can sit down at my computer at home, go through sites, and find what I'm looking for. In the long run, it might even take a little bit longer than going to a store. I don't care. At least I'm sitting down at home.

CONSUMER: I hate going to stores. When I'm walking through a store I feel like a zombie aimlessly walking around and looking at stuff. So my main motivation for online shopping is to keep myself out of stores.

TIME-PHASED MARKET SEGMENTS

As discussed in chapter 1, we have noted that the amount of experience consumers have on the Web has an impact on their online behavior. Therefore, another way of understanding the new consumer segments is based on their experience levels, as shown in figure 2.10.

THE ANXIOUS SHOPPER

The newbie online consumer tends to play it safe and avoids treading into waters that are uncharted. We call consumers in this group Anxious Shoppers. These people lack the confidence in their ability to use the Internet successfully and are fearful that something will go wrong. Still in the earliest days of their Internet adoption, they are not yet shoppers, as they are still too fearful to buy anything online. Consumers in this group are the target customers of America Online, which designs its site to be easy, friendly, and comprehensive in terms of content, functionality, and features. The Anxious Shopper, who never dares to venture

FIGURE 2.10: THE NEW CONSUMER SEGMENTS BASED ON EXPERIENCE LEVEL

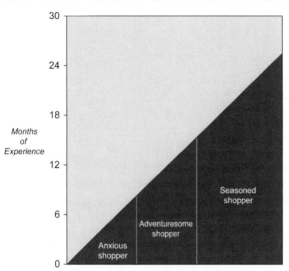

beyond AOL, can become a shopper within the confines of the AOL experience. The goal of AOL is to provide a home that the Anxious Shopper never has to leave. Some Anxious Shoppers, in fact, reach a comfort level and never venture outside the safety net of this familiar environment. Others build their confidence, overcome their apprehensions, and venture out into the wide world of the Web.

THE ADVENTURESOME SHOPPER

We term consumers with newfound confidence and freedom Adventuresome Shoppers. These consumers are confident in their abilities to explore and are free to roam. They enjoy the benefits of the Web: product selection, cost savings, and convenience. They revel in the empowerment they have discovered. Adventuresome Shoppers talk about the Web with their friends, they notice billboards, scan ads, and read Web site reviews. They are seeking sites that will provide a higher potency of benefits—better prices, better selection, and more convenience. As these shoppers increase their expertise and experience levels, they develop strong preferences and habitual behavior. At this point, they cross into the Seasoned Shopper segment.

THE SEASONED SHOPPER

Seasoned Shoppers are solidly entrenched in their Web behavior, they have been using the Web for several years, the Web is highly integrated into their lives, and they spend a significant amount of time using it. As discovered in a study conducted by Stanford University,[4] people spend more hours on the Internet the more years they have been using it. Seasoned Shoppers have strong preferences on how, when, and why they use the Web. They have routine activities for which they always use it, such as reading news, tracking stocks, communicating with colleagues, and shopping for certain types of products and services.

The Seasoned Shopper can be intrigued by new sites, and is less dependent on positive recommendations from friends to try new things. This shopper is also more likely to use advanced technologies to make their online experiences more productive, such as profiling, shopping bots, and digital wallets. Seasoned Shoppers are also more intolerant of spam and other online promotional schemes, because their longevity of Internet use causes them to be subjected to many untargeted and unwanted offers. It is important to appeal to the Seasoned Shopper, not just because of the opportunity to sell to them, but because these are often the opinion leaders who make recommendations to their less-experienced friends.

Implications for Business

Attracting and retaining larger volumes of customers requires online brands to remain devotedly customer-centric, as Web users continue to demand more from their Web experiences. The emergence of these segments, and those that will follow, are a clear indication that online retailers must work to comprehend the factions within their target consumer base and consistently deliver to their specific demands. The implications for e-businesses are significant. A one-size-fits-all Web strategy will not fly among the increasingly diverse Web shopping audience. E-businesses must identify their target customers and offer value proposi-

A one-size-fits-all Web strategy will not fly among the increasingly diverse Web shopping audience

tions that will appeal to their unique audiences. One may choose to address multiple segments, but realize that the same offerings and commerce approach will not appeal to all shoppers. Shotgunning the entire market—meaning trying to be all things to all people—will be increasingly challenging as greater proportions of the mass market come online. Not focusing may result in hitting no volume market at all.

We also believe, however, that the practice of one-to-one marketing is, pragmatically, as flawed as a one-size-fits-all approach. While, in theory, providing uniquely tailored offers to customers based on their preferences is compelling, the obstacles to executing this vision are often too overwhelming. One of the discouraging realities of one-to-one marketing is that targeted offers are only as effective as the quality of data available on the target consumers. Increasingly, consumers are reticent to provide the kind of personal information that is needed to make compelling offers, due to fears of exploitation. And the information that is obtainable—that which gives a history of previous e-purchases—is often irrelevant to future purchase needs. Making promotional offers to customers based on their past behavior is like navigating a car by looking in the rearview mirror. There's only a historical view and since Web customers' attitudes change very quickly, relying on history can be misleading.

As one consumer expressed it, "Human beings aren't databases. We change our preferences all the time. If Web businesses are customizing sites based on our past behavior, then they've really limited their ability to change and make choices, which is the natural tendency of humans."

In addition, most e-businesses today are not prepared to create truly unique and special offers for individual consumers based on consumer profile information. In fact, most companies are still only capable of offering relatively simple solutions based on customer preference data. Truly creating uniquely customized offers to target individuals requires better data—not just about the customer's preferences, but about the products as well. Maintaining the required intelligence about product sales histories, customer responses to promotional offers on those products, and matching product features to customers' benefits requirements goes well beyond most companies' current data mining competencies. And most companies are not prepared to make uniquely different product offers to individual customers due to product manufacturing limitations. As a result, under the moniker of one-to-one marketing, most companies are still delivering a one-to-many value proposition.

CONCLUSION

All Web retailers must provide those components that create a good consumer experience to establish Web brand loyalty and remain competitive. Internet shoppers have indicated that they will accept nothing less. How well individual Web brands meet these customer expectations will determine who keeps users loyal, and who will fall prey to more savvy competitors that lure customers away by offering more of what they want online. The game is just beginning. The struggle to acquire and retain customers will define the e-marketplace of the future. And as more new consumers enter the market, due to the stepped-up efforts of corporations and governments to give more United States citizens Internet access, understanding consumer segmentation and tailoring Web experiences to their relative needs will separate winners from losers.

E-businesses must understand new consumers in multiple dimensions: the motivating benefits of Web usage and consumer experience levels with the Web, as well as more traditional targeting characteristics. E-businesses should also realize that when viewing the new consumer population from a benefit orientation, the proportion of these shoppers will shift as more people come online. Early adopters of the Web embraced the vehicle due to time deprivation. Classically more affluent, their loyalties were won based on convenience and familiarity. We predict, however,

The struggle to acquire and retain customers will define the e-marketplace of the future

that as a wider range of demographic profiles join the Web-initiated, segments such as the Price-Sensitive Shoppers and the Comparison Shoppers will become more prevalent. Loyalty-building strategies and tactics should be adjusted to appeal to the soul of the *new* new consumer.

3

The Challenges of Driving Traffic, Closing Sales, and Retaining Online Customers

As any business professional knows, the fundamental reasons for marketing are to attract prospects, convert them to customers, and retain them for life. Marketing is not only tasked with succeeding in that basic cycle, but with making it happen as rapidly and cost-efficiently as possible. It's not enough to get a prospect's attention and induce them to take your offer. The marketer ultimately only succeeds if he has created a brand-loyal customer—one that is committed to purchasing your brand time after time, regardless of competitors' actions.

The key question that e-business marketers are grappling with is: in this age of new consumers, does that kind of brand loyalty exist? As we discussed in chapter 2, traditional customer loyalty seems to be on the road to extinction, at least for many e-customers. New consumers are being clustered into benefit-oriented segments that define which sites they patronize and to which they *might* be loyal. Early adopters of the Web who were time-deprived and affluent exhibited loyal behavior to sites that were familiar, while price sensitivity was of secondary importance. But as more people come online, other segments are emerging that are motivated by low prices and deals, and that patronize whomever offers the best price—a loyalty attribute and differentiator that is almost impossible for any dot com to sustain.

Thus the *new* new consumers represent a greater marketing challenge than the first wave of adopters. The competitive

The effectiveness of marketing will ultimately make or break the e-business

environment is fierce, and newly empowered customers are lured away by cheaper prices, better offers, and compelling Web experiences. And yet, e-business marketers must continue the uphill battle of attracting prospects, converting them to customers, and retaining them for life. The endgame hasn't changed, but the mountain is steeper— the battles are bloodier, and the outcome is more ephemeral.

In fact, we believe that the role of marketing has not only become decidedly more difficult, it has also become more critical to success—indeed, to survival—in the world of e-business. We are playing a business game that is not just about a better Web site or a better online experience. The effectiveness of marketing will ultimately make or break the e-business.

In this chapter we look at how the topline goals of marketing have changed in e-business. We examine the importance of building online consumer confidence for e-business success and the necessity of marketing in creating confidence. We analyze how marketing strategies differ in attracting and retaining Web consumers, as compared to more traditional business environments. We review what online consumers say about the effectiveness of marketing communications and promotional vehicles. And we discuss the emergence of a new phenomenon we see in the Web world: customer entitlements.

How Marketing Is Different in the Web World

In the Web world marketing is different in many important ways. Why? Because the consumer comes to the online world with a different set of fears, attitudes, and expectations than they have in other aspects of their consumption. The fundamental marketing challenges continue to exist—attracting prospects, closing sales, and retaining customers. But there are several unique attributes of e-business that make the process of marketing substantially more difficult than it is in other business environments. The first has to do with the need to create consumer confidence. The second relates to customer retention.

THE CONFIDENCE GAME

There's a basic e-business condition that is true for all dot coms: they don't exist in a way that consumers can physically validate. In cyberspace, consumers can't really see the credibility of the Web brand. There is no physical context for the company. While new consumers can see the Web site, they can't see the company behind it. They don't know the business practices of the company, the authenticity of their claims, or the legitimacy of the value proposition. They have to take it on faith that what a Web site says it will do is in fact what they *will* do. That's a very different situation, as compared to the ways consumers conducted the consumption part of their lives prior to the Internet.

This was a challenge that the direct marketing industry faced when the practice of direct sales advertisements was introduced to the market. The barriers to entry were very low. All a company needed to do was to design an ad and buy space in a print publication. Because the barriers were low, virtually anyone could claim to be a business with a compelling value proposition. Consumers had no proof of credibility of companies' claims and were reluctant to buy. That reluctance was reinforced when trusting consumers were defrauded by fly-by-night businesses.

While the direct marketing business succeeded in the catalog industry for years, the direct-response advertising business was different. The physical catalogs provided some sense of credibility for the companies who mailed them, even though the consumer literally couldn't *see* the company. The consumer knew that there were some barriers to entry: the cost of printing and mailing catalogs can be significant. But the direct-response advertising business took years to get traction and build the trust of consumers because there was no physical proof of credibility. Trust was required for the transaction to take place—a condition that takes many years to develop.

There are many parallels in the kinds of market development challenges the direct-response advertising industry initially faced and those confronting e-businesses today. While the costs of creating a Web site far outweigh the

Dot coms don't exist in a way that consumers can physically validate

costs of creating and placing a print ad (for serious e-businesses) there are still ways that companies can put up Web sites with little investment, and consumers know that.

Consumers are becoming increasingly savvy about the Web, and feel confident about online commerce in general. However, believing in the credibility of the specific brand is a hurdle that all Web shoppers must clear the first time they do business with a new Web site. Moreover, it's a hurdle that consumers must be able to clear every time they do business with a Web site if that e-business is to retain them as customers.

Because of the new and virtual nature of the Web, building consumer confidence is an important overarching goal of e-business marketing. Marketing programs such as advertising, PR, and promotions carry the burden of proving the company is for real, creating trust in the brand, and building an image of stability and credibility. While one could argue that these have always been objectives of marketing, in the Web world it should be considered a dramatically more critical marketing objective than in the analog world. Marketing strategies and expenditures should be made accordingly.

To illustrate our point, let's contrast the first-time opening of a specialty storefront versus the launch of a new Web site. Let's assume that the storefront and the Web site both offer the same products, brands, and prices, and are launching at the same time. When a new store opens in the physical world, marketing plays the vital role of making people aware of the new store, hooking their interest in it, and driving traffic into the store. Communications vehicles, such as newspaper advertising, direct mail, and local publicity, are used to build awareness of the new store and to encourage people to visit. Promotional vehicles such as grand opening events, special prices, and free gifts are used to entice people to come visit, thus pulling traffic into the store.

Once the consumers are in the store, they judge for themselves if the store truly delivers on the promises made in the advertisements. They make that judgment based on the appearance of the store, the style of its merchandising techniques, and the physical quality of the goods being sold. The physical store carries the burden of proving the enterprise's ability to deliver on the promised value proposition; the store has substance, and, thus, credibility. The physical act of successfully purchasing and carrying products home legitimizes the existence of the new enterprise. The proof is in the physical experience. In other words, consumers might walk away not being very impressed, but they don't walk away from a new retail store wondering whether it truly existed.

In contrast, the launch of a new Web site—with the same products, quality, and prices—is very different. Marketing communications vehicles must still serve the role of building awareness, piquing interest, and driving traffic, but there's another critical dimension. Marketing has to build a solid impression in the mind of the consumer that the Web site will credibly deliver what it says it will deliver, when it says it will deliver it, and that it won't rip people off. Marketing has to convince consumers that the new Web site is legitimate.

Consumers are savvy enough to realize that they can't judge a company's legitimacy by its Web site; they know the barriers to creating a Web site are low. Anybody can do it. Anybody can say they deliver. An ethical company and a fraudulent company can look the same when viewed through a browser. Anybody can be fooled, at least once. Interestingly, while the Web is becoming a widely accepted commerce vehicle, the need to build consumer confidence will increase because the next wave of new consumers will be less adventuresome, less affluent, and more technology averse than the Web consumers we have known to date.

How do you get the vote of confidence from these new consumers? Clearly, you must deliver what you promise, so that word of mouth is

Marketing has to convince consumers that a new Web site is legitimate

NEW SITE ANXIETY

MODERATOR: Did you ever worry about whether or not your online shopping was going to work or whether you could count on it?

CONSUMER: I was really worried because of all the bad publicity. For instance, at Christmas, some sites were saying they couldn't make the deadlines, so I was concerned whether or not they could really deliver.

CONSUMER: I ordered a video for my father from a sort of obscure site, so I didn't know if I'd actually get the video or not. I wasn't sure if they were for real. Even though it wasn't that much money, I was really taking a risk with my credit card. And since it was Dad's Christmas present, I was risking not having something for him on the big day.

MODERATOR: What makes you feel better about online shopping now versus a year ago?

CONSUMER: Positive word of mouth, just in general. So many people seem to be shopping online these days. If you don't do it, you're kind of out of it.

CONSUMER: Before, the Internet was still in its infancy and you were always hearing about credit cards getting stolen and things like that. You don't hear about those problems much anymore, so I feel that online shopping is safer. I've gotten over being worried.

CONSUMER: Everything is better now. I notice that things are quicker on the Internet. There are more choices, more Web sites, more sales, and better prices.

CONSUMER: I worry about going to new sites, too. But I feel better about shopping online now than I did last year.

MODERATOR: What makes you feel better about specific sites?

CONSUMER: Some of the sites have customer ratings where people can actually get on and put ratings in. There's always one camp of people who are real jazzed about what they've bought. But I look for the negative things. And if there are products that don't have anyone griping about them, it makes me feel better than seeing all the glowing reports.

CONSUMER: If I see it listed in a newspaper or a magazine article that says, "Try this site; it's great," then I feel better, particularly if it's in the business section. If it's creating a buzz. That'll pique my interest.

CONSUMER: When the site says, "This is a secure site. Do you want to continue?" It makes me feel more secure.

CONSUMER: I just won't go any place that I really haven't been referred to. That's a big thing. I will look and check out prices, but I'm not going to buy unless I've spoken with someone who has actually bought there.

positive. You must use advertising to create a sense of presence and substance. And, you must actively and relentlessly work the influencer community—including press, analysts, and luminaries—so that the site is positively reviewed and recommended. Marketing has to spend big and spend wisely to build consumer confidence. But the most important first step is to realize that creating confidence is the challenge. Which marketing vehicles to use and when to use them are the subjects of subsequent sections in this chapter.

THE CUSTOMER RETENTION GAME

The other major area in e-business in which marketing challenges are more daunting than in traditional business situations is customer retention. We believe that customer retention in the Web world is more difficult, more expensive, and more cutthroat than any other business environment in history. Is customer retention in the Web world really more difficult and expensive than in the analog world? Are online consumers more fickle than other customers? Does the lack of a personal relationship and consumer anonymity in the online environment contribute to decreased loyalty? Does it matter which benefit segment they identify with? The answers are yes, yes, yes, and yes.

There are really two primary reasons for the online customer retention problem. One is that the Web empowers people, giving them ready access to more choices—and they like that. The second is a market condition that the gold-rush, venture capital, IPO, dot-com frenzy created for itself. Simply put, there's been too much money chasing too few online consumers, in too short a time period.

In the frenetic attempts to drive consumers to the Web and encourage trial usage of their Web sites, well-funded dot coms have quickly and exponentially raised the bar on what they are willing to pay to acquire customers. It's not just that multimillion-dollar advertising campaigns have become the norm. Online consumers have been given

Customer retention in the Web world is more difficult, more expensive, and more cutthroat than in any other business environment

There's been too much money chasing too few online consumers, in too short a time period

all kinds of free stuff as rewards for their first-time purchases: free shipping, free gifts, big discounts. Some sites even pay consumers to read online ads!

The vast amount of capital available to dot coms has created a market condition that's unnatural to our capitalistic system. These promotional offers don't need to make good business sense in any near-term time horizon; dot coms are not attempting to be profitable or necessarily to break even at this phase in their market development. They just need to build a customer base and show their investors some trendlines toward profitability.

The double whammy of consumers loving their new-found empowerment on the Web, and the ever-seductive promotional offers made by dot coms desperate to show positive sales direction, has created a situation that makes customer retention nearly impossible. There's always a competitive dot com that is willing to buy a customer with short-term offers that the consumer cannot refuse—even though the dot com can't afford to sustain the offers in the midterm. The customer is effectively enticed, because there are no barriers to brand switching on the Web. It's convenient to change. There are no personal relationships to give up, no guilt of desertion. All it takes to switch sites is a few extra minutes to key in a new credit card number, shipping address, and other essential transaction information, and it's done. The new consumer is in control and they can win in a big way. It's inevitable that there will be e-business casualties, however, because customer retention in this market landscape is untenably and unsustainably expensive.

Where will it all end? Will customer retention overtake customer acquisition in terms of marketing spending? Will companies have to buy customer loyalty in *every* transaction? Will the mad frenzy to acquire customers dissipate as the industry matures and consolidates? How can dot coms afford customer retention once the funds from the investment community are exhausted? These are some of the questions that should be giving e-business executives sleepless nights.

To better understand the soul of the new consumer and how to market to him in this wild and crazy Web world, we find it useful to examine the process that people undergo when making purchase decisions. Regardless of the types of products or services a consumer is purchasing, there are common phases they experience before coming to a final decision.

First, we'll look at the traditional model of consumer-purchasing decision making and what marketing strategies were appropriate and when prior to the advent of the Web. Then we will focus on how the decision-making process has changed in the online world and the marketing strategies required to survive in this new consumer age.

The Consumer Purchase Decision Cycle— A Quick Review of the Basic Model

There are basically six stages in an individual's purchase decision cycle. This cycle applies to buying just about everything—cars, clothes, toys. As shown in figure 3.1, the steps in the cycle are both from the consumer's and the merchant's point of view, representing the actions consumers take as they move through the purchase decision process, as well as the actions merchants take in winning customers. There are variations on the theme—sometimes steps are collapsed or skipped. But basically the steps are sequential behavioral stepping-stones along the way to a purchase.

FIGURE 3.1: THE TRADITIONAL CONSUMER PURCHASE DECISION CYCLE

STIMULATE	CONSIDER	SEARCH	CHOOSE	BUY	BUY AGAIN
Consumer Behavior: First realize need	Consumer Behavior: Collect ideas for potential solutions	Consumer Behavior: Choose category	Consumer Behavior: Make selection	Consumer Behavior: Make purchase transaction	Consumer Behavior: Repurchase as needed
Merchant Goal: Raise awareness	Merchant Goal: Get on list of alternatives	Merchant Goal: Differentiate within category	Merchant Goal: Differentiate within category and get chosen	Merchant Goal: Deliver on promise	Merchant Goal: Ensure positive experience to achieve repeat purchases

Historically, this traditional marketing model has been helpful when developing strategies and programs because it clarifies the consumer actions we are attempting to motivate throughout the decision-making process. It also gives guidance about which marketing vehicles can be most effective to prod people through the cycle. We believe, however, that marketing to e-customers necessitates some changes to traditional marketing. To understand how marketing in the Web world is different, let's refresh our memories by briefly looking at this classic marketing model.

In the Stimulate stage, the consumer first discovers he has a need and that there are ways to satisfy that need. The role of marketing in this step is to raise awareness among consumers that the marketer's company can provide a solution to satisfy the consumer's need. Typically, marketing vehicles such as advertising, direct mail, and trend stories in the press are most effective in the Stimulate stage of the cycle.

The next stage is the Consider stage. Now that the consumer is aware of the problem, or need, he considers the alternative solutions. Sometimes, there are multiple categories of products or services to fulfill the need. Other times, alternatives are multiple brands within one product category. The goal of marketing in this stage is to get on the list of alternatives that the consumer is considering. Marketers strive to be mentioned in trend stories that talk about new product categories and seek public endorsements from influential people and celebrities. In addition, well-targeted direct marketing and participation in events or trade shows can be very effective.

The next stage is the Search stage. Here the consumer is choosing among various category alternatives and deciding which category best solves the problem. Sometimes the Search and Consider categories blend together when the volume of category alternatives is small. At the end of the Search phase, literally or conceptually, the consumer forms a "shortlist"—a list of the product options that appear to be finalists as potential solutions. Marketers want to ensure that their products are well-differentiated among competitors in this phase, so that they actually make the shortlist. Therefore, marketers want their solutions to be well featured whenever their product category is mentioned or when competitive comparisons are made. For certain types of products, in-store and point-of-sale demonstrations are also important to make an impression in the Search phase.

In the Choose stage, the consumer decides which of the shortlist alternatives to buy. Here, positive word of mouth is critical, so the marketer seeks to develop positive references from other customers and focuses on getting good reviews from influential press. Creating a sense of market momentum is important in this stage to assure the customer of the rightness of his decision. Special incentives to encourage the consumer to buy one brand over another are often effective.

In the Buy stage, the customer makes the purchase transaction. The marketer works to ensure that the customer feels positively about his decision and overcomes any cognitive dissonance or buyer's remorse. Ensuring positive attitudes around the final buying decision is imperative to maintain positive post-purchase attitudes.

Finally, the Buy Again phase focuses on keeping the customer happy. This is important not only for repeat sales and customer retention, but also because happy customers make good references and stimulate positive word of mouth to new customers.

Of course, this is a cursory and oversimplified review of a classic marketing construct. There are countless arguments one could make about whether direct marketing is more effective in the Choose versus the Stimulate stage or if advertising plays a role in the Buy Again stage. Our point here is not to debate the classics but to talk about what we believe is a permanent change in consumer behavior, which gives rise to new theories.

The Consumer Purchase Decision Cycle in the Web Context

How does the consumer purchase decision cycle change in the Web context? Well, let's first talk about what is similar. The consumers are generally the same, they have the same needs with the same amount of money to spend. But in the Web world, the decision cycle becomes more compressed because information is so readily available. The consumer is empowered and is often reached via new mar-

In the Web world, the decision cycle becomes more compressed because information is so readily available

keting vehicles. The steps blend together into fewer discrete phases.

In the Web world, there are really three addressable purchase decision cycle phases, as shown in figure 3.2: the Stimulate/Consider/Search stages merge into one, and we call this the Confidence Building phase; the Choose/Buy stages morph into what we refer to as the Skirmish phase; and the Buy Again/ Retention stages become what we label the War phase. In each of these phases, there are significant differences in the marketing tactics used to guide the consumer through the cycle.

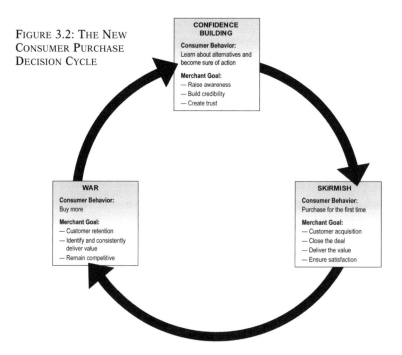

FIGURE 3.2: THE NEW CONSUMER PURCHASE DECISION CYCLE

The Confidence Phase: Building Awareness and Trust in the Site Brand

The confidence phase compresses the Stimulate, Consider, and Search consumer behaviors into a quick, nearly simultaneous succession. It could be argued that the Stimulate is still an initial and separate phase relying primarily on traditional mass media vehicles to raise awareness. The danger in that thinking, however, is missing the importance of search engines in creating initial site awareness. Consumers become aware of sites through many different means—suggestions from friends, search engines and portals, newspaper and magazine articles, and advertisements. Sometimes consumers are "stimulated" or become aware of Web sites through more traditional means, such as print or broadcast advertising. Other times, the stimulus occurs simultaneously with searching as consumers discover new sites through search engines, portals, and links. Whatever the sequence in this compressed phase of Stimulate, Consider, and Search, the sources with the most influence are those that are perceived by consumers to be the most trustworthy.

The reliance on trusted sources is very apparent when consumers name their preferred sources of information for learning about new Web sites. We believe that these sources will continue to be critical for a very long time. As shown in figure 3.3, the three most important information sources cited by respondents are references from friends (100 percent), magazine and newspaper articles (95 percent), and search engines and site links (83 percent). People perceive these sources as credible and are comfortable with references from people and places they trust. Print and broadcast advertising also play an important credibility-building role. Therefore, these sources wield the most power in building the consumer's confidence.

FIGURE 3.3: HOW USERS FIND OUT ABOUT WEB SITES

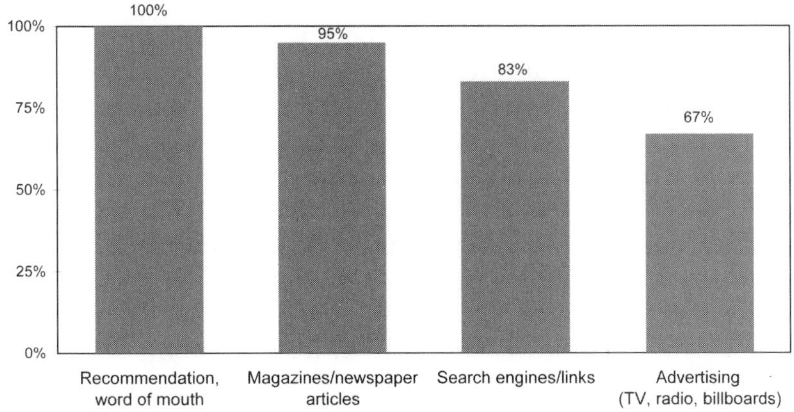

Note: Multiple responses possible.

Source: Pulse of the Customer

FINDING OUT ABOUT WEB SITES

MODERATOR: How do you find out about the Web sites you frequent?

CONSUMER: I go to Web sites when friends e-mail the addresses to me.

CONSUMER: Search engines.

CONSUMER: Reading the business page.

CONSUMER: I think the most successful sites are the ones using multiple media: online banners, print ads, television advertising, and radio.

CONSUMER: Magazine articles. I figure if the magazine thinks enough of it to write an article, it must be OK. But I still get nervous if I've never heard of the site before.

CONSUMER: I just won't shop from a site that isn't personally recommended to me by someone I know and trust that has actually used the site without problems.

MODERATOR: What makes you trust new Web sites?

CONSUMER: I'm less apt to react to an advertisement, but if I hear good word of mouth, I'll definitely look into it.

CONSUMER: I like it when magazines and newspapers do one-page summaries of recommended Web sites by category, like getting a loan or trading stocks online. These are not advertisements but actual reviewed site recommendations. It's nice having a piece of paper that I can stick in my drawer and refer to whenever I need.

Once a consumer has become aware of a site, he actively "considers" the site by searching for it, finding it, and confirming the validity of the site's existence. When the consumer hasn't had the benefit of a direct reference from a trusted acquaintance, sometimes that validation is obtained by checking reviews on other sites, querying people in chat rooms and user groups, or reading articles in the media.

One unique aspect of consumer behavior in this phase is that all of this can happen very quickly. The marketer needs to create marketing strategies and invest in programs in anticipation of many different potential scenarios. For example, as we see on the chart, consumers find out about new sites through friends. Friends often send each other hot links in e-mails or they may send a message to a friend from the actual site, a feature that more sites are offering during the online purchase process. This positive word of mouth is generally stimulated through other means of marketing, such as PR, presence on portals and search engines, and advertising.

THE IMPORTANCE OF PUBLIC RELATIONS IN BUILDING ONLINE CONSUMER CONFIDENCE

A major source of credible and influential information where people learn about sites is articles in newspapers and magazines. That means that proactive public relations efforts need to be aggressively funded in the prelaunch and launch phases of a site, as well as throughout the lifetime of a site. Creating a presence in the press and influencer communities takes a significant amount of time, patience, and financial commitment. These influencers need solid proof of credibility before they are willing to risk their reputations by giving positive reviews. Web sites must be prepared to demonstrate (not just talk about) their value propositions, prove that real customers are successfully using the site, and clearly communicate the differentiation of their site versus those of their competitors.

Press and analysts in the e-business community have become jaded because they have heard myriad pitches from countless dot coms desperate for publicity. Unfortunately, some of those dot coms could not deliver what they claimed, damaging the credibility of the industry and making the press and analysts even more skeptical. That's an old axiom in PR: "Any publicity is good publicity." This is simply not true in the world of e-business. In this era when confidence building is of paramount, strategic importance, bad publicity can kill a Web site.

There's another old axiom in marketing that purports that PR is free. This is also inaccurate. Good publicity is not cheap. It requires spending substantially—both internally and externally—to wage ongoing, compelling publicity campaigns and to hire competent PR professionals. Effective PR programs that are not just launch-, news-, or

Spending on PR to build confidence is absolutely essential to succeed with new consumers

event-driven must be ongoing. Unlike advertising campaigns where you can control when and what is said by buying ad space, PR happens at its own pace. Too many companies make the mistake of underfunding PR programs or cutting budgets because they are discouraged by a "lack of results." Underfunding or prematurely cutting a PR program can also kill a company. Getting positive reviews or inclusions in trend stories comes from systematic, relentless, and focused PR. Spending on PR to build confidence is absolutely essential to succeed with the new consumer.

THE IMPORTANCE OF SEARCH ENGINES AND PORTALS IN THE CONFIDENCE BUILDING PHASE

There are other important places to spend marketing budgets in order to build confidence. Remember in figure 3.3 that consumers indicated search engines and portals as the primary ways they found out about new Web sites. This tips off the e-business marketer to take several strategic and tactical steps. The least expensive action is to ensure that Web site metatags are strategically selected and constantly updated. Metatags are words or short phrases that are embedded in Web pages so that a Web site will be found when a consumer enters a keyword search on a search engine. This is a basic process in the Web world, but one that is vital because so many consumers find sites through routine searches. Each search engine in the market performs searches in different ways, so it is important to understand the best ways to create metatags in order to anticipate different search techniques. That is a technical discussion that goes beyond the goal of this book, but marketers and e-business executives should make sure that executing a metatag strategy is a priority for the site development and marketing teams.

The other—and more expensive—approach to leveraging search engines and portals in the Confidence stage of the consumer decision cycle is to create a presence on consumers' favorite portals. In this context, search engines and portals are synonymous. For example, many consumers have set Yahoo.com as their "home page," which is where the browser first goes when it makes an Internet connection. Some have set their home pages to Web sites that present content they care most about, such as news sites or their stockbroker sites. Other consumers have never bothered to change the default home page that came with their computers, operating systems, or browsers. So whatever was originally there as the home page—which is generally a portal—is still there. That's why there's such high customer traffic claims from portals such as AOL.com, MSN, and NetCenter—consumer inertia!

The implied association of having a brand presence on a trusted portal builds consumer confidence

Whatever the reason consumers use portals, the portal plays a powerful role in building customer awareness and confidence in Web site brands. When a consumer comes to the portal site, her "eyeballs" are captured at that moment. The buttons, offers, and brands she sees on that portal can make an impression and potentially stimulate a consumer to click. In addition, if the consumer trusts the portal, the implied association of having a brand presence on a trusted portal builds consumer confidence. Of course, portals are not naïve to their powerful positions with consumers, so buying a presence on these portals is wildly expensive. But, as shown in consumers' reports of their preferred information sources, portals are a marketing vehicle that Web sites can't afford to ignore.

IMPORTANCE OF AFFILIATION ENDORSEMENTS IN BUILDING CONSUMER CONFIDENCE

Some e-businesses have used a strategy of affiliating with name-brand people or organizations that lend credibility to their otherwise unknown brand. This can be effective in creating a sense of legitimacy, especially for fledgling dot coms. Some companies have built credibility by having well-known people and companies as investors, board members, or executive team members. Others have associated with companies to add value to the site proposition, such as creating content or special functionality. Still others have hired famous people to be their spokespersons in advertising and in the media. Leveraging the fame and reputation of credible people is not a new concept in advertising and PR, but it can be effective in short-cutting the confidence building process in the fast-moving world of the Web. Leveraging people's celebrity has really caught on in sites of every variety. As more sites adopt this strategy, however, the ante gets higher and higher. For example, OneNetNow.com, a Web portal for the urban market, signed up not one celebrity but many to sit on their board—including Sammy Sosa, Jesse Jackson, Edward James Olmos, Andrew Shue, and Babyface.

THE IMPORTANCE OF ADVERTISING IN THE CONFIDENCE BUILDING PHASE

The tactical maneuvers deployed to get consumers' attention and stimulate their consideration of a specific brand have turned to traditional marketing communication vehicles like TV, radio, billboards, and direct mail. Spending in these marketing vehicles also plays a vital role in building consumer confidence. Back in the early days of the Web, some experts believed that the best way to drive traffic to a Web site was through Web advertising and promotions. Today, we know that is no longer adequate. Because the consumer cannot be assured through physical validation of the site, as discussed earlier, the advertising and PR has to do the heavy lifting of creating a credible company image. This isn't just about the marketing "message" or differentiated value proposition. The noise level—frequency, intensity, consistency—all contribute to building a sense of company substance. While the site experience and its offering certainly have to fulfill consumer expectations once they have arrived, the marketing strategies have to focus on creating consumer confidence.

The noise level—frequency, intensity, consistency—contributes to building a sense of company substance

The Q4 1999 and Q1 2000 advertising glut made consumers more confident in e-commerce, even though they complained of dot-com advertising fatigue.

IMPACT OF ADVERTISING ON NEW CONSUMERS' CONFIDENCE

MODERATOR: How does the amount of dot-com advertising you see these days impact your confidence in e-commerce?

CONSUMER: All the dot-com advertising you hear these days! I don't always pay attention to the name of the site, but I'm really aware that there are dot coms everywhere. That makes me feel like the Internet has really arrived.

MODERATOR: Do you think that dot-com advertising is effective in getting your attention?

CONSUMER: Yeah, but they can go overboard. "Dot com" has become like a SATURDAY NIGHT LIVE skit or something. It has become a cliché.

CONSUMER: I get tired of it after a while. After all, there are other things in life.

CONSUMER: You can't get away from it (every radio station, every bus billboard, every TV commercial), it's dot com, dot com, dot com.

CONSUMER: It's not just billboards, it's paper bags, it's sides of buses, it's everything! It's everywhere.

URL RETENTION

Getting the marketing communications mix right is not the only challenge e-businesses face in the Confidence Building phase. Online consumers discuss a challenge that is unique to dot-com marketing and one that has become more acute in the face of proliferating Web sites and advertisements—getting the name right (a similar challenge faced by 800-number businesses). Usually, the consumer is not at her computer when she experiences the TV, radio, or print ad or when a friend mentions a site in passing; therefore, she is not in a position to immediately visit the site. By the time she is at her computer, she often has difficulty remembering the URL or dot-com company name she learned about in the advertisement, creating a gap in the effectiveness of the advertising. Since getting the name right is essential to finding a site, consumers often don't wind up visiting the advertised site, even when it is interesting to them.

To work around this "URL retention" problem, some consumers go to search engines and try typing in what they remember, hoping that they'll get it partially right so they can find it in the search results. Some carry notepads or scraps of paper when they read, listen to the radio, or watch TV so they can jot down the URL for future reference.

Instead of getting cues from advertising, others rely on URLs that have intuitive and memorable meanings, like wine.com or drugstore.com, or familiar brand names like Macys.com.

Dot-com companies have become acutely aware of this issue, which has created a massive rush to register Web site names that are intuitive to the value proposition. And it has created a sideline industry of "cybersquatters"—individuals who were the first to register URLs with the intent of subsequently selling the rights to those names to new e-businesses. This is a practice that has been quite lucrative for these opportunistic types. In fact, companies have been known to pay millions of dollars to buy intuitive-sounding monikers for their domain name from cybersquatters, such as Business.com, which paid $7.5 million.[1] There is even a company, which, in 1995, had registered the URL Music.com because the word "music" was an acronym for the name of their business.[2] When they realized several years later that the URL, Music.com, was a powerful name for an e-business delivering music to consumers, the company changed their business and became a music distributor. This is an unusually dramatic example of the importance of having the right URL!

URL RETENTION PROBLEMS

MODERATOR: After seeing an advertisement or reading an article, how do you remember the names of Web sites you want to visit?

CONSUMER: My monitor is literally papered with post-it notes with Web addresses written on them that I never end up getting to.

CONSUMER: I tear out magazine and newspaper articles that mention interesting Web sites. So far, that's the only way I've managed to remember a URL so I could look up a site later.

CONSUMER: I keep a little notebook and pencil when I'm listening to the radio and if I hear a site that I'm interested in, I write it down right away.

CONSUMER: Some of them I remember because the name of the site is the name of the product. Other names are similar enough to the product that I can find them through search engines, or they're a brand name that I recognize, like Target.com. Other than that, it's hard for me to remember.

MODERATOR: When you hear about an interesting site, say on the radio when you're driving or you're somewhere where you can't write it down, how do you remember the site names?

CONSUMER: I don't.

CONSUMER: I say, "Screw it. The commercial will come on again sometime."

CONSUMER: If it piques my interest, I'll remember the subject and go to the search engine and find it that way.

MODERATOR: So the name matters as far as getting to the site?

CONSUMER: Yeah. It helps if the name correlates to the site purpose. Like WebMD, things like that help me. There are some kooky ones you just can't remember. Wine.com, yeah, you remember that.

CONSUMER: What's the sports one? Quonoff, Quackoff? I mean, how would you spell it right when you typed it in?

CONSUMER: People need to relate the company's name with the Web site.

New dot coms face an interesting challenge as they enter the market at a time when most memorable product and service category domains have already been registered.

THE EFFECTIVENESS OF ONLINE ADVERTISING IN THE CONFIDENCE BUILDING PHASE

Is online advertising—banner ads, e-mail marketing, etc.—an effective way to get consumers' attention in the confidence phase? There are certainly Web site–traffic tracking services that will say so—whether a site received good click-throughs, a lot of eyeballs, and so on. But many consumers argue that the message isn't getting through, complaining about unfocused offers, being pestered with unsolicited promotional e-mail and distracting banner ads. In reality, we think the jury is still out on the effectiveness of online marketing and there is further evolution to come. We predict that untargeted, undifferentiated methods of online marketing will be deemed ineffective and will significantly diminish or go away. In their place will be personalized offers tailored to the individual consumer based on her personal preferences. Consumers are anxious for this to happen, as they are growing weary of the constant barrage of online stuff that invades their space.

ABOUT BANNER ADS

MODERATOR: Do you ever click on a banner ad?

CONSUMER: I know banner ads are really advertisements. So when I see them, they bug me. I might be in the middle of trying to read something on a site and this banner ad is flashing at me, trying to get my attention. Banner ads feel like intrusions that are trying to manipulate me.

CONSUMER: I'm totally desensitized to them. I don't even look at them anymore.

CONSUMER: I've learned to block them out. It's kind of like getting up to get a sandwich during the commercial on television. It's just not there.

CONSUMER: I'm afraid of them.

MODERATOR: Why are you afraid of banner ads?

CONSUMER: I don't know where they are going to take me.

CONSUMER: I'm always afraid that they'll take my information and I'm going to say yes to something that I didn't want to say yes to.

MODERATOR: Have you ever acted on online marketing offers?

CONSUMER: Occasionally I see something that interests me if it's something I've been thinking about and so I might respond to the ad by further clicking. But usually banner ads are not very directed. I would actually prefer to get fewer offers, and more directed advertisements, than get so many that have nothing to do with me or my interests.

CONSUMER: Banner ads are difficult to target because effective offers must meet the needs of an individual. Everyone is looking for something different—price, capabilities, new products, auctions—so few offers meet a person's individual needs.

EVALUATIONS/COMPARISONS IN THE CONFIDENCE BUILDING STAGE

While still in the Confidence Building stage, the consumer performs evaluations comparing sites based on prices, special offers, and product selection. Making products easy to find and information complete while having compelling offers (discussed further in the next section) are key to winning customers.

In addition, ensuring the sites are listed and evaluated by consumer review sites is important in the Confidence Building phase. While the Web site may not have control over what is said in the reviews, it is important to be present—to be positioned as a critical player in the market landscape.

IMPLICATIONS OF THE CONFIDENCE BUILDING PHASE

In acquiring online customers, the goal is to build consumer confidence

Looking at the record spending on dot-com advertising in recent quarters reminds us of an unavoidable fact: building confidence in the world of dot coms requires megabucks. The bar has been raised by the number of online companies that have devoted significant resources to building brand awareness and driving traffic to their Web sites. Companies that intend to build an online brand now need to plan for significant marketing investments to fund a mix of both offline and online initiatives that will create consumer confidence in their brands.

The upshot is this: In acquiring online customers, the goal is to build consumer confidence. In fact, confidence building is never really finished, and so programs must be continually funded throughout the purchase decision cycle. This requires spending on marketing vehicles that go beyond the traditional advertising investments that normally drive behavior in the early phases. It requires continuous and intensive PR campaigns, knowing how to exploit search engine technology, and ensuring a presence on sites that target consumer eyeballs. Once brands are well enough known that confidence is built and positive word of mouth is continuously flowing, marketing strategies shift focus to the ever-present challenges of winning the skirmish and waging the ongoing war for the soul of the new consumer.

The Skirmish Stage in the Web Context: We've Only Just Begun to Fight

The Skirmish phase represents the melding of the traditional Choose and Buy stages of the consumer purchase decision cycle. When contemplating the new consumer purchase decision cycle, we decided to call this the Skirmish phase. Why? Because in the grand scheme of business-to-consumer e-business, getting the customer to buy the first time is just a preliminary competitive conflict. The real battle comes in the War stage (more on that later.) That's not to say that the Skirmish stage is easy or non-strategic. It's just that the fight has only just begun in this phase. The marketing investments made to reach consumers in the Confidence Building phase are critical to success during the skirmish stage. Companies who have won the trust of consumers in the earlier phase will compete much more effectively in the Skirmish. In fact, if the consumer's confidence hasn't been won at this point, the company is unlikely to get the opportunity to be a contender in the Skirmish. The cumulative impact of actions in the Confidence Building phase will be effective in winning the skirmish, as well as moving the process along as quickly as possible.

The Web world moves so fast that there's little distinction between choosing and buying. It's so easy to make the online purchase with a few clicks once the choices are narrowed down. In fact, often the morphing of phases is even more extensive. The Confidence Building and Skirmish stages can sometimes blend into only one phase because there are no time or space constraints to impede the process, nor any logistical barriers between first knowing about a site and purchasing something from a site. It can all happen in one Web session—in a matter of minutes. The trick is to have a unique and compelling offer that motivates the consumer to buy.

It's useful to look back at the 1999 Christmas holiday season to learn about what it took to get consumers to choose and buy. This strategically important time period not only saw an unprecedented amount of advertising spending, but there were also massive amounts of loss-leader freebies designed to lure the customer to buy. As shown in figure 3.4, consumers reported that they responded to promotional offers quite heavily. Seventy-one percent say they bought from Web sites that offered free shipping with their purchases. Another 54 percent admitted that they had responded to offers of a discount on their first purchase, and 40 percent say they used online coupons. Shoppers indicate that these promotional discounts definitely had impact on what sites they chose to patronize in the holiday season.

Why were dot coms giving away so much free stuff? Holiday 1999, for the first time in e-business history, had the promise of enough overall purchase volume to get a clear picture of its status and to chart when many "b-to-c" (business-to-customer) e-businesses would become profitable. In fact, the advertising and promotional spending was driven by the dot coms' frantic need to capture sales and prove positive trendlines toward profitability.

The 1999 legacy was that online consumers were trained to expect free stuff

But while dot coms have been frenetically spending to capture customer loyalty and establish an optimistic trend-line, we believe a downside to the promotional spending developed. The 1999 legacy was that online consumers were trained to expect free stuff—shipping, gifts, discounts. In our research, fielded after this critical shopping season, consumers indicated that they expected to continue to get free stuff on future purchases. In fact, we believe that new consumers now think of free stuff as an entitlement. Delivering what consumers consider as entitlements will be very challenging for dot coms in the future, and is a dilemma that the entire industry will have to reckon with.

FIGURE 3.4: INCENTIVES THAT DROVE FIRST-TIME WEB SITE VISITORS IN HOLIDAY 1999

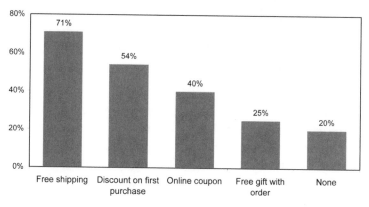

Note: Multiple responses possible.

Source: Pulse of the Customer

The free stuff keeps on coming—it wasn't *just* a Christmas holiday season aberration. Seasonal events such as Valentine's Day, Easter, and Mother's Day have rapidly become causes for special online promotional offers. And some sites don't even require a special occasion. Free stuff is the essence of some dot coms, such as iWon.com, promising big rewards from daily drawings and monthly jackpots just for clicking through their advertisements.

THE POWER OF INCENTIVES

MODERATOR: Describe the promotional offers that have appealed to you.

CONSUMER: Free shipping. If I can't find it at one site, I'll just go to another that offers it. If I can't find free shipping online at all, I'd just as soon shop at the mall.

CONSUMER: I respond to discounted products. It's really noticeable. The discounts just keep getting deeper and deeper.

CONSUMER: Low prices make me try anything, look at anything.

CONSUMER: It only seems like a good deal if there's free shipping and handling.

MODERATOR: Does any particular offer stick in your mind?

CONSUMER: I bought a toy from Amazon and the reason I did is because I got an offer for $10 off, so that was the incentive. And if it wasn't for that, I wouldn't have bought it from them.

CONSUMER: One site got me to go there because of the specials, such as the free shipping and the great vitamins. They had a good offer. I'm not really a vitamin person, but when I heard the advertisement and the way they described the offer, I thought maybe I should start using vitamins!

CONSUMER: I got this $10-off coupon in the regular mail for a Web site. I remember it had a really nice envelope made of rice paper, and it impressed me. I actually used the coupon.

Of course, promotional offers are not the only critical elements in capturing the first-time purchaser, and neither are the confidence building tactics that carry over from that first phase of the cycle. The effectiveness of the Web site, the quality of the experience, the value of the content, the product selection, the prices—these elements are just as critical for getting customers to buy for the first time.

The fight for customer retention will be very expensive for an indefinite period of time

But the level of promotional spending to capture the first-time customer sets a pace for the third phase—the War stage. Because of that, the fight for customer retention will be unrelenting and it will be very expensive for an indefinite period of time.

The War Stage: It's an Ongoing Fight

In the cutthroat Web world, retaining customers has become as difficult as acquiring them—maybe even more so. Customers who are primarily motivated by convenience and timesavings will become a decreasing, yet still important part of the Web population. But these consumers are not the most difficult to retain. The greater challenge comes as more and more new consumers join the Web force who are highly motivated by low prices and deals. This is causing a need for e-businesses to reexamine their assumptions about what is required for customer retention. E-businesses need to focus on what it will take to retain the *new* new consumer. Strategies for e-customer retention need to be built with as much focus and financial commitment as consumer confidence building and acquisition programs.

What's making e-customer retention so challenging is that dot coms have been making outrageously expensive freebie offers to acquire customers, as discussed in the previous section. The theory was that free offers were the first-time price of customer acquisition and that once the customer was acquired, customer retention could be achieved through offering good Web experiences and competitive prices. But in the fickle world of e-commerce, customer loyalty is an ephemeral and elusive concept. The after-effect of too much money chasing too few customers in the acquisition phase has resulted in raising consumer expectations for ongoing customer retention. In retrospect, the recent dot-com, promotional, loss-leader tactics may prove to be a double-edged sword. This has created the difficult situation that marketers face in the War stage of the consumer purchase decision cycle.

Promotional offers have been successful in getting customers to buy, but they also created customer expectations about entitlements in online shopping—a proposition that dot coms can't afford to maintain as part of customer retention. Some

In the fickle world of e-commerce, customer loyalty is an ephemeral and elusive concept

shoppers believe, however, that these incentives should become permanent benefits on Web sites. And they frankly don't care if a company loses money because of it. If shoppers visit a site again expecting the discount, free shipping, or gift and is disappointed, consumers indicate that they will simply find another site that offers a better deal. And, for the foreseeable future, they will be able to find that better deal.

When consumers were asked what they expect to find online while shopping in upcoming seasons, the most frequent response was free or low-cost shipping from their preferred Web sites, as shown in figure 3.5. It seems that promotional offers are moving beyond the customer acquisition realm and will become a requirement for maintaining customer loyalty.

FIGURE 3.5: EXPECTATIONS FOR ONLINE SHOPPING IN 2000

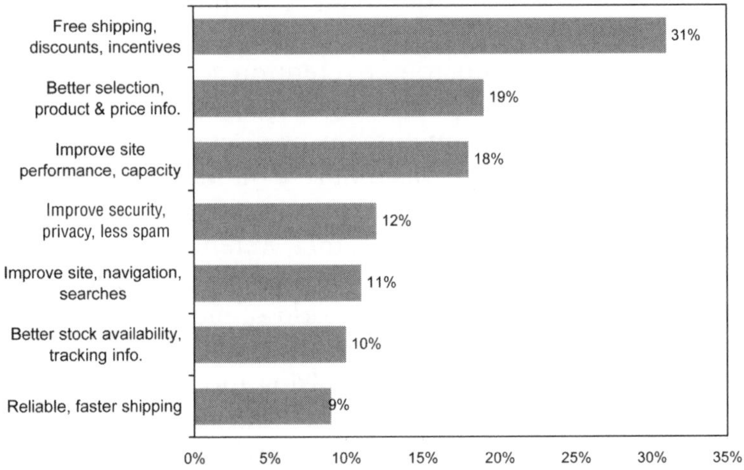

Note: Multiple responses possible.

Source: Pulse of the Customer

There is also a desire for even better product selection and price reductions, including coupons and incentives. Site performance issues, system capacities, and site navigation are also expected to improve as technology becomes more sophisticated. Other expectations for the future include faster and more reliable shipping, as well as better stock availability and merchandise tracking information, as mentioned previously.

CONSUMERS' RECOMMENDATIONS TO E-BUSINESSES

MODERATOR: What do you recommend that sites do to keep your business?

CONSUMER: They have to come up with something to compete. I mean, if it isn't low prices, then they'll have to offer something to draw people in and make them always go back to the same place, because the Web enables you to go anywhere.

CONSUMER: I don't know. There are so many other sites that lowball the prices, trying to steal your loyalty away from others.

CONSUMER: On the Internet, you can literally go and comparison shop until you drop. So there better be some motivation for a site to keep my business, like frequent purchaser points or something.

CONSUMER: I would be loyal if I could put in a bunch of information about myself, my desires, what I want, and the site would create a custom solution for me—kind of the way that investment and news sites do it today. If I could add things that I'm interested in when I go to the site and it would only bring up those things that I care about. You know, if it automated the display of products for me.

The net result is that promotional offers are moving beyond the customer acquisition realm and have become a requirement for maintaining customer loyalty in many market segments. E-businesses will have to be very inventive and competitive in building customer loyalty programs to make customers want to stay. As we discussed in chapter 2, a good Web site experience has become a hygiene factor, or a price of e-business entry—it's not enough to retain e-customers. A bad experience, however, will cause e-businesses to lose customers. What will make customers stay as the bar keeps getting raised?

The key is in understanding the target shopping segments and why they buy online, and then creating customer entitlement programs to appeal to consumers' primary online shopping motivations. For example, if the target customer is a Comparison Shopper (as profiled in chapter 2), offering deals every time she comes to the site and reinforcing the perception that the site consistently offers the best deals would appeal to the primary motivation of that shopping segment. Another example when targeting the Convenience Shopper is to create functionality and special

> *Value propositions must be so compelling that customer loyalty can effectively be earned on every visit and during every transaction*

offers that make the experience easier and faster. Amazon.com's 1-Click[SM] Ordering[3] is an excellent example of a feature aimed at improving convenience. It is also an example of how quickly the competition responds to new ideas given the number of Web sites that quickly added this feature, despite Amazon's legal efforts to protect their patent.

In reality, every site has a mix of shopper types. The marketing challenge is to determine which types a company is best positioned to serve and then create programs, features, and offers that constantly re-hook the customers' attention. What's most important in winning the war is to be ever vigilant in tracking competitors' innovations in customer retention programs, as Andy Grove says in the title of his best-selling book, *Only the Paranoid Survive.*[4] Realize that customers can be lured off the hook very quickly. In fact, it's probably best to assume that long-term loyalty doesn't really exist, so that marketing strategies must be so compelling that the loyalty is effectively earned and re-earned on every visit and during every transaction.

WHAT CUSTOMERS EXPECT NEXT

MODERATOR: What do you predict will happen in online shopping this year?

CONSUMER: I think there will be a lot more people saying good things about online shopping and as a result, more people will do it. And there will be a lot of price reductions, specials, and promotions.

CONSUMER: It depends on the specials and promotions. If Web sites have incentives and sweeteners, online shopping will do well. But if Web sites expect that everyone is just going to come, and it's the same as going to a regular store, I don't think it will grow.

CONSUMER: E-businesses can't continue being unprofitable forever; they'll get bought or merged. There will be bigger corporations and more mergers.

Implications for Business

The days of launching a Web site on a shoestring budget are fading into Web folklore—that is, if such days ever existed. For brands that are trying to establish broad market penetration in the Web world, the unexpected net result is that it is more expensive to build consumer confidence and achieve customer retention with an online brand than to do so in the analog world, at least in the foreseeable future.

Does customer loyalty really exist? Does a dot com have to buy customer loyalty on every transaction? How do we get customer entitlement expectations under control so that dot coms can show P&Ls that are trending toward profitability? When will the period of fast and furious promotional spending end? What will it be like when it is over? Will only the cash-rich survive? These are the key questions e-businesses must quickly address to sustain viability and become legitimate, long-term market players.

Companies face a real catch-22 in meeting the challenges of building consumer confidence, acquiring customers, and retaining them. If every transaction represents a loss because of the expense of acquiring customers and fulfilling entitlement expectations, the gross margins will be unacceptable. And the picture never gets better. In this scenario, the business can never make it up in volume.

The new consumer wants to be bought, but the recent past has created expectations that cannot be sustained. Companies that want to retain customers need to find non-price-related incentives to stimulate repeat purchases.

4
The Threat of Invasion

In this chapter, we focus on the perceived threat of online invasion—consumers' concerns that their space, their privacy, and their well-being will become victims of unwanted and unethical online business practices. Several factors have contributed to this sense of foreboding. The well-publicized security breaches in early 2000 that caused name-brand Web sites to crash created alarm throughout the business community and among consumers. In addition, stories of blocks of credit card numbers being stolen from e-commerce sites put a halo of apprehension over the e-business industry. Lawsuits filed by consumers claiming that e-businesses illegally collected and used personal information have created further anxiety. We have arrived at a critical yet fragile juncture in the development of the Internet. As consumers become more experienced, they become more confident in their abilities to successfully use the Web. But, at the same time, as the Internet becomes more pervasive, more vandalous hackers in more countries are committing online crimes. The new consumer has reason to be anxious about the threat of invasion.

Where are consumers' boundaries? What is privacy in the Web context and why are people concerned? In this chapter, we look at how privacy anxiety impacts consumers' Web behavior and what constitutes stepping over the line of acceptable business practices. Critical topics are explored, such as who's in control of the online experience, how do people feel about registering at Web sites, the concept of "personalization," and the fear of spam.

Privacy: An Issue to Be Taken Seriously

Privacy is generally defined as "the state of being apart from observation," as well as "the freedom from unauthorized intrusion."[1] The United States government has a more specific definition, stating that privacy includes: "intrusion on one's seclusion, publicity that places one in a false light, misappropriation of one's name or likeness and public disclosure of private facts."[2] Both meanings of privacy are relevant in the Internet context.

When we talk to consumers about online privacy, the conversation gravitates to three key concerns: the degree to which their online activities are known to others; the amount of control they have over the dissemination of personal information collected online; and the level of intrusion they experience from outsiders invading their space with unsolicited communications.

WHO KNOWS WHAT—WHERE THE LINE IS DRAWN

Concerns about privacy in the Web world are very real—and for good reason. Not only is the media filled with stories of personal information being sold by Web sites, unbeknownst to consumers and without their permission, every day consumers experience unwanted intrusions pushed on them via spam by overly aggressive direct marketers. According to Simson Garfinkle, in his book titled *Database Nation: The Death of Privacy in the 21st Century*,[3] the main threat to privacy does not come from an Orwellian totalitarian state, but rather from commercial interests. There are several ways that commercial enterprises intrude on consumers' online privacy. These days no one is immune to these industry practices.

Some industry pundits take issue with the assertion that spam is indeed a violation of one's privacy. In an editorial written by columnist John C. Dvorak, the author opines that spam is an annoyance, but not an invasion of privacy.[4] He believes this for two reasons: because the senders don't know who the people are to whom they are sending unwanted e-mail, and because the data used to create the offer is anonymous information stored in massive databases accessed by throngs of Web sites. His concern is that labeling such pesky practices as privacy violations serves only to trivialize the importance of privacy.

The line gets crossed, however, when those giant databases of customer information are no longer anonymous—when the information about online and offline purchase behavior is correlated with a person's actual identity. In a lawsuit filed in early 2000 by a California resident against DoubleClick, the allegation was exactly that—the company had crossed the line, and was charged with alleged violation of privacy rights and deceptive business practices.[5] The suit claimed that DoubleClick reversed its policy of providing only anonymous data about Web surfers to marketers and began combining its online profiles with information from direct mailers and others that helped to determine the actual identity of the Web surfer.

By combining its data with the information from a company it had acquired, named Abacus Direct Corp., DoubleClick knew the name, address, phone number, and the online shopping behavior of its customers. This enabled DoubleClick to offer highly personalized, and, in this case, evidently offensive, offers to consumers. This is an example of stepping over the line, at least in the opinion of the plaintiff, as well as a breach of the privacy policy that the consumer had agreed to when signing up for the DoubleClick program.[6] The reaction of privacy advocates who protect the personal information of online shoppers spurred the Federal Trade Commission and the attorneys general in Michigan and New York to launch investigations.[7]

Regardless of whether pundits agree that these types of marketing schemes qualify as invasion of privacy, consumers clearly seem to feel violated when advertisers relentlessly track them down. Consumer attitudes and behavior have evolved quite rapidly to deal with these online privacy violations. In the best of circumstances, consumers ignore the intrusions until they become weary of the constant bombardments and then stop doing business with offending vendors. In the worst case, some get so turned off by the incoming spam that they abandon using the Internet altogether.

Concerns about privacy in the Web world are very real—and for good reason

PRIVACY POLICIES—ARE CONSUMERS PAYING ATTENTION?

One of the questions we have is whether consumers really read or care about online privacy policies. In a recent study performed by Louis Harris & Associates on behalf of IBM[8] it was found that more than half of Web visitors have indeed noticed privacy policies on Web sites. Although these policies are not usually compelling reading material, 38 percent claim to always read the policy statements, another 56 percent sometimes read the statements.[9] Still, consumers wonder if they can trust Web sites to comply with their privacy policies. As *Business Week* points out, what sites say and what they mean in their statements can be very different. For example, in an article titled "Privacy: The Outrage on the Web,"[10] the authors say that typically site policies make statements such as "we could exchange your name with another company whose products and services interest you." They assert that frequently in practice, however, the policy really means "the site could be selling your information to anyone—other sites, online advertisers, or direct marketers." It's no wonder that consumers are skeptical.

Many get increasingly paranoid about using the Web because they are not sure how information gets collected. They realize that arcane technologies like "cookies" and "sniffers" surreptitiously gather personal information throughout the site surfing, browsing, and shopping process, but they are not sure exactly what data is being gathered, or how to stop it from happening. Net net: Web consumers' daily online experiences reinforce the notion that privacy is up for grabs and that anything goes in the world of e-marketing. Some people will turn away from the Web in disgust; others will slog through it, developing their own clever tactics for avoiding the increasingly disturbing barrage of junk. We strongly believe that, collectively, the e-business industry must change its intrusive business practices or we may be facing a cyber–ghost town in the near future.

Collectively, the e-business industry must change its intrusive business practices or we may be facing a cyber–ghost town in the near future

THE VALENCE OF PRIVACY ANXIETY

In our research, we found that even among veteran Web shoppers—people who have shopped on many occasions and have at least one year of experience under their belts—the concerns about privacy are very real. It's an apprehension that does not dissipate with experience. In fact, because of the unrelenting stream of spam that arrives in an e-mail box once a Web site becomes aware of one's identity, and the longer a consumer has been using the Web, the greater the concerns for privacy become.

FIGURE 4.1: CONCERNS ABOUT THE USE OF PERSONAL, FINANCIAL, AND PURCHASING DATA

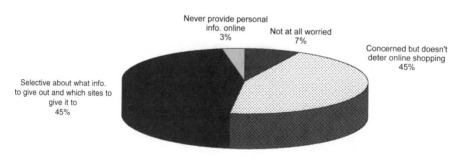

Source: Pulse of the Customer

When asked what barriers, if any, would prevent these experienced e-commerce consumers from shopping online in the near future, 32 percent indicated that privacy issues would indeed inhibit their future shopping. These privacy anxieties, by the way, are not to be confused with online security concerns, an issue that troubles another 34 percent of online shoppers.

How do privacy concerns translate into actual online behavior? As shown in figure 4.1, only 7 percent claim that it doesn't alter their behavior at all and that they are not worried about how Web sites use personal, financial, or purchasing data. Among the much larger pro-

Consumers do business with sites they trust—who have trustworthy brands and have proven that the information provided is not exploited

portion who *are* worried, close to half assuage their concerns by being selective about what information they give out and to whom. They do business with sites they trust—who have trustworthy brands and have proven that the information provided is not exploited. Another 45 percent have concerns, but they are not deterred in their online shopping behavior. A study conducted by Privacy and American Business, a nonprofit research group, corroborates our findings. It found that most Internet users (75 percent of those polled) give personal information to Web sites that display their privacy policy. Thirteen percent reported not to even care about privacy policies and only 11 percent believe that disclosing personal information violates privacy.[11]

The experiences of these consumers have shown that the benefits of online shopping offset the risks of privacy violations. So they forge ahead, hoping that sites will be ethical, and feeling that at any time they can change which sites they patronize. These more sanguine consumers are the ones who feel that they are in control of their Web site experiences and the ways in which their personal information is used.

PRIVACY CONCERNS

MODERATOR: What's the worst thing that could happen if you gave your information to a Web site?

CONSUMER: They might sell my name to another company and then I'm going to get junk e-mails or calls to my home.

CONSUMER: It's a waste of time. It's been my experience that they've been totally wrong in the offers they made to me.

CONSUMER: They would intrude on me. I don't want intrusion into my private life or my business life.

Our research reports on consumers' attitudes based on their past experiences. But we notice that consumers' privacy concerns are increasing over time. As e-business practices evolve, certain databases may be able to store medical histories, driving records, financial reports, or biometric identification, such as DNA, fingerprints, or iris patterns. How personal should information be before privacy advocates file suit against companies that sell information about consumers? Our expectation is that consumers' concerns will become more grave as technology evolves in the future.

New Consumers Want Control

As discussed in chapter 1, this is the age of the empowered consumer—a time when customers have unprecedented access to a seemingly infinite amount of choices. It's no coincidence that the Web consumer is the most empowered customer on the planet: it's because of the Web that so many choices are available to such a large number of people.

As empowered customers, consumers want control of their own Web experiences. Consumers' Web site evaluation criteria—those which determine customers' acceptance or rejection of a vendor—all relate to who's in control of the user's experience.

It's really quite simple *in theory:* Consumers want to control their Web site experiences. In a market-driven economy, the natural and logical conclusion is that vendors should give consumers what they want. Vendors should *enable* users' control rather than fight the customer for it. They should make it easy for consumers to control their experiences, and they should make consumer empowerment work for the vendor as well as for the consumer.

Unfortunately, many companies cannot make the psychological leap to loosen control over the customer relationship. Many companies have roots in an earlier time—a time when companies decided what the market demanded. The company, after all, knew better what consumers wanted and needed than the consumers themselves. Sure, marketing textbooks and market theorists touted "the customer is king," but, in reality, the company has been in control of prices, information, and product availability ever since we can remember. The consumer hasn't been in control—the company has.

> *Vendors should <u>enable</u> users' control rather than fight the customer for it*

We believe that in the world of the Web, companies must face the power shift that the Web has created and think about control differently. In this new age, vendors' control comes from enabling consumers to successfully shape their own Web experiences. It's a whole new way of thinking.

The Four Elements of Control

What do online consumers specifically want control over? What do Web sites need to give consumers control of? For the new consumer, control comprises four key elements: exploitation, exposure, functionality, and content.

- EXPLOITATION is about how personal information is used, and by whom. Consumers want control over who has access to their personal information. They abhor the notion that their information is sold to others without their permission. They also want control over how the information is used. Will it be used to offer better Web site experiences and truly targeted offers, or will it be used to send undifferentiated, intrusive, direct-marketing gimmicks?

- EXPOSURE involves how and when the customer is subjected to, or has access to, personalized offers or content. In other words, which actions are enabled by the site, and what are the options the customer has throughout the site experience? Are special offers presented in a tasteful and relevant context, or are they distracting and annoying?

- FUNCTIONALITY encompasses the features and capabilities of the site and the options the customer has throughout the site experience. This includes being able to view product recommendations based on previous purchase behavior or based on the purchases of people whose profiles are similar. It also includes whether a site offers the ability to create customized pages, such as My Yahoo, a feature many consumers appreciate. And it encompasses features that, with permission, enable the site to notify consumers when certain events occur, such as a low airfare to a specified location.

- CONTENT includes the topical information presented in the experience. Content control provides consumers with the ability to be selective about what content is displayed on a page and how often it is updated, tailored by consumers to fit their special set of interests.

The degree to which vendors allow customers to control the way their personal information is exploited, as well as their exposure, their use of functionality, and the content available makes all the difference between customers' acceptance and rejection of the Web site relationship. Companies are engaged in a continuous balancing act between presenting offers to customers that they want them to buy and allowing them control over their own site experiences.

Online Registration and Trust

Consumers realize that certain information must be provided if they are shopping online. That's common sense. Many face a trade-off—a lesser of two evils. Do they trust a Web site with the required information to make a purchase, such as name, address, e-mail address, and credit card number, or are they so anxious that they would rather shop in some other way? Chances are that many of the consumers who don't shop on the Web fall into the latter bracket—their privacy anxiety keeps them away.

Beyond the obvious "have to or else can't buy online" reason for providing personal information to Web sites, close to 60 percent of the e-consumers we talk to say that there is a very important benefit of Web site registration: it makes future shopping easier and more time efficient. This is not a surprise, as we know that many Web consumers like to shop on the Web because of its convenience and timesavings. A smaller proportion of consumers recognize the other benefit of Web registration: that it enables companies to offer customized promotions, sales incentives, and giveaways.

Many consumers who don't shop on the Web are anxious about maintaining their privacy

Despite misgivings about privacy, almost 70 percent of the e-shopping consumers we polled have provided Web sites with information about themselves so they could set up an account or profile on the Web site of choice. As shown in figure 4.2, most of the information provided is pragmatic: e-mail address, shipping address, billing address, and credit card number. But we also see that many have also provided information that can help the site do a better job of customizing the experience and extending the convenience benefit, such as buying preferences, clothing sizes, and important dates like birthdays and anniversaries.

FIGURE 4.2: TYPES OF INFORMATION PROVIDED WHEN REGISTERING ON WEB SITES

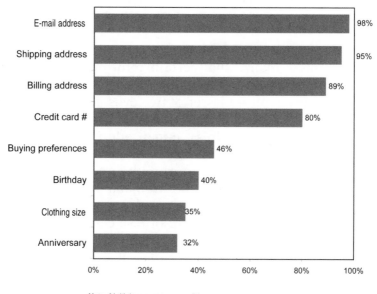

Note: Multiple responses possible.

Source: Pulse of the Customer

Many Web users don't trust sites and are reluctant to provide personal information in the registration process. As seen in figure 4.3, most of the reasons for not providing personal information to Web sites come from trust. Many have concerns about privacy. These consumers feel that personal data that is not related to the transaction they are making should not be necessary for the registration process. Others are worried about credit card fraud, so they don't choose to store their credit card information on Web sites, even though they may prefer to buy from those sites. About 20 percent have "fear of spam," and so they refrain from registering on Web sites.

Many Web users don't trust sites and are reluctant to provide personal information in the registration process

FIGURE 4.3: REASONS CONSUMERS GIVE FOR NOT PROVIDING PERSONAL INFORMATION

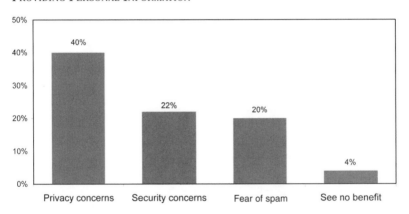

Note: Multiple responses possible.

Source: Pulse of the Customer

In the Louis Harris & Associates study (on behalf of IBM)[12] it was found that people's attitudes about providing personal information were partly influenced by the type of site they were visiting. For example, among the consumers who visited financial services sites, 64 percent said they refused to give information because it was too personal and unnecessary, and, consequently, 61 percent said they didn't use the financial services offered because they were unsure how their personal information would be used. Fifty-eight percent had a similar response regarding insurance sites and their willingness to use online insurance services. Another 57 percent expressed these same sentiments regarding retail sites.[13]

Other Web consumers simply don't see the benefits of providing personal information to Web sites. They feel that site registration often wastes their time and does not result in delivering a compelling enough experience to justify the efforts. To these consumers, the benefit is perceived to be more for the vendor than for the customer, so they choose not to divulge personal information. Many online consumers, believing that too many Web sites have misused personal data, are hesitant to register online unless required to do so to gain access to crucial information or services.

FIGURE 4.4: FACTORS THAT HELP CONSUMERS FEEL MORE COMFORTABLE WITH PERSONALIZATION

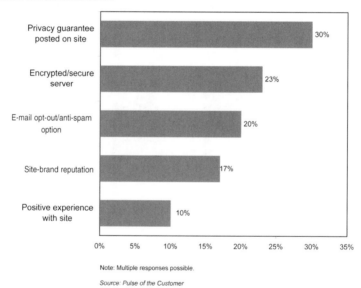

Note: Multiple responses possible.

Source: Pulse of the Customer

There are actions that Web sites can take to allay consumers' privacy concerns. As shown in figure 4.4, consumers feel more secure with companies that have privacy guarantees posted on their sites promising that personal information will not be misused or sold to other parties. This is especially true among sites they trust, either because they have had positive experiences with them in the past, or the companies have earned a good reputation and positive word of mouth in the market. In addition, consumers feel more reassured when the site has secure, encrypted transaction technology designed to prevent credit card fraud. Consumers want to have control over whether they will be receiving future e-mails and spam. They want an "opt-out" option on the registration form so they can avoid unwanted marketing campaigns. This opt-out option is especially effective if consumers can choose which marketing programs they are subjected to. Many times, consumers are interested in selecting a limited set of offers from the full array of a site's product categories, because too often they are inundated with untargeted offers, which becomes overwhelming.

For some customers, companies have already gone too far. They are reticent to give information about themselves, fearful they will lose control and fall prey to unwanted solicitations. Their trust has been violated and there's no turning back. For others who have had good experiences with vendors, they see the benefits of providing Web sites with personal information.

ONLINE REGISTRATION

MODERATOR: Let's talk about your concerns about registering on Web sites. Why register at all?

CONSUMER: Many of today's sites require registration. If you don't register, you don't get access to their information—for example, software upgrades. So I have to, but I don't like it.

CONSUMER: I'm definitely open to providing personal information to sites that make it obvious they are helping me with something. I need to see that it's improving my experience, and that I'm getting something back for providing the information. I only respond to offers that I asked for in some way.

MODERATOR: Why don't you like registration? What's the downside?

CONSUMER: Registration drives me crazy because it leads to marketing intrusions. And it's not just spam. These days, Web sites have telemarketers calling after you've registered. It's a waste of time to have to be on the phone with someone giving me their thirty-second sales schpiel. There should be a way to say that you don't want to be contacted and that you don't want your information given out to others.

CONSUMER: If I could trust that all I was going to get was customization and not tons of junk e-mail, I would be much less paranoid. But I just don't trust them.

CONSUMER: If I knew the information I gave on a Web site was going to be used to provide me relevant, directed marketing offers, then I would give it. But I have probably received only one out of a hundred offers that fall into that category.

CONSUMER: Every time I give my information, I cringe, because I anticipate my e-mail box just being filled up with spam. When it doesn't happen, I'm pleasantly surprised.

MODERATOR: But what if you are offered something of value? Is it a fair trade, your personal information for something you want?

CONSUMER: Generally, it's not a fair trade to provide a site with personal data for a chance to win something. What are the odds—four million to one?

CONSUMER: I don't mind registering to win a free trip or something, but nothing ever comes of it. If I'm not going to get any cool stuff for my efforts, why should I bother registering?

Unsolicited E-mail—A Growing Problem

Unsolicited e-mail is considered an invasion of privacy and has actually become a serious problem for some customers, particularly really busy people. It often impacts people's willingness to register on sites, and in some extreme cases, has prevented people from buying online. Many consumers are fearful that opening unsolicited e-mail will result in getting a computer virus. So they simply delete e-mail when they don't recognize the sender.

Only telemarketing is seen as more intrusive than unsolicited e-mail, as represented by the Intruso-Meter in figure 4.5. And when telemarketing and e-mail are combined, the result is doubly infuriating. Customers indicate that telemarketing follow-up to Web site registration adds insult to injury. They resent it when vendors barrage them with telemarketing calls based on information derived from Web site registration.

Unsolicited e-mail is considered an invasion of privacy and has actually become a serious problem for some customers

SPAM

MODERATOR: So what's so bad about spam? What's the big deal? It's only e-mail. What's the worst thing that can happen?

CONSUMER: Just because I've gone to a particular Web site once, does not mean I want them to target me for the rest of my life. Too many sites mistarget their messages.

CONSUMER: I'm afraid of computer viruses being sent to me via spam.

CONSUMER: As soon as I place my order or request information, I always envision my name being shot out to about 18 billion other people who want to know what I'm interested in. I fear I am going to be spammed to death.

MODERATOR: But we've been getting junk mail for years through the U.S. mail. Why is e-mail different?

CONSUMER: People don't get unsolicited junk mail through the U.S. mail that is offensive. There are laws that govern the distribution of pornographic material via the U.S. mail. But you do get that with e-mail. You get tired of receiving it.

CONSUMER: I have more control over my regular mailbox. I can easily sort the mail and toss the stuff I don't want. But with e-mail, I have to deal with everything that comes in my e-mail box. And sometimes, there's so much stuff that I miss something I really cared about.

FIGURE 4.5: THE INTRUSO-METER OF UNSOLICITED MARKETING VEHICLES

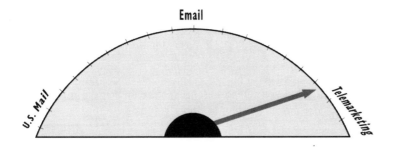

Email

U.S. Mail

Telemarketing

SALES-ORIENTED E-MAIL IS ON THE RISE

Intrusive, sales-oriented e-mail is an increasing problem for many people. A majority of consumers indicate they have seen a marked increase in sales-oriented e-mail in recent months. What are customers' attitudes about sales-oriented e-mail? In our qualitative research, we see a polarization on this topic—few people are neutral on the subject.

One-third say they dislike sales-oriented e-mail so much that it actually makes them avoid the vendor who sends it to them. Based on those comments, we predict that companies may be losing business by taking this type of marketing action.

People are creating ways of avoiding these e-mails, not only by using e-mail filters, which are common features of most popular e-mail software, but also by using alternative e-mail addresses when registering on Web sites. In fact, consumers say that one of the key benefits of free e-mail these days is to have an address that they can use to register on sites without having it be the primary mailbox—an increasingly common workaround to avoid getting unwanted e-mail solicitations.

ACTIONS AGAINST SPAM

MODERATOR: What do you do about unwanted e-mail?

CONSUMER: If a company sends me unsolicited e-mail, I won't do business with them.

CONSUMER: I set up a Hotmail account, and if I get too much spam, I close it.

CONSUMER: If I don't recognize the person that is sending it, I just delete it.

CONSUMER: I don't want to encourage it [sales-oriented e-mail]. It's bad enough my AOL account gets up to a dozen adult-type e-mails a day. It's a hassle and a waste of time. There should be ramifications for this type of conduct.

CONSUMER: I frankly have a dummy e-mail account that I provide to sites that insist on getting personal information from me just so I can look around and browse.

WHEN SOLICITED E-MAIL CAN BE HELPFUL

Consumers find some company-originated e-mail helpful, if well targeted and used in moderation. Interestingly, they want companies to send e-mails that focus on their specific interest rather than promoting all products and services, and that provide important product-usage content, but no more frequently than once every sixty days.

Some people indicate that they like getting sales-oriented e-mail. This is a more common attitude among people who view the Web as a leisure or entertainment activity; therefore, they are more tolerant and open to receiving unexpected, new information. Among all customers, sales-oriented e-mail is most effective when it is sent by companies from whom they have requested information or whose brand name they trust. Even then, consumers want the ability to opt-out of getting solicitations when registering. When consumers receive unsolicited e-mail from companies they don't know, consumers claim they do not read them, they just delete them.

WHEN VENDOR E-MAIL IS WELCOME

MODERATOR: If you could tell an e-business what they should do about sending you e-mail offers—solicited or unsolicited—what would you say?

CONSUMER: It boils down to being responsible versus irresponsible. If the sender is doing their homework and the offer really matches your lifestyle and your criteria, then you're going to appreciate it because it saves you time. If they don't do that, they've just lost my business.

Personalization—A Good and a Bad Thing

Matching offers to consumers' preferences requires the use of a technique called personalization. In this context, we are using the term "personalization" as a broad euphemism for companies' efforts to passively, reactively, and proactively reach and target Web visitors. The term includes current business practices such as profiling, page customization, targeted offers, and use of e-mail for marketing and sales purposes. We found in our research that customers' acceptance of personalization is not a binary issue—it's not an either/or thing. There is, in fact, a continuum of vendors' e-marketing business practices that can dramatically impact consumers' attitudes toward specific site brands.

Web site personalization is perceived as both a benefit and a detriment, depending on how much control the user is given over the exposure, functionality, and content on a Web

Web site personaliza-
tion can be both a
benefit and a detri-
ment depending on
how much control the
user is given

site. Whether personalization is seen as a good or a bad thing depends on if customers feel they are the ones controlling it and making the decisions about how it is used. Consistent with our observations about consumers' needs for control, the majority of consumers we polled (90 percent) prefers a broad range of choice in their Web site experiences over vendor-controlled personalization. So personalization techniques should be applied with the intent to let consumers drive their own experiences.

PERSONALIZATION—THE PLUSES AND THE MINUSES

MODERATOR: What do you think about personalization? Is it a good thing or a bad thing?

CONSUMER: It's nice if it's convenient. It speeds things up, as long as it doesn't get too personal.

MODERATOR: How do you feel about sites anticipating what you might be interested in, based on your previous activities and stated preferences?

CONSUMER: If I can look at it when I'm ready to, I'd be more willing to accept it than having it placed in front of me when I don't want to be bothered with it.

CONSUMER: I would prefer that vendors use one-to-one marketing information to make it easy for me to find what I want when I want it, rather than offering me what they think I want, whether I want it or not.

CONSUMER: I shop for many different reasons. Sometimes I shop for myself, but other times I am shopping for somebody else. It's very difficult for a business to customize a site experience for a user when they don't know what the person's intent is when they visit the site to shop.

MODERATOR: Is giving personal information and getting a more personalized experience worth the effort and risk of being exploited?

CONSUMER: If you choose people who are responsible with your information, you're actually going to benefit from personalization, and can save a tremendous amount of time.

GOOD PERSONALIZATION

Types of personalization that customers appreciate include being able to: design their own pages, control what information and content is presented to them, request specific information, and link to other sites that interest them.

Customer recommendations, popularized by organizations such as Amazon.com, are perceived to broaden consumers' exposure to new things. Consumers like this feature as long as it does not drive *all* content on the page, and as long as they can control when they view the recommendations.

BENEFITS OF PERSONALIZATION

Consumers cite two key benefits of personalization. One is that it saves them time by helping them navigate through myriad content and shopping options. As we have seen in previous chapters, timesavings is one of the top reasons why consumers like using the Web. The other key benefit of personalization is that it broadens their exposure. Sites that make recommendations based on personal profile information educate consumers about options they otherwise would not have known about, such as a book on a related topic or a vacation bargain to a favored destination.

EFFECTIVE USE OF PERSONALIZATION

MODERATOR: What are some examples when personalization has been effective?

CONSUMER: Egghead allows you to customize the content that appears on your opening page if you're interested in a specific type of merchandise. It's a great feature.

CONSUMER: Dell's premier sites are a good example of site customization that works. When I enter the site, it tells me very quickly what I've ordered from them over the last few years, so I know what I should add on to my current order.

MODERATOR: What is it that you like about personalization?

CONSUMER: Customized content gives the appearance of personal attention. Whenever the customer has that perception, it creates a better relationship between buyer and seller.

CONSUMER: I like getting recommendations about what other people have liked who have bought similar things as me. I found myself being exposed to some new and pretty neat stuff that way. But I want the option of when I go there and how it is presented to me.

CONSUMER: I use a travel site that provides me with pricing updates via e-mail based on vacation-preference information I have given them, and I love it. I wish other sites did that for me.

BAD PERSONALIZATION

The dark side of personalization is when vendors attempt to control the user's experience and exposure. At the

The dark side of personalization is when vendors attempt to control the user's experience and exposure

most basic level, consumers don't want companies to decide what gets offered to them. They want to see their choices.

The positive benefits of personalization are too often neutralized by the objectionable business practices of some vendors. Consumers make this association—we call it "the personalization downward spiral": If I register (or buy) something online, then they know who I am and how to contact me. That means they will bother me with things I don't want and maybe even sell my name to others. The result is the customer stops buying online. This downward spiraling attitude is likely to gain momentum if companies continue to exploit the data collected from customers and prospects to sell more goods and services against consumers' wishes.

THE DOWNSIDES OF PERSONALIZATION

Customers say that the biggest downsides of personalization fall into four categories. First, consumers feel the ongoing siege of unsolicited e-mails is intrusive and wastes their time. While not all personalization results in intrusive marketing efforts, many vendors are not mindful enough of consumer's privacy when fielding e-mail marketing campaigns. Similarly, consumers feel that poorly executed personalization is an invasion of their privacy. Consumers resent feeling someone is watching them. In addition, consumers believe that if personalization means that a vendor chooses what is offered to them, they will miss something they care about. Conversely, consumers complain that companies are not focused enough in their offers and do not give them the option to pick which products they want more information about.

The benefits and drawbacks of personalization are depicted in figure 4.6. The challenge for all businesses is to create that critical balance of delivering timesavings while broadening consumers' exposure to new and interesting things, without being intrusive and unfocused.

THE NEGATIVE ASPECTS OF PERSONALIZATION

MODERATOR: What don't you like about the concept of personalization?

CONSUMER: I don't want a Web site to hold my hand as I wade through information—that would really turn me off.

CONSUMER: Why should online shopping be different than going into a retail store? When you go into the store to browse, you don't have to say who you are.

CONSUMER: It feels like Big Brother all of the time. Nothing is sacred anymore. Nothing is private.

CONSUMER: I feel like asking, "Why do you want to know? Why are you asking me that?"

MODERATOR: What are some ways that companies could do a better job with personalization?

CONSUMER: It'd be nice if the site could somehow figure out that a visitor wasn't interested in a certain type of content or offer, and stop offering it.

CONSUMER: If I could turn it on just for one product that would be fine. But instead I get information on too many products that I don't care about.

CONSUMER: Sometimes a site will ask me for personal information too early in the process, before I've even decided that I might shop there. That turns me off real fast.

FIGURE 4.6: BENEFITS AND DRAWBACKS OF PERSONALIZATION

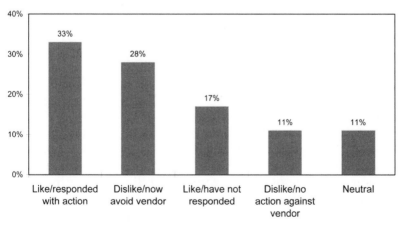

Note: Multiple responses possible.

Source: Pulse of the Customer

Implications for Business

Consumers' preferences discussed in this chapter suggest that businesses face a critical challenge now that the Web has penetrated so many aspects of everyday life. We predict that control of the Web experience will increasingly shift from the company to the customer—consumers will demand it. Organizations must face the power shift that the Web has created and think about control differently—enabling a wide range of user control, rather than wrestling the customer for it.

We predict that the model of vendor-controlled marketing is coming to a slow and painful halt in the context of the Web. Web customers enjoy their newfound power and they want vendors to play by a new set of rules. E-businesses have to approach the challenge differently or the Web experience will be ruined for everyone.

Companies can improve their Web site offerings and address consumers' concerns about privacy by:

- Clearly stating privacy policies and registration procedures up front and adhering to them
- Providing robust, customer-controlled personalization
- Offering nonintrusive, targeted, sales-oriented e-mail
- Using both online and analog marketing vehicles to stimulate consumer awareness, increase site traffic, and build up brand-name recognition and loyalty
- Monitoring customer needs and expectations on a regular basis, then offering site experiences that foster trusting relationships

Consumers' objections can be overcome to some extent by explaining data collection, direct marketing, and registration policies up front—and complying with those policies. Since trust is essential for registration and personalization efforts to succeed, sites should offer consumers the choice of whether or not they want to be subjected to marketing promotions that rely on registration data. And remember, all consumers want the ability to opt-out of getting solicitations when registering.

Whether or not a company can relinquish control, the truth is the consumer always has the right to vote with their eyeballs. In the absence of government intervention or improved business practices by the entire industry, the ultimate outcome of constant and unbearable exploitation of the Web as a promotional vehicle will be the new consumers' passive rejection. And that will result in e-businesses spending lots of money to reach consumers that simply look the other way.

E-businesses have to respect consumers' privacy or the Web experience will be ruined for everyone

We believe that the best-positioned companies going forward will be those that accommodate and respect the privacy concerns of their users, enabling a shift of control from the company to the consumer. Offering value-for-value information exchange and requesting voluntary disclosure of personal information for targeting purposes only, is clearly the way customers want to be addressed.

If e-businesses don't do a better job of respecting the new consumers' boundaries, and if Internet vandals are not thwarted, will consumers scale back their online activities? The answer is: it depends on how offensive companies become and the level of peril consumers face due to security breaches. If consumers' responses to the early 2000 Web site crashes are any indication, we believe that most new consumers will roll with the punches. Web site traffic at the compromised sites returned to normal almost immediately after the well-publicized hacker attacks. It seems that the Internet has become such an integrated vehicle for managing our daily activities that we have no choice but to hang tough. However, e-businesses shouldn't take new consumers' resiliency for granted by continuing objectionable business practices. In fact, because of the growing dependency on the Web, the threat of invasion to the soul of the new consumer can become an issue of gigantic proportions.

5 *Room for Improvements*

Consumers are becoming increasingly comfortable with shopping online, as we have discussed throughout this book. The majority of shoppers say that the Web meets their expectations, most of the time, for purchasing certain categories of products and services. Consumers say, however, that there is definitely room for improvement. Any e-business that becomes complacent about consumer satisfaction and stops upgrading their value proposition will lose out. There's always a clever, well-funded company that can invent a better mousetrap to lure customers away and capture their attention. On the Web, the work is never done. Consumers' expectations know no boundaries.

So while e-commerce has gotten better, more functional, and more fun over the last year, there are still plenty of opportunities to make it better. In this chapter we discuss online disappointment, from the new consumer's perspective. What happens when things go wrong between the consumer and the Web sites? Where do improvements need to be focused and what can companies do to continue to meet and exceed customers' expectations? What are the barriers to the next level of growth in business-to-consumer e-commerce?

> *On the Web, the work is never done. Consumers' expectations know no boundaries*

New Consumers' Disappointments

Looking at online shopping on a broad level, most new consumers will say their shopping experiences meet their expectations. Despite glitches and specific site problems, overall it's working—at least well enough to be a viable solution for solving a subset of consumers' shopping needs. While expectations are often met, it is important to understand what happens when consumers are disappointed. What causes the gap between the desired experience and the actual experience?

When asked to list why their expectations were not met, shoppers predictably focus on e-businesses' failure to deliver the advantages they have come to expect online: items took too long to be delivered; products were out of stock or hard to find; they did not find lower product prices; and sites were too slow, crashed, or were too difficult to navigate. These and other reasons are shown in figure 5.1. It is interesting to note that 68 percent of consumers report nothing has been "really disappointing" in their recent Web experiences—even though they are quick to name some trouble spots and areas that need improvement.

FIGURE 5.1: REASONS WHY ONLINE SHOPPING EXPECTATIONS WERE NOT MET

Reason	Percentage
Nothing was disappointing	68%
Product out of stock	40%
Poor customer service	38%
Shipping expensive	38%
Site slow	37%
Order damaged, incomplete	36%
Site crashed, lost order	32%
Order arrival not as promised	31%
Privacy misuse	31%
Gift wrapping options inadequate	29%
Product did not meet expectations	29%

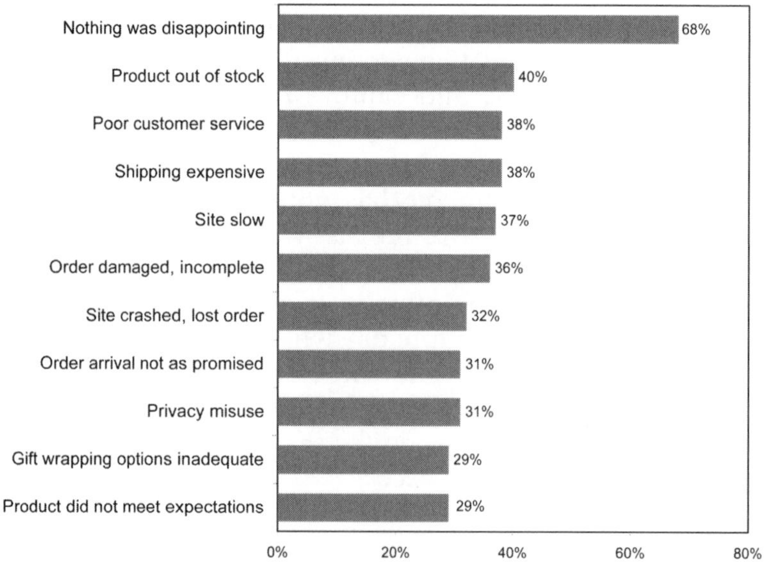

Note: Multiple responses possible.

Source: Pulse of the Customer

These trouble spots cluster around five primary themes: product availability, site performance, shipping, customer service, and invasion of privacy. Let's examine each to understand the key issues.

PRODUCT AVAILABILITY AND CONSUMER DISAPPOINTMENT

Dissatisfaction among many consumers is stimulated by product problems, the most common being the lack of availability of the desired items. Especially during high-traffic times, such as holiday shopping seasons, consumers get frustrated when products are out of stock. They go to their favorite Web sites, select an item, and learn that the product is back-ordered or even permanently unavailable. Customers never like to hear that what they want isn't available, especially if they have invested online shopping time and learn about availability problems late in the shopping sequence. Worse still, consumers complain that product availability information isn't always accurate on Web sites. They complete the purchase transaction process assuming the products are on the way, and learn after the fact that the product isn't actually available—creating great inconvenience and frustration.

Some consumers have had problems with orders that arrive damaged or incomplete. Of course this can happen during shipping due to faulty packaging or rough handling; poor packaging is an issue that e-businesses must address. But sometimes orders arrive incomplete because of the product availability problems mentioned above. Some Web sites don't bother to tell their customers that an order will be shipped incomplete due to out-of-stock items until the customer actually receives a partial shipment. The unsuspecting customer opens the box to find that key items are missing, adding insult to injury. This is especially disastrous for the consumer who is counting on the on-time arrival of the full order for a special occasion, such as for a birthday gift.

Another reported product problem is that the purchased items do not meet the consumer's expectations. This broad complaint usually boils down to one cause: the online information about the product is too limited or imprecise. For example, consumers comment that online product photographs are not true representations, or that adequately

When products don't meet expectations or when desired products are not in stock, the value of online shopping is greatly undermined

detailed depictions of the actual products are not provided. Sometimes size calibrations of small, medium, and large do not match the norm. Consumers also find that the quality or colors of products are misunderstood because of the visual limitations of the site, resulting in dissatisfaction.

When products don't meet expectations or when desired products are not in stock, the value of online shopping is greatly undermined. Since many consumers shop the Web because of convenience and timesavings, not having the product when the consumer demands it is not only disappointing, it's really inconvenient.

WHEN PRODUCT AVAILABILITY IS THE CULPRIT

MODERATOR: What are some of the problems you've experienced in product availability?

CONSUMER: This year, I ordered all the presents for my nieces and nephews from one site and was so happy that I was done with my Christmas shopping. I didn't know until I actually opened the box that one of the items was out-of-stock. They didn't bother telling me before then. I just found this ugly little printed notice inside the box, one day before Christmas, that said "Sorry. . . ." I was frantically searching the malls at the last minute to replace the missing gift, which was the main thing I was trying to avoid by shopping online in the first place!

CONSUMER: I ordered from a company that didn't send my order and I had to initiate an e-mail to get an explanation. Then they sent me an e-mail back stating that they had run out of the item and would not be able to fill my order. I ended up going to the store at the last minute.

CONSUMER: I was told several days after buying them online, that my products were on back order. I'm still waiting for some items to be shipped and it's next to impossible to find out when or if they'll ever be shipped at all.

MODERATOR: When is the right time for them to tell you about product availability?

CONSUMER: If the product isn't in stock, they should tell you right then when you are trying to buy it, not two days or even two hours later.

CONSUMER: I need to know while I'm still in the process of shopping. If it's not in stock, I need to go find something else, right then. And I really would like sites to recommend other products when the ones I want aren't available. That would help.

SITE PERFORMANCE AND CONSUMER DISAPPOINTMENT

Many times, there's an inverted relationship between the success of the e-business and the performance of Web sites and the Internet in general. In other words, the more traffic, the worse the performance. Consumers complain about several aspects of performance, but they all roll up into one common ailment: "It takes too long!" The vast majority of e-shoppers make this complaint.

Some problems that are reported emanate from sites being too busy when consumers want to visit, and so the site isn't available. Simply getting access to the site can be a problem, especially during peak times driven by advertising, events, or season. In addition, some consumers complain that they can't effectively access a site because the site requires more advanced technology than the consumer has on his computer. This results in the consumer not being able to use the site. As to be expected, if consumers can't even reach or read the site, they become frustrated—and they certainly can't buy anything.

Once on the site, consumers complain that pages load too slowly. This is not just a function of bulky graphic files that are slow to download; it's also a site scalability issue. Often, sites are not planned to handle the amount of traffic at peak times and thus serve content up slowly. This happens because many e-businesses have not effectively determined how much site traffic to expect and how to scale to the site volume requirements. Sometimes e-businesses underinvest in the required technology in the interest of saving money. This can become a case of being "a penny wise and a pound foolish," especially when the marketing department and the site operations department are not in sync. For example, a ridiculous faux pas committed by several dot coms during their Super Bowl 2000 advertising campaigns was that their Web sites were not able to handle the traffic generated by the advertisements. These companies spent millions of dollars to drive traffic to their sites and almost 25 percent had some kind of performance problem in terms of page-download times, according to Keynote Systems, a San Mateo firm that specializes in Internet performance.[1] The worst cases were page-load times that went from 5.5 seconds at a normal time, to sixty-two seconds during the peak. Another site was completely inaccessible in the middle of the game. In both cases, these companies lost prospective customers and squandered their advertising expenditures by offering unacceptable site performance. At $3.2 million per thirty-second advertisement, that is an expensive lesson to learn.

SITE PERFORMANCE PROBLEMS

MODERATOR: What are some of the technical problems you have experienced while shopping online?

CONSUMER: I have problems with compatibility of my browser and some sites I try to visit. For example, I don't like it when sites expect me to be able to accept JavaScript. I don't have it on my browser, I don't want it on my browser, so there's no way I can see what is on some sites.

CONSUMER: Yeah, sites should have a baseline, or some simple way of looking at what they have, not just the fancy flash.

MODERATOR: Beyond problems with browsers and advanced technologies, what other problems have you experienced?

CONSUMER: I get really mad when I can't even get on a site. On one site, I tried at least ten times to access the site. Finally I gave up and ordered from their mail-order catalog and their 800 number.

CONSUMER: I had a real problem with a well-known retailer's site. It wouldn't load up; after the third try, I went elsewhere.

Consumers sometimes comment about the sluggishness of shopping carts. Depending on how the shopping cart functionality is set up, purchasing items can be very tedious. Some sites make the mistake of not taking the shopper back to the place where they were when they made a product selection. We call this contextual shopping and some sites do a really bad job of it.

For example, a customer may be shopping for a back-to-school outfit on an apparel Web site. After answering myriad questions about size, gender, and style preferences, the site recommends and displays the full ensemble: pants, shirt, sweater. That's great, but each item is sold separately. When the first item is selected and placed into the shopping cart, the recommendations page is lost and can't be retrieved. To access the same recommended items in order to buy the next piece in the ensemble, the consumer has to go through answering all of the questions *again* because she has no easy way of identifying and finding those items through other means of site searching. This process must be repeated for all three items!

SITE FUNCTIONALITY PROBLEMS

MODERATOR: Have you run into any issues while in the actual process of buying?

CONSUMER: Sometimes the shopping cart moves way too slow. On the Gap site, it took me almost two hours to buy twelve items, because each time I clicked, it took several minutes to load the page. I was furious by the time I finished.

CONSUMER: On one site, I didn't find out that they did not accept American Express until the end of a lengthy order process. I had to go back and put in another credit card and do the whole thing again.

CONSUMER: I get mad when Web sites change their format. I am used to using a site one way and then all of a sudden, I click to it and it looks completely different. I try and try to find what I usually buy and it takes five clicks to get there. Shopping at that site used to be so much easier. I just stopped shopping there.

CONSUMER: I wanted to buy thirteen items from a site but it wouldn't let me. It would only let me put twelve items in my shopping cart. No explanation why. It just wouldn't accept a thirteenth item.

Another real-life shopping scenario that consumers complain about is when a Web site has many different product sections, such as a department store that sells books, music, toys, electronics, tools, and so on, but the shopping process is not fully integrated. For instance, the consumer goes to a Web site that sells a wide variety of product types, wanting to buy several jazz CDs. He goes through several clicks to get to the music section he seeks, he selects jazz music, selects the desired artist, picks the first CD to purchase, and puts it in his shopping cart. When he clicks on the "continue to shop" button, he is transported to the main menu of the site—not the music department, not the jazz section, not the artist's selections—but the opening page of the Web site. The shopper then has to go through all the same clicks to get back to the desired

E-businesses are thinking about the easiest way to develop the site, not the easiest way to use the site

Cumbersome online shopping processes infuriate customers

section. Even though he can use the same shopping cart for whatever he might buy from that site in that session, he loses the context of where he was on the site when he made his purchase, which is very annoying to consumers.

There are many Web sites—like leading brands—that function in these unacceptable ways. Why does this happen? We believe that problems like this occur because the site developers are not keeping the consumer in mind when they create the shopping process. They are thinking about the easiest way to develop the site, not the easiest way to use the site. These types of problems could easily be discovered through conducting usability tests with target consumers. In other cases, problems occur because the sub-sites within a site are not yet fully, technically integrated, due to companies acquiring other companies and not having adequate time to re-architect the sites for integrated shopping. Integration is a task that will get done, in due time.

From an internal perspective, e-businesses may have plenty of justifications for why the shopping processes on their sites are cumbersome, but the bottom line is that it infuriates customers. Poorly designed shopping processes waste consumers' time. Site gaffs like these are really maddening. It's not a good time to anger consumers—while they are in the process of selecting products to buy!

Some unlucky consumers have had sites actually crash during or after the shopping session, and totally lose the order. Again, it's not surprising that these types of site-performance problems make bad impressions on customers and foster negative word of mouth.

SHIPPING AND CONSUMER DISAPPOINTMENT

Some consumers have had real nightmarish experiences when it comes to the shipping link in the e-commerce value chain. Blame gets placed on the Web sites in some cases, on the shipping companies in others. But regardless of who is held accountable, it spells bad news for the consumer.

Even though consumers realize that shipping is a necessary expense in online shopping—that is, if they buy from a site that doesn't offer free shipping—they still comment that the expense of shipping is a disappointment in their online shopping experiences. The fear of shipping costs can impede consumer behavior

Some consumers have had real nightmarish experiences when it comes to shipping

in several ways. It impacts what they choose to buy, picking only products that they are certain will not need to be returned. They pick products that they assume will not be difficult to ship, shying away from bulky, heavy items. And when available, they pick sites that provide free shipping.

SHIPPING ISSUES

MODERATOR: What kind of problems have you encountered with shipping?

CONSUMER: I've had problems with the delivery companies following my instructions about where to leave packages that I bought online. That may not really count as an Internet problem, but it was still a part of the whole process.

CONSUMER: I had the same product shipped and billed to me twice. I'm still trying to get it all sorted out, but I guess it's better than not getting anything at all.

MODERATOR: How did the shipping problem impact you?

CONSUMER: I have thirty days to read a book for my book club. So I ordered in the beginning of the month but it never came. They said it shipped but it didn't. I had to call several times. I finally got it with one week left to read my book. I barely finished in time and it took all the fun out of my book club that month.

CONSUMER: I didn't get what I bought when I wanted it. That was the problem. I was pretty disappointed.

MODERATOR: How did you resolve the problems?

CONSUMER: I ended up canceling an order because they said they would ship it in a certain number of days and then didn't. When I called, it still hadn't shipped. I avoid that Web site now for that reason.

CUSTOMER SERVICE AND CONSUMER DISAPPOINTMENT

Another center of gravity in customer disappointment is customer service. Interestingly, this is an area in which consumers report significant improvements in recent months. Evidently, many sites have substantially improved the way they handle service for online customers, which is good news for everyone in the industry. Nonetheless, there is still room for improvement.

CUSTOMER SERVICE IMPROVEMENTS

MODERATOR: How did customer service this year compare to last year on your favorite Web sites?

CONSUMER: Customer service was a lot better on many Web sites this year than before. I really like getting e-mail within minutes of ordering something, confirming my order, and then getting follow-up e-mail when it has been shipped.

CONSUMER: This year it was better. They actually had a phone number on the site!

It used to be that Web sites were a little online obsessed, meaning they believed that if customers were going to shop online, then they should be serviced and supported online as well—to the exclusion of other methods of customer service contact. While this makes sense for some types of situations and can be effective in solving some problems, it doesn't fit all consumer requirements. Increasingly, the customer service solutions to e-consumer problems are not delivered online.

Most consumers (80 percent) have communicated via e-mail with a Web site when they needed customer service, as shown in figure 5.2. Most frequently, the types of issues

FIGURE 5.2: CHANNELS USED FOR CUSTOMER SERVICE BY WEB SHOPPERS

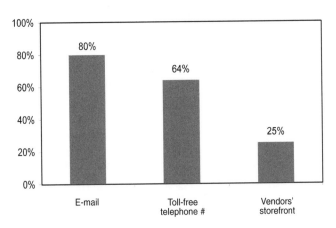

Note: Multiple responses possible.

Source: Pulse of the Customer

that are resolved via e-mail are standard, frequently-asked questions that are not time-urgent or mission-critical. Sometimes, issues

Resolving problems via e-mail is often not an effective process

can be resolved by pointing consumers to relevant content on the Web site or responding to customers' questions by sending standardized, templated responses. Often, however, resolving problems via e-mail is not an effective process.

Consumers claim to prefer speaking to a live customer service representative, to ensure that their customer issues are resolved, especially during times like a hectic holiday season. Many of these shoppers report negative experiences with e-mail requests in terms of meaningful and timely resolution. Often, consumers get what appear to be "form-letter" e-mail responses that are not effective in resolving their problems. Consequently, e-shoppers will resort to calling e-businesses' toll-free call centers to solve their online shopping frustrations, as it is not always apparent that there is a human being awaiting their e-mail at the Web site.

CUSTOMER SERVICE DELIVERY PREFERENCES

MODERATOR: What is your preferred method of getting customer service when you shop online?

CONSUMER: I've had good luck with e-mail. Like on Schwab.com, I talked to some advisors online back and forth. It works like a phone call, basically.

CONSUMER: I get my problems resolved by phone. I haven't used e-mail much for customer service. E-mail seems more casual.

CONSUMER: E-mail customer service doesn't work for me. I like to vent to real people. Little exclamation points in an e-mail don't really cut it. I like to yell at somebody and apologize later.

MODERATOR: Have you had trouble finding a phone number for an e-business?

CONSUMER: Not anymore. After I paid for my product purchase, the site sent me a confirmation number and the phone number was there. So, I called them.

CONSUMER: Yes, and I hate it when there isn't any phone number or contact information on a Web site. It's really frustrating when you keep clicking through to reach "Contact us" and it's all just e-mail addresses.

CONSUMER: I hate it when they offer a phone number and it's always busy!

Toll-free call centers for e-businesses are a relatively new phenomenon. When talking to consumers as recently as 1999, the number-one complaint about e-commerce service was the lack of telephone customer support. Consumers groused that telephone numbers were totally absent from Web sites. Try as they might, consumers could not figure out how to reach a human voice when they were having problems with their online transactions. Clearly, many of the leading Web sites got that message loud and clear. Now, a large proportion of e-consumers report using the newly available toll-free numbers offered by e-businesses. In fact, some companies provide integrated telephone support so that consumers can talk to a customer service representative while online and the representative can actually view the shopper's session from their own computer. Based on consumers' attitudes expressed about the frustrations with e-commerce customer service, innovations such as this should be effective in continuing to build consumers' confidence in online shopping.

Many consumers would like to use a storefront in combination with a Web site to get customer service, but this is still a nascent trend. Recent polls show that only 25 percent of consumers visit a vendor's storefront to rectify their online shopping customer-service issues—for good reason. Most dot coms today don't have storefronts, and many brick-and-mortar stores have not offered online shopping to their target customers. This is an area of opportunity to serve online customers better, as consumers say they like using the vendor's storefront for customer service when it is an option.

Consumers also appreciate apologies when something has gone wrong in their online shopping experiences. Apologies are particularly powerful if they include a token gift or discount on future purchases.

RECTIFYING MISTAKES

MODERATOR: What about when a Web site made a mistake? What did they do to rectify it?

CONSUMER: Most of the time, I got some gift certificates or discounts when a site screwed up.

MODERATOR: Did that make you feel better?

CONSUMER: Yes, that definitely eased the pain.

INVASION OF PRIVACY AND CUSTOMER DISAPPOINTMENT

Chapter 4 focuses on the topic of privacy; therefore, we won't go into depth about privacy here. But it is important to repeat that consumers remember the times they are intruded upon and are very motivated to discover who is responsible for the intrusion. E-businesses should keep this in mind and follow acceptable business practices to avoid creating consumer resentment and tarnishing the brand.

PRIVACY AND DISAPPOINTMENT

MODERATOR: You say your sense of privacy was abused. Who did it?

CONSUMER: I don't know. I never give any personal information to Web sites. But, somehow they get it anyway. I don't know how they do it, but they get it. If I knew who was doing that, I'd figure out a way to stop it.

CONSUMER: I went to a site that already had information on me and I had never even been there before. I think they bought it from Safeway. It made me really not want to go to that site. That's an invasion of my privacy. And now, I'm mad at Safeway, too.

When Buying Online Is Just Too Hard

When new consumers are repeatedly disappointed, they can conclude that the end does not justify the means and that online shopping is just too hard. Figure 5.3 illustrates the areas in which consumers commonly run into difficulties when trying to buy online.

Sometimes the difficulty is product related, rather than about the way a Web site performs. When products are difficult to buy online, it is often because the consumer needs to see, touch, or smell the product before buying. We will discuss which products are seen as most difficult in the following section.

But there are other issues beyond the need to "experience" the products that make online shopping difficult. Consumers report that product information is often inadequate, obstructing the ability to make a final purchase decision. Consumers complain that too often, sites are missing key purchase information such as physical dimensions or product availability. Also, most sites only have front-view photos of the product, which is often woefully inadequate when purchasing a three-dimensional item.

FIGURE 5.3: WHY SOME PRODUCTS ARE DIFFICULT TO BUY ONLINE

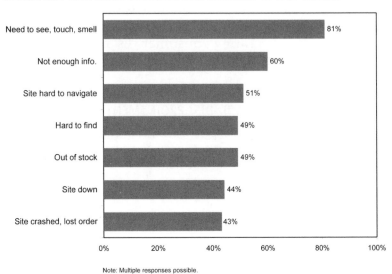

Note: Multiple responses possible.

Other issues that make products difficult to buy online are more related to site problems, rather than to product problems, as previously noted. One of the interesting complaints that consumers often make is that Web sites change the navigational schemes too often. Consumers get annoyed when they have to re-learn a site's layout. This is particularly frustrating to Convenience Shoppers who are looking for the fastest way of accomplishing the task. Frequent changes in site design diminish the benefits of the online shopping experience. Consumers appreciate the need to constantly update sites in terms of content, and they value fresh, up-to-date information. They don't understand, however, why the page layouts, navigation bars, and frames are altered so frequently. Change is good, if the right changes are made.

Product availability resurfaces when consumers talk about the difficulties of buying online. Frequent complaints are voiced about products being out of stock. As a result, popular items are very hard to find—even in the vast world of e-commerce.

SOME PRODUCTS REQUIRE A PHYSICAL EXPERIENCE

Consistently, we hear consumers voice this thought: some products require physical examination before they can be bought. This desire to "experience" particular products is pervasive in certain product categories, and has been a challenge since the inception of e-commerce. Here again, we see the consumers' confidence as a key factor in online purchase behavior.

THE NEED FOR RICHER EXPERIENCES

MODERATOR: Why are some products especially hard to buy online?

CONSUMER: In my case, I couldn't hear the product. I was on an auction site trying to find a drum set. They had five hundred drum sets for sale. I was going through it and realized I don't really know what any of these sound like. I'm not really much of a drummer, but I still wanted to try it out and make sure it sounded good.

CONSUMER: I need to see the front and the back of a product to feel comfortable buying it, since when I'm wearing it, both sides will be visible.

CONSUMER: If I'm going to spend a lot of money, I want to do more than just see a picture of it. I want to learn how to use it. I want to be sold.

CONSUMER: I would never buy something mechanical on the Web. I've only made purchases that are really no-brainers.

CONSUMER: Sites should give a little more explanation, detail, illustration, and pictures. Sometimes I go to a site and look at something I want, but there's just a two-sentence blurb about what it is and you don't really know what you're getting. So you're hesitant to buy it, even if it costs only $20.

Some consumers say they "cannot imagine" buying products such as apparel, food, jewelry, or furniture online because they fear that the products may need to be returned if they are not satisfied. The obstacle is clear. Consumers continue to only purchase products that they are confident will meet their needs and, therefore, not need to be returned. "I'll only buy what I'm sure to keep" is the guiding principle of many online shoppers.

For more complex products like consumer electronics, machines, and tools, consumers often require an expert to demonstrate the product, as well as teach them how to set up and use the product. Therefore, they feel more comfortable dealing with personnel at retail stores. For these types

Consumers only purchase products that they are confident will not need to be returned

of items, product breakage in the shipping process is also a concern.

Some of the problems that consumers mention can be addressed by improving online merchandising techniques. By giving consumers more extensive information and richer visual experiences, some of the "tactile" barriers can be overcome. We are already beginning to see this with consumers that have DSL or cable modems. It's important to remember, however, that there is a balancing act to maintain, as better audio and visual information lead to larger graphic files and longer page-download times. The need for faster site performance, as described in earlier sections, must be balanced by consumers' desire for better visual information. Sites should offer consumers the option to view information in either a text or graphic mode to address the needs of both consumer factions.

THE HASSLE OF RETURNS

MODERATOR: So what is the big deal? You can always send it back, right?

CONSUMER: It's a problem because when something goes wrong, you just can't get it corrected right away. It's not like a store where you can always go there to take it back. But when you've bought it online, you have to ship it back, and they charge you for it, or even if they don't, it's a hassle.

CONSUMER: Yeah, so then you go to the post office, take a number, and stand in line. It's a hassle and a big waste of time.

CONSUMER: You don't always get a good perspective of products online. I ordered a basketball and hoop for my son, and when it showed up, it was probably one-tenth of the size of the real thing. So, I had to return it and then I was short a birthday gift.

"DIFFICULT" PRODUCTS AND THE "NEED TO TRY" CONCEPT

Many products are well-suited for e-commerce, such as books, CDs, toys, and software. These are usually "low involvement" products that have two common attributes: they don't require a tactile experience before purchase and there is a low likelihood that they will need to be returned.

These are the product categories that have become standard e-commerce fare.

Low-involvement products are popular e-commerce fare due to the low likelihood of returns

When consumers are asked to select those products they specifically find difficult to purchase online, the general tendency is to name "high involvement" products. Typically, high involvement products are those that are relatively expensive, bought infrequently, risky, and highly self-expressive.[2] Examples of these items are shown in figure 5.4, such as apparel, jewelry, furniture, cars, and art. Risk in this context has several dimensions: the risk of the e-business being fraudulent; the risk of the product being of unacceptable quality; and the risk of the product not fitting the target application, i.e., the living room or the human body. The latter two risks give rise to concerns about having to return items.

FIGURE 5.4: PRODUCTS REPORTED AS DIFFICULT TO BUY ONLINE

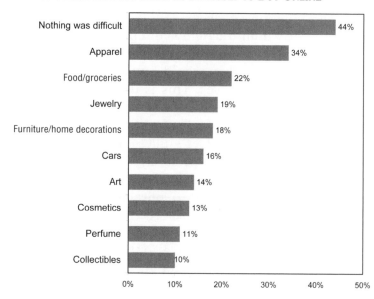

Note: Multiple responses possible.

Source: Pulse of the Customer

SPECIFIC PRODUCT TYPES ARE THE CHALLENGE

MODERATOR: What are the product categories that you can't imagine buying online and why?

CONSUMER: To me, art is an experience. I can't even imagine buying a piece of art after only seeing it on a small computer screen.

CONSUMER: I don't like to buy cosmetics online. I can't because I need to go to the store, talk to the salesperson, try things on my face, and see how I like them. They may look beautiful on the site, but when I put them on, they look awful on me.

CONSUMER: Cars would be hard to buy online. If there's something wrong with it, you want to take it back to a dealership or the person you bought it from, so you can go yell at them. I mean, it's a person. And anyway, how does the car get to your house?

CONSUMER: I can't buy apparel online. I have to know how it'll look and it's such a pain to send it back.

Over one-third of the respondents rank apparel as being the most difficult item to buy online. Interestingly, apparel falls into both the high- and low-involvement categories, based on how consumers think about e-shopping. It depends on for whom the item is intended, how important "fit" is, and how well the item is merchandized online. Some consumers say they would buy apparel online as a gift, but not for themselves. This is understandable, considering that shoppers are often guessing size when the apparel is a gift, whether they buy online or in a store. But when buying for themselves, unless they have a clear understanding of what the product will be—a previously purchased style and size of brand-name jeans, for example—shoppers are reluctant to purchase clothing items online. Consumers need to check the fit of the garment as well as the fabric and quality before buying.

Cosmetics and perfume are also thought of as difficult to purchase online, especially for first-time purchases, as the product selection process is dependent on the olfactory and tactile senses. Once brand preferences are established, after-market sales for these categories are well-suited to e-commerce channels.

APPAREL

MODERATOR: Let's talk more about apparel. What is difficult about buying clothes online?

CONSUMER: Most of the time when I'm shopping, it's usually for clothes and I like to try on clothes. I like to feel what the fabric is. Over the Internet, you can't really tell what kind of fabric it is, you can't try it on to see how well it fits and you can't get a real grasp of the color—the true, actual color.

CONSUMER: Sweaters I'll buy, but other clothes I won't buy online. You don't know what a "medium" or a "large" is in many items.

CONSUMER: I tried on six pairs of pants at the store the other night before I found one that fit. There's no way I want to go through that nightmare on the Internet. Having them sent to me, try them on, send them back. It's not going to happen.

Furniture and decorative items are considered to be challenging to purchase on the Web. This is not just because of the need for a richer visual and tactile experience, but it is also due to concerns about the expense and inconvenience of shipping and returning large, bulky items.

FURNITURE

MODERATOR: Let's talk some more about furniture. What's the obstacle there?

CONSUMER: I have to shop for things like furniture and linens in the store. I need to be reassured about the quality of the fabric and the dimensions, because it might be bigger or even smaller than it looks online.

CONSUMER: I want to sit on it, touch it, and decide if I could really take a nap on it.

CONSUMER: I'd be worried about what you do if you don't like it. How do you ship it back? I can't imagine what kind of hassle and expense that would be.

It's also interesting to note that food and groceries rank relatively high as products that are difficult to buy online. This isn't because food fits the classic definition of "high involvement." Interestingly, many consumers don't trust online grocers to select the right products on their behalf, especially product categories such as produce and meats where selection is very subjective. In addition, we suspect that for some consumers grocery shopping is indeed an expressive, individualized task, and one that is reluctantly relinquished to strangers.

Making It Easier to Buy Online

Some of the problems with buying high-involvement products online can be solved by leveraging traditional distribution channels in the online consumer offering. Strategically, companies can deliver to the e-customer those online benefits they've come to expect, while overcoming the concerns they have about needing to experience the products.

CROSS-SHOPPING

One of the ways to overcome the need to experience a product is to offer consumers channel alternatives within a retail brand. As discussed more deeply in chapter 6, consumers wish that any channel—retail stores, catalogs, or the Web—would offer multiple purchasing options. For example, shoppers may rely on the Internet to provide product information, pricing, and selection, but will go to the retailer's storefront to make the final purchase. Others indicate that they will perform the "touch" test at the store, then return to the Web to look for the best price or a desired style and color.

These emerging cross-shopping preferences will continue to evolve and will drive retailers in all product categories to provide multiple shopping channels within the same brand. This could indicate a potential advantage for brick-and-mortar retailers who execute their e-commerce strategies well.

ONLINE EXPECTATIONS OF BRICK-AND-MORTAR RETAILERS

Consumers say that a solution to breaking through the experience barrier for online selling of high-involvement products is for brick-and-mortar retailers to get involved in the dot-com world. In fact, consumers expect their favorite retail brands to offer online alternatives. The news media is filled with stories of companies making this transition. Brick-and-mortar retailers can leverage the advantage of a physical environment by adding an e-commerce alternative or by partnering with dot coms, thus providing consumers with multi-channel alternatives—commonly known as a "click-and-mortar" strategy.

In a click-and-mortar environment, consumers often expect a Web site to contain at least the same number of product categories and a better product selection than its brick-and-mortar counterpart. Most consumers indicate, however, that this expectation is rarely met by retailers today. Realizing how quick-

Consumers expect Web sites to offer equal or greater product selection as their brick-and-mortar counterparts

ly consumers' expectations become requirements, it is likely that last year's more patient click-and-mortar consumers will become next year's frustrated customers. New consumers are increasingly demanding better online product selection and will desert those retailers who fail to bring their full product inventory online.

WHEN CROSS-SHOPPING IS NECESSARY

MODERATOR: What are some examples of how you would like to combine online and offline shopping?

CONSUMER: I visited a number of dealer sites when I was shopping for a car, but I still had to go to the dealership to have a test drive. I just couldn't experience that online.

CONSUMER: I've checked out furniture and home accessories in the store and then tried to find them online, hoping that I could get a better price.

MODERATOR: Do you find acceptable cross-shopping alternatives?

CONSUMER: Not enough are out there. I read about some clothing that I wanted to purchase in a magazine, which wasn't available in the stores in my area. I went online, hoping I could purchase it there, and they didn't have an online store. That not only disappointed me, but it actually made me mad.

CONSUMER: I find that many online stores only sell a few of the products they offer in their retail stores. It frustrates me when I know the store carries what I want, but they won't let me buy it online. Most of the time I won't even go to the store to follow up on it.

CONSUMER: I expect to find more online, lots more. But I don't see that, most retail stores aren't selling all of their products online.

Future Barriers of Online Shopping

To comprehend the impact of customer disappointment, it's important to know what consumers consider to be bad experiences and how those experiences will impact their future actions. When experienced shoppers are asked which barriers, if any, might prevent them from making more online purchases in the near future, the need to touch, feel, and try on products was the most common response, as shown in figure 5.5. Web retailers choosing to carry high-involvement products will continue to struggle with the consumer's need to "experience" these types of products in the coming year.

These high-involvement retailers should seek ways to provide target customers with the required tactile information to overcome the barriers to the sale. Whether addressed through the use of better graphics technology and higher bandwidth or through click-and-mortar, multichannel alternatives, the issue must be addressed to break through current barriers.

FIGURE 5.5: BARRIERS TO PURCHASING MORE ONLINE IN 2000

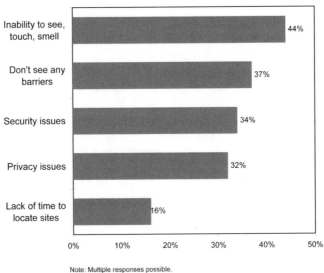

Note: Multiple responses possible.

Source: Pulse of the Customer

Even though e-customers are becoming more and more comfortable with providing credit card and personal information online, security and privacy issues are still seen as barriers to e-shopping in the future. Dot coms need to be sensitive to consumers' reluctance to provide their personal information online. One way to gain consumers' confidence is for Web retailers to address the issue up-front with reassuring security and privacy policy statements. Furthermore, it is imperative that companies abide by those policies. While there are still barriers to break down, 37 percent of consumers remain optimistic and report that they did not anticipate *any* barriers preventing them from buying more online in the next year.

Implications for Business

We have outlined the key areas for improvement on which every e-business should focus. That is, however, only looking at the goal of customer satisfaction and retention through the rearview mirror. Looking forward to the near-term future, several areas should be addressed for improvement.

An issue that is rapidly developing into a key e-customer expectation issue is the delivery of accurate online product inventory information. According to our research, shoppers expect the inventory information that appears on e-commerce sites to be an accurate representation of current product levels. While many inventory database systems update product availability records at timed intervals throughout the day, this data becomes stale with every passing minute. Web shoppers of the future will not be satisfied with old data; they fully expect that the product inventory listed online is in fact "real-time." Anything less than real-time will be unacceptable. This is a customer-relations management issue that deserves to be given much closer attention. Companies who don't take this seriously will lose business.

Consumers express disappointment when making their purchase decisions based on the availability of a product, only to find the product is out-of-stock or back-ordered because the system had outdated inventory levels. Notifying shoppers of product availability problems after the purchase process is complete is deemed unacceptable even if it's just a few hours later. Shoppers want to complete their shopping experience so they can "check it off their list." If the site reports product unavailability after the fact, the shopper has to start over, which is seen as a waste of time.

Many of the problems and bottlenecks that consumers currently experience will be solved with pervasive adoption of higher-speed connections

Another area for future improvement is in online merchandising techniques. As high-bandwidth connections become a reality for a larger proportion of the United States population, significantly improved techniques for displaying three-dimensional products will be possible. Using technologies such as immersive video, consumers will be able to interactively experience products in the intended environment before they buy. Consumers will understand products better when they can see every side by rotating the product on screen, watching it move, and even listening to it. The visualization technologies to perform these tasks are available today; the problem is getting the "last-mile" bandwidth into consumers' homes. Many of the problems and bottlenecks that consumers currently experience will be solved with pervasive availability and adoption of higher-speed connections. These technical solutions will go a long way in broadening the categories that consumers will consider buying online. Until that day comes, e-businesses should continue to incrementally improve site experiences and meet the ever-expanding set of expectations of the new consumer.

6

The Impact of the Internet on Other Aspects of Consuming

The acceptance of the Internet by consumers as a vehicle for commerce and consumption has not occurred in a vacuum. For every action, there is a reaction. Internet adoption has had—and will continue to have—a ripple effect throughout our systems: economic, communications, cultural, and societal. This wave of change is impacting some of our capitalistic institutions quite dramatically and visibly. The effects on other aspects of life are subtler—in some people's opinions, more insidious. The more hours per week consumers use the Internet, the more significant the changes in social, communications, and shopping behavior.[1] Whether viewed as a favorable or unfavorable change, the impact of the Internet is certainly pervasive.

Regardless of one's opinion about the upsides and downsides of the Internet phenomenon, in reality it is here to stay. We must adapt to it and learn to benefit from the changes it is creating throughout the business ecosystem (defined as the interdependent environment and business community interacting and functioning as a unit.) The Internet changes how we do things—how we begin our daily tasks. The Internet also changes how we do other routine activities of life, which has impact on the institutions with which we have grown up.

In this chapter, we explore some of the aspects of day-to-day consumer behavior that have been altered by the Web. Specifically, we address how the Internet has altered consumers' shopping preferences: where, how, and why they shop. We look at how people view the notion of news and how the Internet has affected the preferred news media. In addition, we explore how the Internet has changed certain preferences for entertainment pastimes, communication vehicles, and financial management.

Where, How, and Why New Consumers Buy

We have been examining consumer shopping behavior from several angles throughout this book. We have primarily focused on what consumers like and dislike about online shopping. But how has the Internet changed the other ways that consumers shop?

To delve into this question and build our context, let's summarize what we know about the new consumers' attitudes about shopping online. The key reasons new consumers say they like to shop online are:

- It's more convenient as compared to other methods of shopping
- It saves time
- They are more empowered because of better product information and the ability to compare offerings among many different vendors
- They find better product selection at better prices

Online shopping, however, so far has not proven to be the panacea for the new consumer's shopping wants and needs. The primary drawbacks to online shopping are:

- Some products are simply not conducive to an online purchase
- Many consumers appreciate and want to experience the "aesthetics of shopping," i.e., touching things and trying items on
- Returning products that don't meet their requirements is a hassle. Customers are reluctant to per-

form online commerce if they don't recognize or trust the company brand

For some product categories, the Internet poses a threat to other shopping channels. We have already witnessed this effect in many industries. At the same time, companies who can address the disadvantages present in the current online shopping alternatives have potential opportunities.

THE INTERNET IS CANNIBALIZING ON OTHER CHANNELS

Consumers predict that they will be buying more online in the near future—to the detriment of other sales channels. Though almost a third of the consumers we talked to claimed to be simply buying more overall when they buy online, figure 6.1 shows how their Web shopping behavior is affecting other channels from which they typically buy. One in five consumers we polled say they are now buying less from printed catalogs due to their online buying activities. Similarly, 13 percent report to be buying less from retail stores, and another 13 percent are buying less from both catalogs and retail stores.

FIGURE 6.1: CHANGES IN SHOPPING BEHAVIOR DUE TO E-COMMERCE

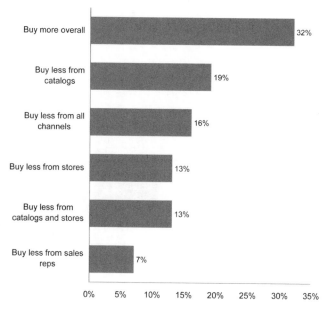

Source: *Pulse of the Customer*

Consumers predict that they will be buying more online—to the detriment of other sales channels

Looking more closely at the impact that consumers predict the Internet will have on their catalog purchase activities, we compare consumers' intentions to increase, decrease, and maintain the number of catalogs versus the number of Web sites from which they shop. This is an important indicator of the changes the two channels will experience as a result of consumers' experimental shopping behavior. As shown in figure 6.2, a large majority of consumers predict that they will buy from more Web sites in the future than they do now. But regarding catalogs, consumers don't plan on much more exploration; in fact, the use of new catalogs appears to be stagnating at 50 percent of the sample, indicating that consumers expect to use the same number of catalogs in the future.

FIGURE 6.2: EXPECTED CHANGES IN THE NUMBER OF CHANNEL BRANDS USED: WEB SITES VS. CATALOGS

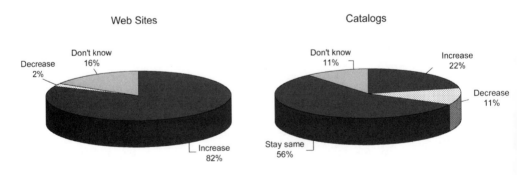

Web Sites

Don't know 16%

Decrease 2%

Increase 82%

Catalogs

Don't know 11%

Increase 22%

Decrease 11%

Stay same 56%

Source: Pulse of the Customer

Consumers' Retail Store Shopping Preferences

Is e-commerce having an effect on retail stores? We think the answer is obviously yes. Do consumers prefer to shop in retail stores over online? The answer is sometimes, for some things. Are retail stores doomed to a long, painful death at the hand of the Internet? We think the answer is—it depends. We don't believe that the Internet will put retail stores, as a category, out of business, just as direct-mail catalogs didn't put retail stores out of business. We do believe, however, that the ways in which the individual retail-store brands react to the Web will determine the survival of those specific individual retailers.

Retail storefronts continue to serve a distinct purpose in the lives of consumers. This is particularly true for high-involvement items that require demonstration and service to successfully complete the transaction, as well as for products that consumers feel require a tactile experience such as clothing, furniture, fragrances, and food. In addition, for items that are needed or desired immediately, retail stores will always provide a good solution. Products that need to be tried out or tried on remain popular retail store items. But for products that are routine, commodity, staple items, consumers report an increased preference to buying them online, resulting in an abandonment of the retail store for those low-involvement goods.

In addition to the need to try before buying, retail stores hold appeal among consumers for other reasons as well. Some shoppers simply enjoy the overall experience of shopping in a store or mall. It's entertaining to look at merchandise, point-of-sale displays, and store decorations. The store ambiance can offer a satisfying, aesthetic excursion. Consumers can keep up with the latest trends in fashion, home furnishings, and electronics by looking at store displays. It can be social, an outing to enjoy with friends. It can even create a sense of community when consumers encounter their neighbors while out shopping.

There's instant gratification when purchasing products in a store—assuming the store has the desired items in stock. The consumer

Products that need to be tried out or tried on remain popular retail store items

can purchase the product and use it immediately. So, not only is there a low risk of return when the product is selected in person, there isn't a time lag in being able to use it. In this world of low tolerance for delayed gratification, immediate access to desired products can be very powerful.

ATTITUDES ABOUT RETAIL STORE SHOPPING

MODERATOR: What do you like about shopping in retail stores?

CONSUMER: Sometimes I just want to be sold to by a real person, face-to-face. Compare products, let me see and hear the differences—especially expensive products.

CONSUMER: Take a bookstore for example. There's something about being able to pick up the book and read something about it, while being around other people who are doing the same thing. There's something about the experience and the feel of it all that you don't get on the Internet. Part of it is emotional. Part of it is product-driven and has to do with your expectations associated with that product.

CONSUMER: When I want to buy something, I want it right now. I don't want to wait for two weeks; I lose interest in it.

MODERATOR: Are you loyal to certain stores? If so, why?

CONSUMER: I'm loyal to stores that I'm familiar with, so I can get in and get out.

CONSUMER: I like Target. They have a good standard of quality. It's good for gifts because you know there is going to be a Target to where you can take it back if you need to.

CONSUMER: I love to go to Wal-Mart for my cleaning stuff. They have good prices.

The balance of consumer demands with the ability of retail stores to meet those demands will cause the retail store channel to endure for years to come. But we believe that the range of products and services procured from retail stores by new consumers will shrink. Not only will the retailers be largely relegated to high-involvement products, but also, in reality, only a subset of the shopping public is motivated by the attributes that make retail store shopping attractive. Given an option, many shoppers would prefer to avoid retail stores. For shoppers who abhor retail stores and who have for years endured the crowds, the noise, and the overstimulation, other methods of retailing—catalogs and online—have come as a welcome relief.

As consumers, we are neither consistent in what motivates us to shop nor where we choose to shop. Each individual can savor the joy of shopping for some types of products and harbor feelings of dread of shopping for others. No one person is the same shopper across categories.

As consumers, we are neither consistent in what motivates us to shop nor where we choose to shop

These dynamic and complex consumer preferences make offering the right mix of retail options very challenging.

Clearly, retail stores continue to have an edge over the Internet, for some people and in some product categories. But new consumers' preferences are evolving quickly. This evolution may impact catalogs more swiftly than retail stores.

IF RETAIL STORES HAD ONLINE ALTERNATIVES

MODERATOR: If your favorite stores offered an online alternative, would you shop online?

CONSUMER: Even if they put Foley's online, I wouldn't shop online. I love going into the store.

CONSUMER: I would if it had the same product selection. I think department stores like Macy's should offer the same or more products online. I would like to completely replace going to the store with buying online. But they only offer one-tenth of what they have in stores online. I find that very frustrating.

Consumers' Catalog Shopping Preferences

When mail-order catalogs were first invented years ago, they were designed to reach customers who lived in places where physically shopping in retail stores was highly impractical. Companies such as Sears & Roebuck and others pioneered the concept of the mail-order catalog in 1895 to leverage the power of the U.S. Postal Service and railroads to expand their geographic market reach without having to build stores. From that point through to the present, the mail-order catalog business has been a growing industry.

The proliferation of direct-mail catalogs was dramatic in the last few decades of the twentieth century. The confluence of many factors created a ready market for direct-

The benefits of shopping via catalog and shopping online are perceived by consumers to be very similar

mail catalogs and the Internet, many of which were discussed in chapter 1. Direct-mail catalogs were well accepted for several reasons: the population became increasingly more time deprived; credit cards were more vastly adopted; delivery systems were more competitive in terms of speed and price; and technology became more pervasive to keep it all managed.

Catalog shopping offered several key benefits to consumers over retail stores: it was more convenient, and it was much more time efficient than physically shopping in a retail store. The range of products available through catalogs proliferated exponentially as new brands were created and brought to market. In addition, catalogs provided critical price information and gave consumers a pricing frame of reference while shopping.

Interestingly, the key benefits that made catalog shopping a viable alternative to retail stores are the same key benefits that online shopping offers. Therefore, catalogs seem to be more vulnerable to e-commerce competition as compared to retail stores, because the benefits of shopping via catalog and shopping online are perceived by consumers to be very similar.

Catalogs continue to have some benefits over Web shopping, according to consumers. When compared to today's generation of Web sites, consumers perceive catalogs to provide better visual representation of products due to the quality of printing and the merchandising context provided by the typical catalog photography. The photos provide a better understanding of the product, since they are presented in a proper scale and appropriate setting. And consumers enjoy looking at the pictures.

For many consumers, catalogs have a more user-friendly format than most retail Web sites. It is easier to view many products on one layout. Flipping through the pages is faster and it's easier to look at many types of products and options in a short period of time. It's easier to mark pages of interest and reference back to those pages. And it is easier to share and show to other people.

Consumers also perceive that catalogs have an advantage over the Web in terms of product selection. When comparing a singular catalog to a singular competitive Web site, some consumers believe that the typical catalog has more product range and depth than its cyber-counterparts.

With direct-mail catalogs, shopping can be more spontaneous than on the Web

This belief is not unanimously held, however, as some believe that product selection is much vaster on the Web due to the massive group of sites available within a simple mouse click.

Lastly, consumers say that another advantage catalogs have over Web sites is the potential for unplanned, immediate stimulation. Because catalogs come to us in the mail, shopping experiences can be spontaneous and we have the potential to immediately view products. As compared to the Web where the consumer must take the action to shop—such as turning on the computer, waiting for it to boot up, dialing up the ISP—with catalogs, shopping experiences can begin with little initiative on the part of the consumer. Of course, the voluminous number of catalogs mailed to United States households today has become unwieldy for many consumers. This advantage of immediate stimulation can backfire when the number of catalogs received per day becomes too profuse for consumers to cope with.

ATTITUDES ABOUT CATALOG SHOPPING

MODERATOR: What do you like about shopping in catalogs?

CONSUMER: I appreciate the creativity of what is presented, especially for gift items. It gives me a lot of ideas on what I can buy. It's really convenient to order and pretty soon it comes.

CONSUMER: With the catalog, I'm more apt to see something I hadn't thought of that I want to buy. And it's easy to show someone else.

CONSUMER: It's the milieu of the pictures, they sort of sell you a fantasy.

CONSUMER: Sometimes you bond with the person taking your order and they tell you about a special.

CONSUMER: With a catalog, I'll sit down on the couch and relax.

MODERATOR: What advantages do catalogs have over the Web?

CONSUMER: It seems more confidential and secure with my credit card, as compared to the Internet.

CONSUMER: It's more spontaneous because you can just pick it up and look at it. Whereas with the Web, you have to say, "OK, I'm going shopping now," and log onto your computer.

> CONSUMER: I interact with catalogs differently. I sit there and just go through it like I'm reading a book. Whereas online, I'm trying to find one specific area.
>
> CONSUMER: The pictures are better in catalogs. They put the clothing on a person. The person is in a pleasant setting. I get a better feeling about it than when the item is shown in a sterile looking picture on a Web site.
>
> MODERATOR: What makes you loyal to a catalog?
>
> CONSUMER: They're the same attributes of loyalty for anywhere I buy. It's consistent quality and good products. In the case of catalogs, it's better products than I can get at the store with better prices, plus the convenience of not having to go to the store to get them.

Comparison of Internet, Catalog, and Retail Shopping

Every retail channel has its benefits and fans; consumers value their chosen channels for many different reasons. While the Internet is not likely to totally eliminate retail channels as we know them today, as we have seen, the Web has already begun to change how people prefer to shop. The next section compares and contrasts consumers' attitudes and behavior across the three primary retail shopping channels—storefronts, catalogs, and e-businesses. We analyze the specific products consumers buy from these three channels, and what motivates behavior in their shopping experiences.

PRODUCTS AND SERVICES PURCHASED BY CHANNEL

As discussed in earlier sections, consumers have strong preferences regarding the types of products they buy from the various retail channels. Illustrated in figure 6.3, there are notable patterns in the reported product purchases by channel. The propensity for consumers to shop at retail stores for high-involvement products is very obvious: 75 percent of the consumers we polled prefer to buy furniture in a retail store, whereas only a small percentage shop for furniture online and in catalogs. Appliances is another category in which consumers seem to have greater comfort buying from retail stores. Consumers are still most likely to purchase food and groceries from retail stores as well. It is important to note, however, that the ability to purchase products online is a contributing factor in this data. Because online grocery shopping is still in the early phases of market penetration, the lower proportions attributed to online shopping can be partially due to the lack of availability.

FIGURE 6.3: PRODUCTS/SERVICES PURCHASED BY CHANNEL

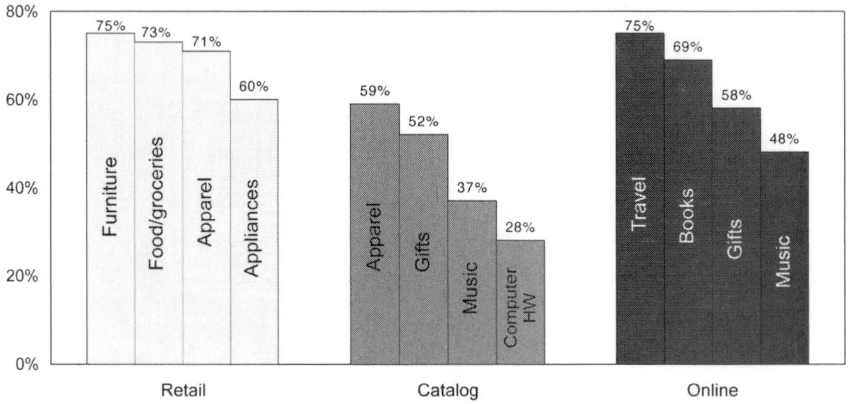

Note: Multiple responses possible.

Source: Pulse of the Customer

In the apparel category, retail stores and catalogs appear to fare much better than online sales. Clearly for retail stores, this is because of the need to see, touch, and try on the product before purchasing. But, interestingly, many consumers overcome these barriers when shopping via catalogs. The hassle of returns is no greater for catalogs than for online shopping, yet consumers report purchasing more apparel via catalogs. Why is this the case? There are several reasons. Apparel catalog brands are more firmly established. As a result, consumers have more confidence in those brands and they are more familiar with the quality and fit of their favorite catalog brand's product lines. Thus, there is less risk associated with purchasing from those familiar brands, based on their prior experience. The second reason that consumers seem to prefer catalogs over online for apparel is that the visual merchandising presentation is better, not just aesthetically but also contextually. Consumers feel they know more about the product when they can see it in context with the other items in the staged photograph.

It is important to note, however, that more than one-third of the consumers bought apparel online. What apparel gets purchased online versus in other channels seems to involve who the purchased item is for, how important "fit" is, and how well the item is merchandised online.

In other product categories, the Internet seems to be stealing consumers' channel loyalty. For travel, books, and computer software, the Internet has gained significant ground over other methods of retailing. Finally, there's a close race among retail channels in categories such as computer hardware, music, and gifts.

PURCHASE MOTIVATION BY CHANNEL

Knowing what consumers prefer to buy from each of the retail channels is only part of the story. It is more important to gain insight into why they prefer the different channels. Figure 6.4 shows the most important factors that motivate consumers to make purchases from the various retail channels. Again, we see some dramatic patterns confirming our previous analysis.

Consumers are primarily motivated to shop at retail stores when they need to touch the product: 75 percent of the consumers we polled say that's why they go to retail stores and, of course, this is a benefit that neither catalogs nor Web sites can offer. Another benefit that some consumers see as unique to retail stores is service: 29 percent indicate that service is their motivator for shopping in retail stores, an attribute that barely registers when they talk about catalogs and Web sites. It is important to note, however, that many consumers complain that service quality in retail stores has deteriorated substantially. What once was a true differentiator is becoming neutralized by poor in-store service and untrained personnel.

Consumers are primarily motivated to shop at retail stores when they need to touch the product

Notably, retail stores are rated low in terms of convenience. As com-

pared to pointing and clicking, driving and parking is much more of a
hassle and time-consuming chore.
Mall management companies are
starting to realize that they need to
address the threat of e-commerce by
making it more convenient to shop
in malls. While they can't change the
fact that consumers must still drive

*As compared to point-
ing and clicking,
driving and parking is
much more of a hassle
and time-consuming
chore*

and park to shop at a mall, the new trend in mall designs is
to cluster competitive stores together, making it easier for
consumers to comparison shop for specific product categories. Given that the number of mall visits consumers
made dropped by roughly 20 percent over the last ten
years, it is not surprising that mall retailers are reexamin-
ing their traditional ways of doing business.[2]

FIGURE 6.4: PURCHASE MOTIVATION BY CHANNEL

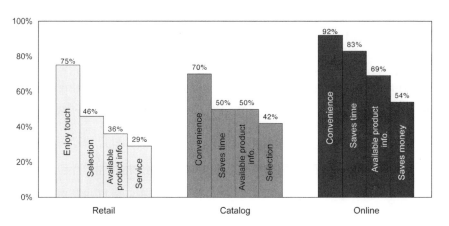

Note: Multiple responses possible.

Source: Pulse of the Customer

Other significant patterns are noticed when consumers talk about the motivators for shopping online.
Convenience, timesavings, and information availability
lead the list of Web shopping benefits, as we have seen in
previous charts. Interestingly, these are the same top
three reasons why consumers like to shop via catalog. It

Catalog sales are the most vulnerable to cannibalization from e-commerce sites is notable, however, that the proportion of consumers who name these as online shopping benefits is greater than those naming these as catalog shopping benefits. We believe the upshot is that catalog sales are the most vulnerable to cannibalization by e-commerce sites.

While there are many similarities in why consumers shop online and via catalogs, there are some distinct differences in the benefits that each of these channels offer. The key advantage catalogs have is the ability to provide better graphic representation of products. By contrast, due to current bandwidth constraints, Web-based graphics are still slow to load. Also, flipping through pages to view a range of products is not as easy as with a printed catalog—a disadvantage that will disappear as higher bandwidth and higher speed network connections are available and embraced by the mass market.

On the other hand, Web sites are thought to offer several key advantages over catalogs. There is a perception that products are cheaper when bought through the Web. Consumers believe—rightly or wrongly—that inventory information is more up-to-date on the Internet than when they call a catalog's toll-free telephone number. And, once the shopping task is complete, consumers believe that shopping online is faster and saves more time.

INTERNET VS. OTHER RETAIL CHANNELS

MODERATOR: What do you think will happen to retail stores due to the Internet?

CONSUMER: I think salespeople are going to have to get smarter if they are going to add any value, because anybody can jump on a computer and research what they are looking for. Consumers are getting better educated.

CONSUMER: Retail stores should sell their products, anything they have, online. The Internet is going to be used more and more. If retail stores want to keep their sales, they're going to have to go that way.

MODERATOR: When does online shopping have an advantage over retail stores?

CONSUMER: The number one reason to shop on the Internet or by mail order is convenience.

CONSUMER: When you are looking for something obscure like a book or CD, you can't always count on a store having it in stock if it's very unusual. More likely, you can find it online.

CONSUMER: Certain stores only stock certain brands, whereas if you go online, you have access to a lot of brands. You might get the breadth of ten different stores.

CONSUMER: In retail stores, they pressure you. The salespeople won't leave you alone. I don't like that.

MODERATOR: What is different about shopping with catalogs versus shopping online?

CONSUMER: When I get the catalog in the mail, I have to deal with it. I can't not look at it. It stimulates my buying. Versus on the Internet, I have to seek it out.

CONSUMER: I like looking at the pictures. When I'm on the Web, I get sidetracked.

CONSUMER: There's more personal accountability. You give your credit card to somebody over the phone and you have their name or their operator number. If you have a problem, you can go back and use that information to start an investigation.

CONSUMER: It kind of gives an experience of window-shopping. I don't find the same satisfaction online.

CONSUMER: Catalogs are more vulnerable to the Internet than retail stores, because you'll always need to go touch something in a store.

Customers choose various channels based on the perceived experience and/or benefit the channel provides. Figure 6.5 offers a comparison of perceived benefits across retail channels. Although similar benefits are cited across all channels, there are some distinct differences as well. Of particular interest is the similarity noted previously between the benefits of online and catalog channels. Although both offer similar benefits, the online benefits of convenience and saving time are reported at a much higher rate, and saving money balances out selection in the catalog channel.

FIGURE 6.5: CHANNEL BENEFIT COMPARISON

	ONLINE *Commodity products & gifts*	CATALOG *Commodity products, clothing/decorative, gifts*	STORE *Big-ticket items, clothing, furniture, food*
+	❏ Convenience (92%) ❏ Saves time (83%) ❏ Available info (69%) ❏ Saves $ (54%)	❏ Convenience (70%) ❏ Saves time (56%) ❏ Available info (50%) ❏ Selection (42%)	❏ Physical contact w/ products (75%) ❏ Selection (46%) ❏ Available info (36%) ❏ Service (29%)
—	❏ Limited product selection ❏ Limited visual experience ❏ Service ❏ Less familiarity with brand	❏ Service ❏ Product availability info. ❏ Telephone hassles	❏ Time intensive ❏ Inconvenient ❏ Deteriorating service

Impulse Purchasing

Another interesting aspect of consumer shopping behavior is the tendency to impulse shop. We find that people have polar opposite responses to the Web versus brick-and-mortar stores regarding impulse purchases.

For some, the drawback to online shopping is the impulse to buy more than they originally intended. These e-shoppers find themselves lured by site links and other products, which often lead them to new Web retailers or different product categories, enticing them to buy. Other shoppers have the opposite opinion and feel they tend to be more distracted when shopping in a brick-and-mortar setting. These consumers are more focused and directed when shopping online.

IMPULSE SHOPPING—WHERE DOES IT HAPPEN?

MODERATOR: Do you think you buy more or less when you go to a retail store versus when you are on the Web?

CONSUMER: I probably buy more at the mall because I don't have to hesitate. I can see what I'm buying and I can get it right then.

CONSUMER: When I'm online, I just see what I came for. I stay focused. The window only shows the products I'm looking at, and I'm not interested in browsing just to see what else might be there.

CONSUMER: I'm just the opposite. I get distracted and tend to buy more when I'm online, because I might see a special offer, or be reminded about something I've wanted in the past but forgot about until I see something that reminds me. Then I might go look for that other product.

CONSUMER: Being impulsive with the Web, you kind of have to re-discipline yourself on how to use your money, since everything on the Web requires using a credit card. In a retail store, I know I have to stop buying when I run out of cash.

MODERATOR: What stimulates you to make impulsive purchases?

CONSUMER: I buy more when I'm in a store because as I walk toward what I'm looking for, I get side-tracked. I buy more things for myself when I'm at the store, because they're right there and I can just take them home.

CONSUMER: I'm very impatient. I want things here and now.

CONSUMER: Online, there's so much stuff that when you get into the Web sites, you just go crazy. It's so easy just to click a button and punch in your credit card.

Emerging Preferences for Cross-Shopping

Considering the emerging channel options and preferences of new consumers, we believe that ultimately the best retailing model will be a multi-channel approach—one that allows consumers to shop across retail methods within one retail brand while they move through the purchase decision cycle. Consumers describe the ideal scenario as a hybrid retailing model—one in which merchants offer customers the option of online, catalog, and/or storefront shopping. There are many permutations to how consumers want to use multiple channels within one purchase decision occasion.

For example, consumers want to perform product research online, and then go to the store of choice to buy the product. These scenarios are most often needed among high-involvement products that require a demonstration or a trial before making the actual purchase. As noted in figure 3.2 in chapter 3, the Web is particularly useful to consumers in the Confidence Building stage of the decision cycle. It plays a vital role in locating retail sources for the desired items, educating on product features and functions, and comparing prices. In addition, a variety of distribution channels can play a key role in winning the skirmish to acquire customers and waging the war of customer retention.

Other consumers talk about flipping through direct mail catalogs, selecting the items, and then going online to buy the product. These people find the product selection experience of the catalog superior to the Web because of the photographs provided in the print medium. But, they believe the order placement experience of the Web is superior to calling a toll-free telephone line because they don't like dealing with the sales reps and, interestingly, they believe that product inventory information is more accurate and up-to-date online than via telephone customer service.

The current trend toward the adoption of the Web into the daily activities of average Americans is forcing the evolution of a new business model. Catalog and retail enterprises should seriously and quickly offer e-commerce alternatives, as

Ultimately the best retailing model will be a single-brand, multi-channel approach

well as continue conducting business through traditional channels. Retail brands offering multiple channel alternatives will be the ones to win and maintain customer loyalty. Companies that don't recognize the power of the Internet in the retailing process will eventually disappear from the consciousness of the consumer.

ADVANTAGES OF MULTI-CHANNEL ALTERNATIVES

MODERATOR: Why does it matter that a retail brand offers you multiple ways of reaching them?

CONSUMER: It saves me a lot of time and hassle in the store. If you go to the Toys "R" Us site, it will tell you where in the physical store you can find the product. It showed me what aisle it was on.

CONSUMER: It depends on my mood. Sometimes I want to go out and shop. Sometimes I want to stay in. I want to have the option.

CONSUMER: I want to be able to choose.

Confusing the Consumer

When retailers offer multiple shopping alternatives, as discussed above, an important strategic element is how each alternative is presented to consumers, relative to all the options. Consumers attempt to understand what the retailers' motivations are and sometimes infer more than might be intended by the retailer. Retailers should realize that when they offer different prices in different channels, consumers are often aware of the differences. Managing consumers' understanding of a retail-brand strategy can be especially challenging when the "dot-com" part of a retail business is separately managed from the "brick-and-mortar" part of the business. Dot coms tend to think their only competition are other e-businesses and may price to be competitive among online retailers. But shoppers will notice the discrepancies and will want to understand what is happening.

When retailers offer different prices in different channels, consumers are aware of those differences

CONFUSED CONSUMERS

MODERATOR: Why is it confusing for retailers to offer multiple ways of doing business with them?

CONSUMER: I noticed Wal-Mart had one price for a product in their stores, and a cheaper price for the same product online. Why do they do that? Are they trying to get me to go online instead of going to their stores?

CONSUMER: I figure, for some reason, companies really do want you to use the Internet. Like at the brokerage places, they charge you more money if you use the phone when you trade than if you do it online. A lot of things are like that. I guess they do that because it's more convenient for them.

CONSUMER: I think companies want you to do business online because it's easier to track who their customers are. It just automatically goes into a database.

The Online Auction Phenomenon

An interesting shopping phenomenon that came about with the Internet is the online auction. The concept was originally invented by Onsale, Inc., now known as Egghead.com, with the notion that consumers and businesses could buy and sell refurbished and closeout items via an online bidding process, at whatever prices the market was willing to bear. Other companies, such as eBay, transformed the auction concept to a consumer proposition in which users buy and sell personal items in an auction format. Others quickly followed suit.

Two forces were at work in creating consumers' proclivity to online auctions. First of all, buying other people's junk has been a passion of consumers for centuries. Street fairs and flea markets are found in every culture. These markets serve multiple functions—not just access to goods and services, but entertainment and social interaction as well. The common practice of Saturday-morning garage sales was another unsophisticated precursor to the consumer auction. Secondly, auctions have been a vehicle for commerce for many centuries. The average consumer, however, has often been too intimidated to participate in auctions due to unfamiliarity with the rules of auctions. While auctions have the mystique of offering good deals on unusual items, many average citizens have been too afraid to participate.

In the world of online auctions, the consumer *can* learn how to participate without the pressure of the crowds and fast-talking auctioneers. Consumers can look at other people's junk to their heart's content. The entertainment value, albeit aesthetically different from the experience of wandering through a street market, can be great. But the true benefit of online auctions is the deal. Of the consumers we polled, close to 30 percent claim to participate in online auctions. Most say the key advantage of auctions online is the ability to buy hard-to-find items at low prices.

ONLINE AUCTIONS

MODERATOR: Why do you like shopping in online auctions?

CONSUMER: I like finding things that can't be found anywhere else, and the thrill of an auction is exciting.

CONSUMER: You get the opportunity to bid on something that is hard to come by, or at a cheaper price than at a store.

CONSUMER: Auctions provide the convenience of shopping for a bargain price without going to a store.

CONSUMER: I like the descriptions that people write about their stuff. They are so creative. You feel like you really know the person who's selling it.

MODERATOR: What is the downside to buying via an auction?

CONSUMER: The auction's lack of responsibility results in bogus bidders. EBay claims to take bogus bidder concerns seriously. But in the end, they're powerless to do anything for the sellers who get screwed from false bidders.

CONSUMER: You don't get a chance to examine the goods before purchase.

CONSUMER: Sometimes the merchandise offered is damaged and ruled unavailable for purchase after the bidding is over. I guess it's good that they realize that something is damaged before they send it, but I get frustrated when something I won a bid on ultimately can't be shipped.

CONSUMER: I don't like auctions because there are no guarantees or protection.

MODERATOR: What advice do you have for newbie auction shoppers?

CONSUMER: Always make sure to e-mail the seller with any questions about the item you're bidding on. Only bid on things that you have good knowledge about. Also, only bid on items that have a photo attached.

Consumers' News Gathering Habits

The Internet has had significant impact on how consumers get news—world news, industry news, business news. In fact, the immediacy of news available to consumers through the Internet has practically redefined consumers' expectations of when information is truly news. "News" is defined as "a report of recent events."[3] For many consumers, information is really only "recent" when it is delivered up to the minute and presented directly onto their computer desktops. In fact, according to research by Pew Research Center for the People and the Press, 49 percent of online users believe that Internet news is actually more accurate than traditional news sources.[4]

Of course, the news industry has been very aware of the shift in consumers' expectations and preferences for news channels, which didn't just begin with the Internet. In fact, there has been a steady shift from printed news sources to broadcast news sources since the advent of television, as evidenced by the fact that the daily newspaper circulation in the United States has stayed level during the last twenty years. At the same time, the total population and number of households has been rising.[5] This trend corroborates the Stanford study, which found that one-third of regular Internet users say they spend less time reading the newspaper now than they did before using the Internet.[6]

Many broadcast and publishing companies have invested heavily in the Internet to offset the diminishing interest in traditional news communications channels. We believe that the Internet will not replace newspapers and TV news programming completely, but increasingly, these communication vehicles must carve out a different role for themselves, when reporting on "news" is no longer the function they serve. What is that different role? Consumers talk about reading the newspaper as a leisure activity, one that is associated with relaxing. Feature stories, community interest notices, and local news continue to be the domain of newspapers.

As the consumer need for news migrates away from printed versions (i.e., daily papers), the need for more accurate and focused reporting increases. This is because the volume of news and online news sources is growing at a rapid rate. Consumers like the ability to sort through the

morass of content and select which news is most meaningful, by personalizing pages on search engines or requesting
that daily online versions of trade publications be forward-
ed to them.

INTERNET AND NEWS CONSUMPTION BEHAVIOR

MODERATOR: Has the Internet changed your news consumption behavior?

CONSUMER: Definitely. I keep Yahoo on all day, so I know the news instantly.

CONSUMER: I don't read the newspaper anymore. By the time the newspaper comes out, it's old news already.

CONSUMER: It virtually eliminated the newspaper I read. I get much of my news off of the Internet now. Also, it cut down on my watching television for news.

CONSUMER: I decided, why buy the paper? So, I canceled it.

MODERATOR: In what way is getting news online better than the traditional ways we get news?

CONSUMER: Now that I have personalized news through my Yahoo page, I can get the stories I want without having to look through the whole newspaper to find two or three things of interest.

CONSUMER: I think I wind up reading more news due to the Internet because now I can quickly pinpoint the stories that interest me.

CONSUMER: I go to the Internet for all the latest news. And I can find human interest stuff as well as headlines.

MODERATOR: What are the limitations of news on the Internet?

CONSUMER: It's too global. I'm a third-generation native. I'm very community oriented. Unless you read a newspaper, there's very little local news on the Internet.

CONSUMER: I still enjoy my newspaper. The Internet never gave me enough information. I want to know what the story is and I can read it at my leisure without it changing. And I don't need the most up-to-date news. If I want that, I can listen to the radio.

MODERATOR: For those of you who still read the newspaper, has the Internet had any impact on what you read or how you use it?

CONSUMER: I like reading the newspaper, flipping through it, looking at different things. I use the Internet for reading headlines and stuff like that.

CONSUMER: I don't need to read it every day. So, I cut my newspaper service from daily to Sunday only. The Sunday paper is a ritual. There's something traditional about Sunday morning and a paper.

Consumers' TV Habits

Consumers say their television viewing habits have changed. Some consumers actually believe that because of the Internet, they watch less TV, or are less attentive to it. This claim is confirmed by the Stanford study, which found that 60 percent of regular Internet users say their TV viewing has been reduced due to the Internet.[7] This is happening because, for some people, using the Web is entertainment. They have found that the educational, entertainment, and communications attributes of the Web have replaced the more passive act of watching TV. We believe that changes in TV viewing due to the Internet will ultimately be dramatic, and that TV and the Web will become symbiotic vehicles. The lines between watching and interacting will blur. It is, however, still too early to see this behavior among consumers. The wider availability of cable Web access and information appliances designed as set-top boxes will be important steps in the convergence of TV and the Web in consumers' homes.

THE INTERNET VS. TELEVISION

MODERATOR: Has the Web changed how much you watch TV, or how you watch TV?

CONSUMER: I just don't veg out in front of the TV anymore.

CONSUMER: Now I just have it on for background noise while I'm on the computer.

CONSUMER: I don't watch nearly as much as I used to.

CONSUMER: I don't watch TV at all anymore.

MODERATOR: Why has the Web replaced your TV watching?

CONSUMER: With the Web, I can stay away from TV, find something better to do and something more educational to do. Like maybe I'll be interested in a topic like European wars. You just have so many places to go.

CONSUMER: I can communicate with my buddies or play games online. It's more fun than TV.

CONSUMER: When there's nothing good on TV, I'll get on the Internet and play poker with somebody. I always enjoy talking to guys overseas in Europe and they're always wanting to know what Arizona is like.

How Consumers Communicate

One of the "killer" applications that draws consumers to the Internet is e-mail. The ability to quickly and inexpensively communicate with other people, regardless of distance, is a great draw for individuals of all demographic groups. In fact, some consumers have developed a preference to e-mail communications in lieu of other forms of communication. Some researchers believe that this is not necessarily a positive trend. In the Stanford study, it was found that regular Internet users spend less time with friends and family and less time talking on the phone.[8] But Web users we poll claim that because e-mail is cheaper than long-distance telephone calls, they communicate more often, with more people, over a wider geographic distance.

USING THE INTERNET TO COMMUNICATE

MODERATOR: How has the Internet changed the way you communicate?

CONSUMER: I stay in touch with people more frequently mainly because it's cheaper than making a long distance phone call.

CONSUMER: I communicate with my friends and family on e-mail. I don't send regular mail to them anymore. I only use regular mail if they don't have Internet access.

CONSUMER: I'm keeping up with people that I had lost contact with for twenty years. Somebody sends you a joke, you forward it, and you chitchat. Stuff that's too trivial to call about.

CONSUMER: I have friends and family all over the country. The only way I talk to them anymore is on the Internet.

Sometimes, however, e-mail communications don't bring out the best in human behavior. Flame e-mail—mail that has insulting, derogatory content about specific individuals or organizations—is a way of expressing hostility in an anonymous, or at least nonconfrontational, way. The ease at which negative e-mail can be dispatched has eliminated the barriers to potentially destructive communications. People who perhaps haven't the nerve or conviction to directly express negative sentiments can blast the recipient electronically via e-mail. And these negative feelings can be widely broadcast simultaneously to potentially vast numbers of other people as well. Conventional wisdom says that healthy resolution of interpersonal conflict requires direct and collaborative communication between the affected persons and that if conflict is sufficiently troubling, it deserves to be worked through in a face-to-face encounter. E-mail provides a means of avoiding direct confrontation and allows expression without accountability. This reality does not contribute to healthy personality development. E-mail is a powerful communications device that has many positive attributes. But it can also be a destructive, slanderous vehicle when misused by immature individuals.

On a more positive note, e-mail has given rise to the electronic greeting cards industry. Many companies have been founded that enable consumers to send greeting cards for every conceivable occasion. Consumers like to send electronic greeting cards, as it is often easier to send an e-greeting than to physically purchase and mail a greeting card using the postal service.

In addition to the communications benefits of e-mail, some consumers use the Internet to communicate with strangers through chat rooms. These consumers enjoy the anonymous contact with other people, while expanding their reach to new geographies and new interests.

BENEFITS OF INTERNET COMMUNICATIONS

MODERATOR: What are the benefits of using the Internet to communicate?

CONSUMER: My wife and I get along better now. We've been so busy with jobs and kids, we haven't had much time in the past few years for friends. On the Internet we meet people in chat rooms, vent our feelings about each other, and make friends. It has really helped our marriage.

CONSUMER: I use the Internet to develop relationships with people all over the world.

CONSUMER: My wife claims I quit talking to her. My computer is called the "other woman" in my house.

Of course not everyone perceives communications via the Internet as a positive addition to our culture. Some consumers believe that our society is becoming too dependent on technology to the detriment of our overall development.

INTERNET COMMUNICATIONS—GOOD AND BAD

MODERATOR: Is increased electronic communications a good thing or a bad thing?

CONSUMER: There are people that can't get out for whatever reason, so it's ideal. It's like their lifeline.

CONSUMER: Some people wind up spending more money. Because the Web is not really real, like a store is, it's easier to lose control.

CONSUMER: I think people need to keep it in perspective. I know kids who can't use a hammer, they have no concept of the earth they live on, but they can play computer games. We need some balance here.

MODERATOR: How will the Internet change the way our society communicates?

CONSUMER: I hope it won't change it too much. I still like the social experience of shopping in stores, of talking and getting feedback.

CONSUMER: I really worry that we're going to get too automated and people are going to be sitting in their little houses and never want to go out, that there's going to be too much online.

CONSUMER: I wonder what it's going to be like when people we've relied on are put out of business by the Web, services like insurance agents. We don't mind buying insurance online until we have a problem and we don't have someone to talk to. It's fine as long as there's an insurance agent to go to. But when there are no car dealerships, no insurance agents, no grocery stores, what's it going to be like? I believe a lot of businesses will disappear because of the Internet.

How Consumers Invest and Bank

The Internet has a two-sided impact on the way people invest and manage their money. The emergence of online trading made stock transactions more available, more affordable, and more comprehensible to many consumers. The mysteries of the stock market were unlocked when consumers could more actively participate in making investment portfolio decisions. In fact, close to 20 percent of the consumers we polled indicate they use the Web for stock trading and tracking.

Another 20 percent of the consumers we polled use the Web for home banking and bill paying. Home banking is an application that predated the widespread penetration of the Web, as banks offered private dial-up lines to transact business with consumers through their home computers. Given the relative longevity of home banking, the level of usage, as compared to other Web activities, is rather low. Gomez

Advisors estimates that 11.1 million consumers now use the Web to access their bank account information, with about 5.9 million using online banking at least once a month.[9] And they believe that by 2003, as many as 48.3 million people will use the Internet to do some type of banking.

Why did online stock trading catch fire faster than home banking? The well-publicized launches and IPOs of dot coms made the stock market more attractive to speculative traders. The high valuations and wild volatility of Internet stocks made consumers more and more conscious of the power of the Web in creating as well as annihilating personal wealth. So while online investing has its risks, it is also very sexy and, for some, entertaining. On the other hand, home banking is a more pragmatic application and many systems are still difficult to use. In addition, personal finance is a key area in which consumers are particularly protective of their privacy.

INVESTING ON THE WEB

MODERATOR: How has the Internet changed your investment behavior?

CONSUMER: I changed the way I invest. I do all my investments online. I don't need to do it any other way.

CONSUMER: I never used to play the stock market. Now I can because of the Web.

CONSUMER: You can talk back and forth with traders without ever using the phone.

CONSUMER: I constantly watch how my stocks are performing, all day long. I have them right there on my Yahoo page.

MODERATOR: How do you feel about banking on the Web?

CONSUMER: I pay all my bills online. I have for years. It's really convenient once you get it set up.

CONSUMER: I tried home banking, but it's just too hard. It's easier just to call the voice response system at the bank and check my balance, or go to the ATM.

CONSUMER: I worry about how they'll use the information if I pay my bills online.

Implications for Business

While the impact of the Internet has had a fascinating and significant impact on consumer behavior in news con-

Loyalty in the future will be to the retail <u>*brand*</u>*, not the retail* <u>*method*</u>

sumption, entertainment activities, interpersonal communications, and investing, we circle back to the key focal point of this book—the soul of the shopper. For retailers, whether storefront, catalog, or e-commerce, the implications of consumers' shifting shopping preferences are significant.

We believe that the advent of e-commerce is forcing a redefinition of "retailing." Loyalty in the future will be to the retail *brand*, not the retail *method*. Retailers will be forced to offer multi-channel retail approaches to serve customers' needs and maintain market share.

For pure-play dot-com companies, the race is on to build brand presence and positive word of mouth to overcome the barriers in the consumer market. For existing retail brands, the challenge is to move quickly in offering a value proposition on the Web that leverages and reinforces brand equity already established in the analog world.

These multi-channel models will be the keys to success as storefronts, catalogs, and e-commerce Web sites continue to struggle for channel dominance.

The time for virtually all retailers to reexamine and potentially redefine their model for doing business is now. Adoption of the Web into mainstream America has empowered the customer at an astonishing pace, throwing all sellers into an e-consumer's market. While the specific issues differ with the retail channel—storefront, catalog, or online—each must aggressively court their targeted customers' preferences and deliver them through a hybrid, multi-channel approach.

IMPLICATIONS FOR E-BUSINESSES

While dot-com companies may have the first-in advantage on the Web, it is important to not underestimate the potential for traditional retailers to leverage their well-known analog brands and enter into the Web with a multi-channel approach. E-businesses require more than a Web presence to actively compete with their offline counterparts. To compete with traditional retailers, e-businesses must:

- Focus on the highest quality online service, based on customer preference, and deliver it. Customer contact via telephone is key.
- Compete against the visual and tactile advantages of traditional retailers by building graphical presentations with more context and product content
- Allocate resources toward building e-brand awareness and capturing market share

CONSUMERS' ADVICE TO E-BUSINESSES

MODERATOR: What advice do you have for e-businesses about how to be more successful?

CONSUMER: You don't really know who they are just because they have a site. They need to advertise who they are, and how to find them.

CONSUMER: They should advertise on TV and radio.

CONSUMER: A lot of people don't have Internet access. If they want more of the business, they're going to have to go to different avenues to reach more of the public.

CONSUMER: Focus on site performance, make it faster. And focus on security.

IMPLICATIONS TO CATALOGS

As compared to other retail channels, consumers have higher expectations that catalogs will offer integrated e-commerce. Catalog sales appear to be the most vulnerable to cannibalization by e-commerce because the perceived benefits of buying through catalogs and buying online are similar. But there are some important differences that can give catalogs an advantage. Catalogs can:

- Leverage consumers' perceptions that catalogs provide a better visual representation of products, and use this merchandising experience online for differentiation
- Take advantage of established brands and established consumer confidence
- Provide online and offline ordering channels with excellent customer service
- Utilize knowledge of customer location and purchasing behavior for precision direct marketing

---

CONSUMERS' ADVICE TO CATALOGS

MODERATOR: What advice do you have for catalogs vis-à-vis the Internet?

CONSUMER: Catalogs should integrate with the Internet. If you want more information than what they have in the catalog, you can go online, or if you want to order something you saw in the catalog, you can order it online.

CONSUMER: Catalogs should offer both online and paper catalogs.

CONSUMER: They could send smaller catalogs, serving as a reminder for the Web site. And eventually, paper catalogs will go away.

CONSUMER: They should continue sending catalogs and give people the option to shop online. I like to see the catalog and then go online and order.

IMPLICATIONS FOR RETAIL STORES

Although trends may indicate that commodity products such as books, CDs, videos, and software will recede in importance for traditional retailers, the fact is that there are some products which are not conducive to the entire purchase being completed online. To leverage their real advantages when implementing the multi-channel model, retail stores should:

- Focus on the tactile shopping experience and the variety of choices available. Offering specialty products will become a key benefit.
- Facilitate customer interest in researching in-store purchases. Provide them the information they need to come to the storefront and complete the sale, and/or offer product demonstrations at the storefront and allow for the transaction to be completed online.
- Take advantage of seniority in the market by offering brand-loyal customers an online alternative

---

CONSUMERS' ADVICE TO RETAIL STORES

MODERATOR: What is your advice to retail stores about the Internet?

CONSUMER: Get on the Internet. Expand your reach. Use your name recognition to draw in customers.

CONSUMER: Have the same selection online as in the stores, so that customers don't get confused. Retailers should promote their stores on their Web sites and vice versa.

CONSUMER: They should give price comparisons.

CONSUMER: Along with offering products, they should also offer good online customer support services, so you don't have to pick up a telephone and make a call.

7 *The Business E-Customer*

The purpose of this chapter is to give a high-level overview of businesses as "new consumers," more commonly referred to in a business context as "e-customers." Entire books could be written about businesses as e-customers, and there are several different ways to analyze a business: by industry, size, location, job titles, etc. We do not attempt to be comprehensive in our analysis of business e-customers in this single chapter. Rather, we discuss this important market within the same topical framework we have used to discuss consumers throughout this book. We examine business e-customers in terms of their Web consumption behavior, the benefits they derive from the Web, the components of customer loyalty, their attitudes toward e-marketing, their feelings about privacy, the barriers they see to doing more e-commerce, the impact the Web has on their other modes of business behavior, and their Web wish list for the future.

In this context, we define the business e-customer as a person who buys products and services online on behalf of his company. In large and mid-sized companies, the professionals who fit this description tend to be in procurement, operational, and IT-type jobs. In smaller businesses, these customers tend to be business managers and proprietors. Certainly there are many people with other job titles within businesses using the Internet, for all types of activities. Our purpose here is to zoom in on the act of buying, remaining consistent with the definition of "consumer" used throughout this book. The degree to which other job functions have the right to purchase products and services online is a matter of company policy and varies widely. Therefore, we focus on the more general aspects of business consumption via the Web among the procurement, operational, and IT departments of corporations, as well as of small businesses.

Profile of the Business E-Customer

Many "new consumers" are business e-customers. In fact, many consumers admit that they first used the Web at work before they started using it for personal reasons. Some still prefer to use their work computer rather than their home computer for personal e-commerce because of faster network connections. While there are many common themes in terms of online likes and dislikes that cross the boundaries of personal versus work use, there are also many differences—because of the policies, limitations, and processes that are a necessary part of business organizations.

AN AGGREGATED VIEW OF BUSINESS E-CUSTOMERS

Online buying is the most important Web function for our sample of business users, as shown in figure 7.1. Business e-customers would like to be able to do more e-commerce. The biggest constraint to businesses buying online, however, is in having access to the full range of products they need to buy. Products that have broad market relevance, such as office supplies, computers, and software, are easily found online—a fact that pleases business e-customers. But specialized products are often still scarce on the Web, although this is beginning to change. Business customers use the Web for sourcing and locating products. This is an important precursor to online buying in the business world, as many companies have policies dictating that purchasers get multiple competitive bids before making purchases. In addition, the Web is an important source of news for business e-customers. Many have bookmarked news sites that brief them on industry news, as well as local and world news.

The types of products and services that business e-customers buy online are depicted in figure 7.2. Leading the list are products that relate to most any type of business, regardless of size or industry. Most popular e-commerce purchases are books, computer software, computer hardware, office supplies, and travel. While business e-customers don't express it in the same terms as consumers, the same online purchasing pattern is noted as in the consumer segment: high frequency of buying low-involvement products, with little or no frequency of buying high-involvement products.

FIGURE 7.1: MOST IMPORTANT WEB FUNCTIONS

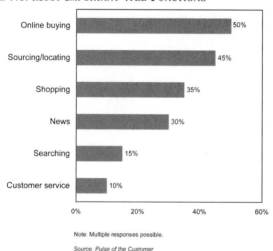

Note: Multiple responses possible.

Source: Pulse of the Customer

FIGURE 7.2: PRODUCTS AND SERVICES PURCHASED ONLINE

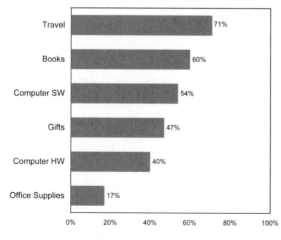

Note: Multiple responses possible.

Source: Pulse of the Customer

Content businesses consider most important is shown in figure 7.3, with product pricing and online catalogs leading the list. At the bottom of the list are content types that are seen as marketing or sales oriented, such as on-site feature stories, promotional offers, and product recommendations.

FIGURE 7.3: MOST IMPORTANT ONLINE CONTENT

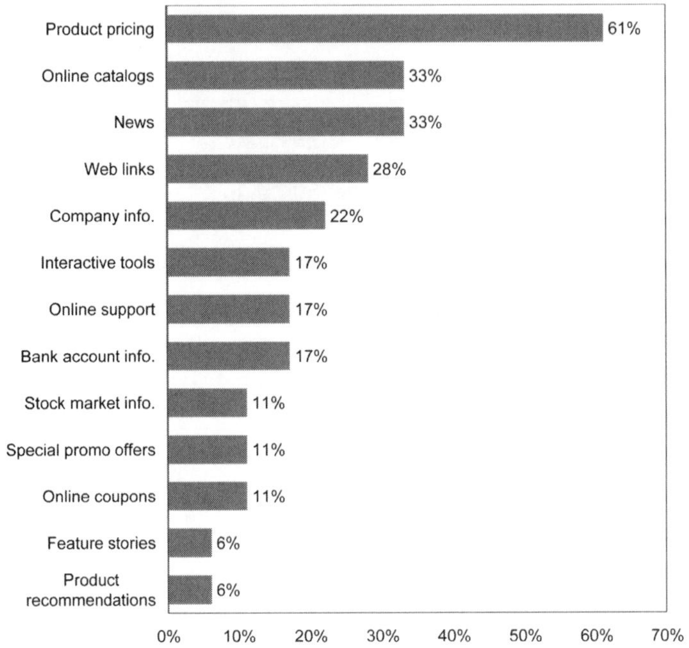

Note: Multiple responses possible.

Source: Pulse of the Customer

THE STRATEGIC STATE OF E-BUSINESS: AN INSIDE-OUT VIEW

Most e-customers we talk to increasingly consider the Web a strategic business vehicle. Overall, these business consumers believe that the Web is an integral part of people's jobs in their companies; it adds to their company's competitiveness, and it is beginning to influence who they select as vendors. The intensity with which they hold this belief is directly related to how important the Internet is in their individual jobs.

People employed in operations management and IT positions are generally upbeat about the importance of the

Web to their companies and to their jobs, especially in larger companies. Procurement professionals are less enthusiastic about e-commerce and indicate that as a general rule, only 10–20 percent of their overall purchasing activities are performed online, although the majority considers it will be important in the future. The reasons for the relatively slow adoption are very valid, and are discussed in the "Barriers to Business E-Commerce" section later in this chapter.

Small business owners are becoming more enthusiastic as more Web-related products and services are being tailored to their needs, and as more of their customers demand to be served online. Even among very small businesses, such as single-location dry cleaners, restaurants, and personal service companies, the adoption of the Internet as a business vehicle is over 50 percent. While many of these users are not purchasing online, they are becoming more reliant on the Web for product sourcing and searching. Online purchasing is only one short step away for small businesses that haven't already taken the step.

It is interesting to contrast the types of Web functionality and preferences that matter to different e-customer professions. In this next section we profile major business e-customer groups by job function.

E-CUSTOMER PROFILE: THE IT PROFESSIONAL

The majority of IT management professionals use the Web as a daily business tool. They are enthusiastic about the medium and feel the Web is a very important contributor to their productivity and success in the workplace. In fact, many indicate that they could not do their jobs without access to the Web. They use the Web to fulfill four primary business-to-business needs:

- Product research (data sheets, service information, price, technical specs)
- Sales and distribution activities (account status, pricing, ordering, shipment tracking)
- Support (customer support, software updates and patches, white papers)
- Tracking competitors

In figure 7.4, IT e-customers rate downloading of software, online technical support, and getting product information as the most important aspects of Web functionality. Web activities, such as being able to track shipping of products online and ordering online, are also considered important tasks. The IT professional indicates a very pragmatic set of priorities in terms of online functionality, a pattern that is to be expected. It's interesting that for these professionals, the Web holds relatively little interest as a social vehicle. Interacting with peers scores in the neutral zones among IT professionals, as does having information personalized to their specific requirements, because they don't see those functions as enhancing their productivity.

FIGURE 7.4: THE IMPORTANCE OF WEB FUNCTIONALITY TO IT PROFESSIONALS

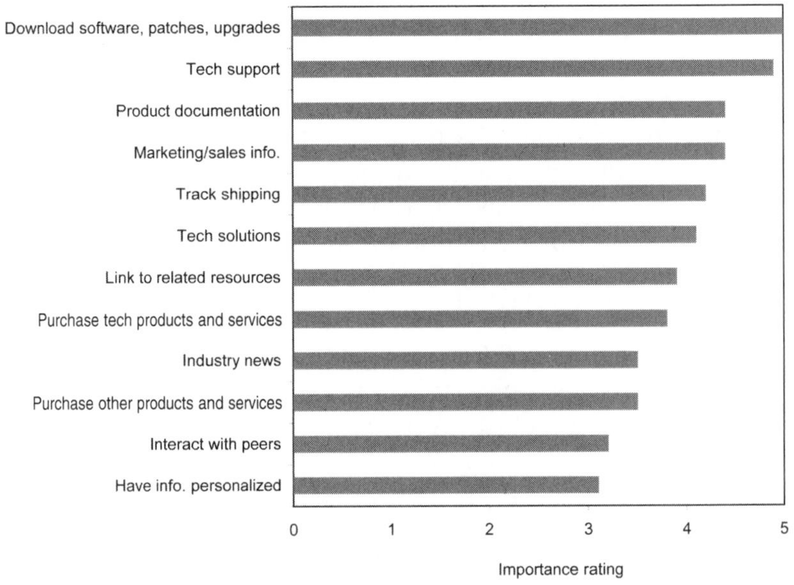

Note: Scale of 1-5, with 5 being "very important."
Source: Pulse of the Customer

E-CUSTOMER PROFILE: THE PURCHASING PROFESSIONAL

Figure 7.5 shows a very different type of user—the person responsible for purchasing for their companies or departments. These people rate tracking of product shipments as the highest, which is logical, since they get pres-

sure from their constituents about product availability.
Online purchasing scores slightly above the neutral zone,
reemphasizing procurement professionals' lukewarm reaction to e-commerce. Social and personalized functionality
scores as neutral among these workers as well.

FIGURE 7.5: THE IMPORTANCE OF WEB FUNCTIONALITY TO PURCHASING PROFESSIONALS

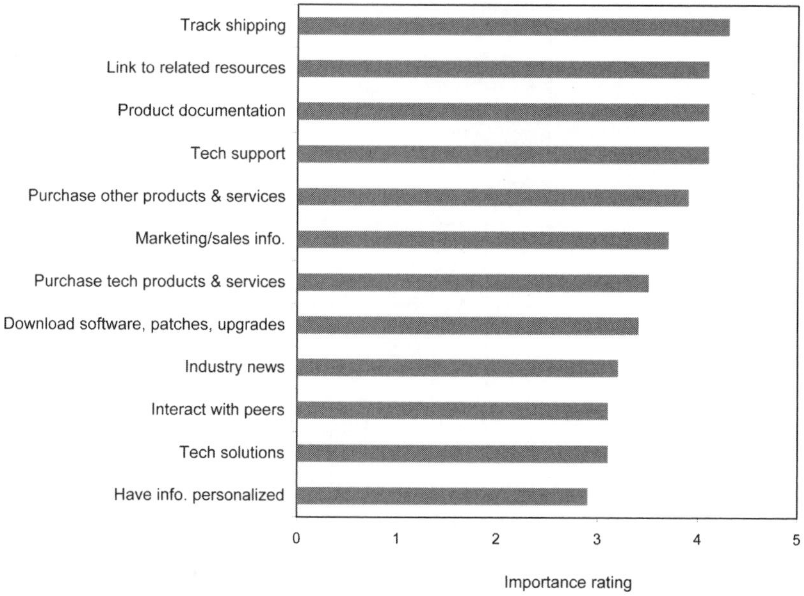

Note: Scale of 1-5, with 5 being "very important."
Source: Pulse of the Customer

E-CUSTOMER PROFILE: THE SMALL BUSINESS

Small business e-customers share common traits with
consumers, as well as with larger businesses. The majority
of small businesses indicate that they use the Internet for
business purposes, although many actually access the
Internet from their homes rather than from their places of
business—especially very small businesses.

The most popular activities performed online by very
small businesses are e-mail and product sourcing, as
shown in figure 7.6. We define very small businesses as
companies with less than twenty employees. The proportion of these companies that report to purchase online is
below 50 percent.

FIGURE 7.6: BUSINESS ACTIVITIES PERFORMED ON THE WEB BY VERY SMALL BUSINESSES

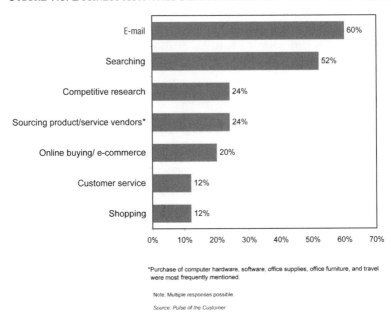

*Purchase of computer hardware, software, office supplies, office furniture, and travel were most frequently mentioned.

Note: Multiple responses possible.

Source: Pulse of the Customer

Small businesses are aware of the wealth of online products and services available to them. Lack of product availability is not a constraint in buying more online. For these e-customers, the issue is their own lack of time to explore. Being an owner of a small business is all-consuming for many of these people.

Benefits of the Web to Business E-Customers

Professionals across all types of business—IT managers, operations and procurement professionals, and entrepreneurs—prefer to buy on the Web for one key reason: it is more convenient and saves them time, thus making them more productive. As shown in figure 7.7, business e-customers are very pragmatic in their reasons for purchasing from the Web and the benefits they derive from it.

Business e-customers want to visit sites that help them solve their problems quickly and productively

For these business e-customers, productivity is a function of the interplay between several attributes: access to the Web (speed and avail-

FIGURE 7.7: MOTIVATION FOR PURCHASING ONLINE

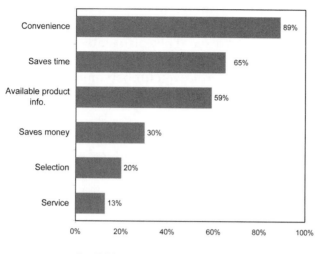

Note: Multiple responses possible.

Source: Pulse of the Customer

ability); the usefulness of the site content; site functionality and navigation; and site organization. Business e-customers want to visit sites that help them solve their problems quickly and productively, which means different things for different job functions. Overall, however, business e-customers say that certain business processes are indeed easier and faster to perform in the Web world than in the offline world. Activities such as order tracking, quick access to product documentation, and customer support are the processes most often mentioned as Web-enabled productivity enhancers.

E-BUSINESS BENEFITS FROM AN IT PROFESSIONAL'S PERSPECTIVE

To IT professionals, reasons for visiting Web sites include more than e-commerce: they are reliant on the Internet to do their jobs. Typically, they access computer-related Web sites and go to the Web for: software updates, Web fixes, patches, technical support, research, pricing information, general knowledge, product specifications, comparative analysis, technical manuals, white papers, and case studies. These types of users feel that technology sites, on the whole, do a good job of meeting their business needs.

IT professionals enthusiastically recognize the benefits of conducting business online. Many believe the Web helps them to improve job performance and makes them more productive in the workplace. They also state that the Web is having ripple effects on their vendor-company relationships, and is bound to improve cumbersome and outdated business processes that hurt the corporate bottom line.

THE IT PERSPECTIVE

MODERATOR: Give me some examples of how the Web has changed your job.

E-CUSTOMER: When our engineers go out to buy something or get materials quotes, they don't use catalogs anymore. They use the Web to find what they need and then get quotes online. We also do a lot of electronic data exchange and have vendors dial in so they can help us manage our inventory. The Web helps to build a more intimate relationship with our vendors.

E-CUSTOMER: Our point-of-sale vendors use the Web. We use it to track open service requests and for selecting services for our remote locations. For example, because we are a movie theater, when we need to change the scripting that prompts our automated theater information service, we can now do that via the Web. A command is entered via the Web that then sends the request to the programmer and to the voice-over talent. Now we know from start to finish where the project stands.

MODERATOR: Your vendors are helping to drive change. Are your customers helping to drive change as well?

E-CUSTOMER: We do a lot of business with the government—many agencies are our customers. In many cases, we now have to conduct business with them over the Internet—doing things such as pricing, interactive quoting negotiations, ordering, and looking up information.

E-CUSTOMER: My clients and I like the idea of using the Web as a collaborative business environment. If my client can access a secure Web site and go over a project with me in real-time, that's where the Web looks very promising for us.

MODERATOR: What are some of the ways you do things differently because of the Web?

E-CUSTOMER: I get technical documents over the Internet now, rather than using EDI [Electronic Data Interchange].

E-CUSTOMER: When we need new hardware, the first place we turn to is the Web. Sometimes we buy direct from the manufacturer and sometimes we buy through an online intermediary.

E-CUSTOMER: We get quotes via the Web, but we still have to go through our purchasing department to buy something.

E-BUSINESS BENEFITS FROM A PURCHASING PROFESSIONAL'S PERSPECTIVE

The two primary reasons why purchasing professionals access the Web is to track shipments of products and receive technical support. But procurement specialists don't always see immediate benefits to conducting business online, because not enough vendors are enabling them to conduct business transactions via the Web. Part of the problem is that old information systems have not been updated.

THE PROCUREMENT PROFESSIONAL

MODERATOR: Why hasn't your job function utilized the Web more?

E-CUSTOMER: Not enough of our vendors are conducting business online; I wish more would. We have a corporate mandate to reduce the number of purchase orders and the number of transactions that our department generates. That mandate pushes us in the direction of Web-based purchasing. Ultimately, online ordering will make my job easier.

E-CUSTOMER: We don't do any online purchasing at this time. Ours is a very paper-intensive organization. It's a bureaucracy and slow to change. We are just now making inroads.

MODERATOR: Do you expect things to change in the near term?

E-CUSTOMER: The Y2K issue forced us to revamp our entire software system, which was an important first step. So we are actively talking to our vendors about implementing some type of Web-commerce system, now that the new software is in place.

E-CUSTOMER: We have a lot of reps who use laptop computers out in the field. It's easier for them to go online and order from a vendor rather than having to write up the order the old fashioned way. I wish more vendors offered online business solutions.

MODERATOR: What are the benefits of doing business online?

E-CUSTOMER: The FedEx order-tracking process is much easier.

E-CUSTOMER: Purchasing PC software on the Internet is a snap. It is easier to find out what's available, and it is convenient because I don't need to talk to some sales rep.

E-CUSTOMER: On the Web, it's easier to access technical publications and to search for specific product information.

E-CUSTOMER: The Web offers a rich environment in which to improve workflow. When managers can audit a project or purchase something direct any time they need to—without going through the purchasing department—it is a huge improvement.

E-CUSTOMER: I like doing business online because it removes the subjective nature of purchasing. The negative side is that it takes negotiating out of the picture. I'm a bit worried that the Web will have an adverse effect on smaller, mom-and-pop vendors.

E-BUSINESS BENEFITS FROM A SMALL BUSINESS PERSPECTIVE

When talking about the Web, small businesses tend to first think of its potential as a customer-facing and promotional vehicle, rather than as a business vehicle. In some cases, the ambivalence they express about the Web is because they are uncertain as to whether it will be valuable in promoting their businesses. They see significant potential benefits in using the Internet to help run their businesses—if they only had the time to make it happen.

MANAGERS OF SMALL BUSINESSES

MODERATOR: How do you use the Internet today?

E-CUSTOMER: I do e-mail with my customers and suppliers.

E-CUSTOMER: We search the Web for auto parts and supplies that we need.

E-CUSTOMER: I keep up with what the competition is doing, who's out there, what kind of coupons they are offering, what they are selling.

E-CUSTOMER: We're a franchise, so we use the Internet to communicate with our home office and to find out about new programs.

E-CUSTOMER: We use it to book our travel.

MODERATOR: What do you see as the main benefits of the Web as a business vehicle?

E-CUSTOMER: I don't think we've even begun to tap its potential. There are many more benefits than I've had time to check out.

E-CUSTOMER: It works the hours I do! I really like being able to use it late at night, after we've closed the restaurant and put the kids in bed. Then I use it for business stuff.

Components of Customer Loyalty

For business e-customers, loyalty on the Web is earned by companies who can directly and consistently deliver the benefits of increased productivity. Business e-customers are very different from online consumers because they are not as susceptible to promotional deals. What motivates business e-customers to repeatedly patronize Web sites is a site's ability to save them time. While getting fair, competitive prices certainly matters to busi-

Business e-customers are very different from online consumers because they are not as susceptible to promotional deals

ness users, they are not as prone to be swayed by free gifts, coupon discounts, and other loyalty-building schemes.

EXAMPLES OF LOYALTY-WORTHY SITES

MODERATOR: Give me some examples of how IT vendors have earned your e-business loyalty.

E-CUSTOMER: A lot of the computer manufacturers such as Dell Computer have created really slick Web sites that allow you to custom-configure computer systems.

E-CUSTOMER: Dell allows its key customers to create custom Web sites that store all of the appropriate account information—including purchasing discount information and who within the company is authorized to purchase what.

E-CUSTOMER: I look for Web sites that build solutions. Cisco does a good job providing that type of information—you can configure different scenarios for your environment. You can also design custom products and get recommendations for configuration.

MODERATOR: Thinking beyond IT sites, how have other types of sites earned your loyalty?

E-CUSTOMER: Boise-Cascade has a nice Web site for ordering office supplies via the Web. They've really simplified the ordering process.

E-CUSTOMER: Office Depot offers a custom online catalog for its business accounts. A company can block employees from ordering certain items, and the catalog that employees upload appears on-screen, minus the items that are not approved. That makes my job a lot easier.

E-CUSTOMER: I like the Printra business card order site. I can scan printable goods and send them to their site. They proofread the copy and farm out the job to various local print companies. The entire process is seamless for the customer.

E-CUSTOMER: FedEx is a good site where tracking packages is simple. UPS and Airborne Express also have good sites.

Marketing to Business E-Customers

Many business e-customers consider themselves impervious to companies' marketing efforts. But they do rely on outside sources to learn about new Web sites, especially those that are seen as most objective. As shown in figure 7.8, the key ways that businesses discover new Web sites is through search engines, recommendations from colleagues, and from articles in magazines and newspapers. Few business e-customers claim to learn about new sites from print, broadcast, or online advertisements.

FIGURE 7.8: SITE DISCOVERY SOURCES

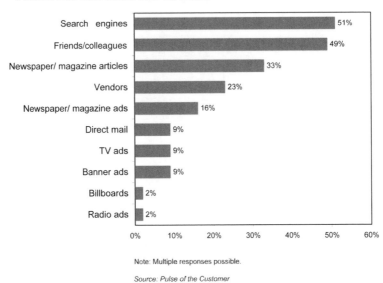

Note: Multiple responses possible.

Source: Pulse of the Customer

Many business e-customers wish they were ignored by marketers because they find marketing annoying. These customers get particularly adamant about the growing use of the Web for marketing. They complain that it impairs their productivity and wastes their time, and that vendors are squandering money in their attempts to exploit the Web for these purposes. Let's look more deeply at these issues.

BANNER ADS: WHAT COMPELS YOU TO CLICK?

Business e-customers indicate that numerous factors influence whether or not they click on a banner ad; but for the most part, they say they do not click on banner ads in the business environment. The predominant feeling is that banner ads are a costly waste of time and that clicking on a banner ad takes the user down a road of trouble.

Business e-customers say they do not click on banner ads in the business environment

BANNER ADS

MODERATOR: What is your attitude about banner ads?

E-CUSTOMER: They are a nuisance. You can't avoid looking at them—they flash and rotate and scream at you to look at them. They are obviously a revenue stream for the operators of the Web site, but that doesn't mean the messages they are trying to convey enter my consciousness.

E-CUSTOMER: I never click on ads that are unclear as to what they are saying or selling. If the message is vague, they won't get my click.

MODERATOR: Why do you dislike them so much?

E-CUSTOMER: The problem with banner ads is that they draw you in three or four levels deep, away from the content you were originally searching for. I don't have the time to follow an ad around. I've got work to do.

E-CUSTOMER: Banner ads usually lead you down an unproductive path.

E-CUSTOMER: Banner ads are tricky—avoid them. They compel you to click on them and then transport you to a marketing site. Banner ads rarely deliver what they promise.

MODERATOR: Do you ever respond to offers on banner ads?

E-CUSTOMER: I only click on banner ads once in a while. The advertised topic has to be something I am really interested in at that time. I might be searching for HP product information and see a banner ad for a new printer. I might click on that ad because I am already searching for HP product information.

E-CUSTOMER: If I saw an ad that looked like it would meet a business need, I might click on it.

E-CUSTOMER: If I see something visually interesting—bright colors, motion, something out of the ordinary—I might click on it.

E-CUSTOMER: I might click on a banner ad during personal use, but not at work. I don't have a lot of time to waste.

Business E-Customers and Privacy

Marketing to business e-customers and privacy are symbiotic topics. Often when business e-customers complain about Web marketing, they are really focusing on the intrusiveness of sales-oriented e-mail—one of the most visible forms of online privacy violations. In this section, we explore how business e-customers feel about privacy, in terms of their attitudes about the use of the Web for sales-oriented e-mail, online Web site registration, and the effectiveness of personalization technology.

ATTITUDES ABOUT SALES-ORIENTED E-MAIL

Business e-customers and consumers have similar opinions on the topic of intrusiveness: they resent being bombarded by communications that add no value and that waste their time. But business e-customers seem even more resentful of the problem and report that the volume of intrusions is growing at an alarming rate. In fact, 60 percent of the business e-customers we talked with say that there has been a noticeable increase in the amount of sales-oriented e-mail they are receiving.

This is seen as a problem even when the e-mail comes from a trusted vendor. Too often, vendors are not selective enough about what they send, or do not even give the e-customer the option to choose what they wish to receive. Any vendor is risking their business relationship with customers when they indiscriminately send unwanted e-mail. More than one-third of business e-customers we talked to say they dislike sales-oriented e-mail so much that they avoid the vendors that send it to them; another 20 percent say they dislike it but haven't taken any actions against the offending vendor.

Interestingly, some business e-customers like receiving sales-oriented e-mail *if they requested it and if it is targeted to their unique interests.* Unfortunately, most sales-oriented e-mail does not fit that description.

ATTITUDES ABOUT SALES-ORIENTED E-MAIL

MODERATOR: Why is sales-oriented e-mail a problem?

E-CUSTOMER: It wastes my time. It fills up my e-mail box with junk and makes me miss the stuff I need.

MODERATOR: What's an example of useful vendor e-mail?

E-CUSTOMER: E-mail from vendors that tells me important information, such as product upgrade availability and promotional offers on the products they know we buy. Those are the types of vendor e-mail that are helpful.

MODERATOR: What's an example of irritating e-mail?

E-CUSTOMER: Sometimes when I buy a software package from a vendor, I'll get recurring e-mail messages for the next thirty, sixty, ninety days about the vendor's complete product line. I don't care about their entire line of products. That type of marketing irritates me and makes me hesitate before buying additional software.

MODERATOR: What do you do to vendors that send you unwanted e-mail?

E-CUSTOMER: If a company sends me unsolicited e-mail, I won't do business with them.

E-CUSTOMER: I stop doing business with them.

E-CUSTOMER: I send them an e-mail saying to remove me from their list.

ATTITUDES ABOUT SITE REGISTRATION

Business e-customers draw the line when sites ask for personal information that is irrelevant to the matter at hand

Many business e-customers recognize the need for a Web registration process to enable business services such as online technical support. They will register "if they must" to get access to job-critical data—e.g. software patches, pricing information, or technical support—but they draw the line when sites ask for personal information that is irrelevant to the matter at hand, such as income, age, education, or home address. Their feeling is that many Web ventures take advantage of their power to collect and distribute personal information for marketing purposes, rather than use the data to provide a more valuable Web experience. They strongly believe that personal information should remain private.

For registration to succeed in the business-to-business environment, trust must be earned and users' rights must be respected. Business e-customers say that businesses need to better explain their data collection, registration, personalization, and direct marketing policies up front. Companies should give users a choice as to whether or not they want to be subjected to marketing promotions that rely on registration data. Businesses should deliver on the registration promise by delivering valuable content to the user exactly the way the user wants it.

REGISTRATION AND PERSONALIZATION

MODERATOR: How do you feel about registering on Web sites?

E-CUSTOMER: Registration is a front for sucking data from the registrant into some marketing department.

E-CUSTOMER: If I'm already a customer of a business, I'm open to registering online. I trust my vendors.

E-CUSTOMER: I never register. I don't want spam. It's not worth the effort.

E-CUSTOMER: I might register if they promise not to sell my name. I don't want junk mail, faxes, etc.

E-CUSTOMER: There is no ROI [Return on Investment] if you register online. None. Zero.

E-CUSTOMER: I register with big company sites, but not small ones.

MODERATOR: What are the benefits of registering?

E-CUSTOMER: Qualifying for technical support access motivates me to register.
E-CUSTOMER: Registering software online so that I can access technical support is worthwhile. But the registration process is redundant and time-consuming. I wish someone would develop a centralized database that stored my basic user-profile information so I could allow a company access to it at the click of a mouse.
MODERATOR: What are the downsides of registering?
E-CUSTOMER: Registration is intrusive. I don't like it.
E-CUSTOMER: It takes too much time. My attitude is just, "Give me the info. Let me get in and get out."
E-CUSTOMER: If they want to know who I am and where I live, I won't do it.
E-CUSTOMER: I don't trust Web sites that say they won't sell my e-mail address to other companies.

ATTITUDES ABOUT PERSONALIZATION

Business e-customers are more likely to buy into the personalization concept if it actually improves business processes. If personalization can make their jobs easier, they are open to the idea. Business e-customers agree that personalization works best when it delivers on the content promise—serving up content that a user needs most. An example of a Web site that delivers these customized benefits is Dell Premier Pages, which retains a company's required configuration, negotiated pricing, and purchasing policies. In this type of application, personalization is focused on personalizing at the company or department level, not at the individual level.

Business e-customers who remain skeptical about the benefits of personalization wonder what content they are missing when they register to receive personalized content. How can an electronic database possibly anticipate their ever-changing content needs and desires? The Web personalization services are only as good as the general predictions and assumptions they make about the user. On the whole, these skeptics do not trust what companies are doing with that data and they are not convinced that personal data is necessary to enhance their Web experience.

Business e-customers understand the concept behind personalization and also recognize the need for organizing information based on direct knowledge of the site user. It is clear, however, that in a work environment, the notion of personalization is somewhat inappropriate—at least at the individual level. Site functionality should be aimed at meeting the customized needs of a user's job function or company, rather than at them as individuals.

Some business e-customers are uncomfortable with the technologies that enable personalization. Many participants distrust "cookies" and say that they disable them on their browsers. In fact, several business e-customers report that their companies have policies against accepting "cookies" for security reasons.

ATTITUDES ABOUT PERSONALIZATION

MODERATOR: When is personalization useful?

E-CUSTOMER: I like personalization. With Dell's site, you don't have to go through the same order entry process with every log on—it saves me time.

E-CUSTOMER: It takes time to personalize a site, time I don't have. But I do like the results.

E-CUSTOMER: If it's used to streamline the ordering and procurement process—to match the PO and the requisition—I'm all for it.

E-CUSTOMER: I like Web sites that let me create my own "Web-bytes," nuggets of data that I need to know about in an easy-to-read format.

MODERATOR: When does personalization become inappropriate?

E-CUSTOMER: I don't want a Web site to control the information I view. I want to choose my information. If I don't get to choose, I wonder what I am not getting.

E-CUSTOMER: Personalization is kind of hokey.

E-CUSTOMER: Office Depot offers personalization features. But the "Good morning, Sam" stuff is not really necessary.

E-CUSTOMER: We have a rule at our company: we will accept no "cookies."

E-CUSTOMER: "Cookies" are difficult to stop. I worry about them because they could cause security problems on my system.

E-CUSTOMER: I would like to know the kind of information that a "cookie" is tracking. I am not comfortable with not knowing.

Online Barriers in Businesses

Barriers to more extensive use of the Web for business-to-business e-commerce are rapidly eroding. Opportunities in the business market have stimulated a proliferation of new products, technologies, and services to

If adopting e-commerce means changing the personal-relationship element of doing business, many customers will not want to change

serve all manners of business. We expect to see dramatic shifts in Web behavior in the short- to mid-term, as common barriers are overcome—industry by industry. At present, there are three key obstacles to buying more online that impact most types of business e-customers.

Product availability is the key reason why businesses don't buy more online—the products and services they need to buy simply aren't available. Unlike the consumer market, where people are hard-pressed to think of products and services that they can't buy online, the business-to-business market suffers from the lack of a pragmatic adoption of e-commerce in the supply chain—at least until very recently. Of course, common products such as office supplies, computers, software, and travel are available online, but the products that comprise the mainstay of business-to-business commerce have not been purchasable via the Web. This includes thousands of materials, parts, and substances that go into manufactured goods. Why is the business-to-business so far behind the consumer market in terms of product availability? Because the infrastructure to make it work is more complex and very difficult to implement.

While the consumer market had a ready method of payment for online commerce—the credit card—most supply-chain purchases are not easily transacted online. As one business e-customer who works for an industrial janitorial service company said, "You can't go online and buy 1,000 gallons of floor cleaner with a credit card." The purchasing procedures of POs, invoices, and Accounts Payable/Accounts Receivable require complex systems to interface between buyer and seller. While these systems are increasingly available and are being adopted, the infrastructure is not there yet to handle the broad array of supply-chain products. The recent emergence of business-to-business exchanges is an exciting development that may prove to be the solution to these problems.

In addition, the accountability embodied in a sales representative is still vital for many businesses. Knowing that a person, with a name, phone number, and a boss, is promising delivery of an order at a specified time and place is critical to many businesses. If adopting e-commerce means changing this element of doing business, many companies will not want to change.

The challenge in business-to-business e-commerce is to deliver the decreased cost of routine business, while still providing the assurance that the quality and timeliness of orders will not suffer. Companies need to offer their business customers a hybrid approach that will improve the tedious aspects of the business process, while still providing the benefits of the human touch.

These general problems apply to virtually every type of company. At the same time, each different e-customer group grapples with problems unique to their job functions. The following section documents the most common barriers that businesses face today by job function.

BARRIERS TO E-COMMERCE USAGE: THE IT PERSPECTIVE

IT e-customers view productive Web sites as places where they can go to get practical content—things like pricing, product specifications, quick and easy access to tech support, comparative analysis, and software patches and upgrades. The principal barriers that trouble IT professionals as Web users are those that make obtaining that content difficult.

But the IT e-customer has another perspective on e-commerce—how they can enable, secure, and control their company's use of technology outside of the firewall. The transactional issues are more critical to these business customers. They indicate that numerous barriers stand in their companies' way of using the Web to conduct business-to-business transactions. The most common barriers are: budgeting, control, procedural, employee skill sets, security, and corporate policy.

Avoiding human contact in the online world is seen as a plus for some IT professionals

Unlike their procurement counterparts, IT professionals are much less concerned about the loss of human interaction in the online world. In fact, avoiding human contact is seen as a plus. Many IT professionals don't want to be bothered by salespeople calling them and slowing down their productivity. The Web solves this problem by empowering IT customers to configure and order their own products online, or to find their own answers to problems they may have.

THE IT PERSPECTIVE ON E-COMMERCE OBSTACLES

MODERATOR: What are some obstacles blocking your company from doing more e-commerce?

E-CUSTOMER: Ignorance, corporate policy, loss of control, fear of credit card fraud.

E-CUSTOMER: Our budgeting department would never grant control of purchasing to an outside resource—such as a vendor's Web site. They want to maintain control over every single aspect of procurement that's more than a few hundred dollars in price.

E-CUSTOMER: The concept of doing business electronically really appeals to me. Procedural barriers such as budgetary constraints or issues of control occur prior to actually placing an order. The real barrier to doing more e-business is that most of the vendors we are dealing with are not there yet—they have yet to develop Web sites that enable us to do business with them.

MODERATOR: Is it just your vendors not being prepared, or is it internal groups as well?

E-CUSTOMER: We must mature internally before we can use the Web. We need more assurance that the Web is the way to go.

E-CUSTOMER: We don't have employees who are savvy enough to go out and discover these new online vendors—they certainly don't have the time to surf.

E-CUSTOMER: We are concerned with what will happen once we have given all of our employees the capacity to connect to the Web from their desktop. How are we going to monitor their usage to make sure they are using the Web for business purposes rather than for playtime? It's a question of management philosophy—do we want to play Big Brother or not? We prefer to treat our employees as professionals.

E-CUSTOMER: Purchasing departments have rules and processes they must follow. A person must first initiate a request, then somebody has to complete a purchase order. It must be approved at multiple levels, then sent off to the vendor. To re-engineer that process within an organization is an extremely difficult challenge. It requires changing mind sets. Most businesses are not quite ready to embrace dramatic change.

MODERATOR: In what ways does the advent of e-commerce make your job more challenging?

E-CUSTOMER: The bar keeps getting raised. Staying on top of everything is very challenging.

E-CUSTOMER: Security and reliability are barriers we haven't yet worked out. I am concerned about the security break-ins—particularly when client data is involved.

E-CUSTOMER: We are working on an internal system where our largest customers will be able to dial in to a proprietary area on our Web site and conduct business transactions with us. Momentum seems to be shifting in this direction for conducting business in the future.

BARRIERS TO E-COMMERCE USAGE: THE PURCHASING PERSPECTIVE

For purchasing and procurement professionals, many organizational and technology infrastructure issues stand in the way of deeper use of the Web as a daily business tool. These business e-customers say that the lack of adequate technology prevents heavier Web usage. Many indicate that their departments are not "webified" because they have not been given the right tools necessary to perform their jobs online, even though they want to be more Web involved.

The technology gap manifests in many ways: lack of ready access to computers; lack of fast Internet connectivity; and lack of necessary technical skills. But more importantly, from a systems perspective, many procurement specialists identify two root causes for not using the Web more extensively for corporate procurement: the inability to technically integrate procurement policies into Web-based purchasing systems; and not being able to interface Web transactions with legacy accounting systems. Even when Web purchasing is an option, using existing EDI systems or ordering via telephone is often easier.

THE PURCHASING PERSPECTIVE ON E-COMMERCE OBSTACLES

MODERATOR: Tell me about the organizational barriers to e-commerce at your company.

E-CUSTOMER: Some aspects of the procurement process will have to be altered dramatically for things to change. We have to get away from matching the packing slip to the invoice before payment is made. As long as businesses rely so much on a paper trail, it will be difficult to do business any other way.

E-CUSTOMER: In our company, the accounting department is based in another state. This means we can only do a limited amount of electronic ordering from our office. We are tied to a sister office that doesn't want to order online.

E-CUSTOMER: Procurement card programs are a problem online. Some banks restrict their use—they can't be used for online orders. That means I have to cut a check for my online orders. Why would I want to go back to the way we used to do business?

E-CUSTOMER: I need to do business with local vendors because when I place an order, I need the items yesterday. All of the online vendors I have seen are based out of state. It's unrealistic for me to do business with them. I wish more local vendors were online.

E-CUSTOMER: I work for a government organization—a very paper-intensive bureau whose philosophy is: Why send e-mail when you can send paper?

E-CUSTOMER: Web solutions must improve on what EDI can offer to get me to switch.

Procurement specialists indicate that real organizational issues stand in the way of their use of the Web as a daily business tool. The specialists we polled use the Web to perform only 10 percent of their daily procurement-related business duties. A lack of adequate technology prevents them from heavier Web usage. We found that those employees whose departments have been provided the tools to access and transact via the Web are more likely to choose to transact online over traditional "paper and telephone" procedures.

Fifty percent of the procurement professionals we polled indicate that the Web is important or very important to them in performing their jobs, but they express concern that the Web removes the "human element" from their daily business duties. Many believe that human relationships, personal accountability, and artful negotiations were important to their work. Not surprisingly, all agree that Web sites have not addressed the loss of interpersonal contact to their satisfaction.

Time barriers exist as well. Getting online is painfully slow for many purchasing professionals. Sixty percent of those we polled said that they use dial-up access to log onto the Web, which is extremely slow during peak business hours. When they are denied access to the Web or when the online connection is slow, they reach for the telephone instead of doing business online. Additionally, many purchasing professionals feel that the Internet actually adds one more job to their daily routine that they don't currently have.

ATTITUDES ABOUT ONLINE ORDERING

MODERATOR: Are you comfortable ordering online?

E-CUSTOMER: We are a small company and we like to do business with local vendors. Local suppliers are more responsible. They are right down the street and they are there to service me. Many of them are not yet online in any significant way. I don't know how a Web site 3,000 miles away can compete with that kind of service.

E-CUSTOMER: Reliability and order confirmation are more difficult online. This is a major problem. When I make a phone call, I can assign a name and date to an individual and get a verbal confirmation. I can examine a paper PO in my hand. I can't do that online.

E-CUSTOMER: Office supplies can be ordered automatically through EDI and it's easy. On the Internet, a user has to go through multiple firewalls. I am not happy that fellow employees can now order office supplies online. There is a serious issue with people buying without need.

E-CUSTOMER: The lack of personal contact concerns me. When I have a problem, I like to know that there is a person I can call.

E-CUSTOMER: It's always beneficial to have a person's name you can write down and come back to if there is a problem. On the Web, I have no idea who is handling my order.

MODERATOR: What is the downside to ordering online?

E-CUSTOMER: I hesitate to purchase on the Web because I can't negotiate terms and conditions with the vendor prior to my initial order.

E-CUSTOMER: What is the incentive for me to order online? What happens when an order is late? Who do I yell at?

TIMESAVINGS BENEFITS

MODERATOR: Let's talk about time constraints. The Web is supposed to help save time. What is the problem?

E-CUSTOMER: I need quick answers and I need them fast. Does the Web really save me time? I don't want to go online and get bogged down filling out forms and all that rigmarole. I have to call about certain things anyway—deadlines, what's in stock, shipping options, the latest price—I'm not convinced Web sites work any better than the telephone.

E-CUSTOMER: So far, the only thing that is easier to do online than offline is order business cards. It's twenty times faster to order business cards online—and for someone like me who is always ordering new cards, this is a big deal.

E-CUSTOMER: I waste a lot of time when I try to order online. Online access needs to be faster and more reliable. Vendors' servers need to be more robust. It is often easier to talk on the phone than to do business on the Web.

The Impact of the Internet on Other Consumption and Related Organizational Behavior

Similar to the impact that the Web has had on consumers, the Web is changing businesses' perceptions of themselves, their organizations, and the way they do business. The Web even impacts a company's choice of vendors.

What other ways has the Internet impacted the consuming function of e-customers? The Internet has changed the mix of channels through which businesses buy. In addition, the Web impacts how companies are organized and how job responsibilities are defined. At the core, it is changing the competitive landscape and what companies must do to build and maintain market share.

IMPACT OF THE WEB ON THE PURCHASE CHANNEL MIX

When analyzing the impact that the Web has had on more traditional aspects of consumer behavior in chapter 6, we learned that the mix of preferred distribution channels changed significantly. That same pattern is seen among business e-customers. Businesses indicate that due to the Web, they now buy less from all other available channels. The most dramatically hit are purchases from catalogs and retail stores, and e-customers predict that trend will continue. More than 85 percent of those we talked to expect to buy more online in the future. As expected, the Internet is used mostly for purchasing low-involvement type products, as compared to more traditional channels for high-involvement products, such as office equipment.

The sales channel that seems to be least impacted by the Internet is that in which purchases are made from sales representatives. While the overall proportion of products purchased through direct reps varies broadly by industry and company size, business e-customers voice a certain comfort level in the personal accountability that is implicit in the direct-sales model. This is especially important for mission-critical purchases that are required for day-to-day business operations.

IMPACT OF THE WEB ON VENDOR SELECTION

While not yet a prerequisite for doing business with all vendors, many businesses indicate that whether or not their vendors have Web sites makes a distinct difference in their overall opinion and selection process. Having a Web site means that a vendor is innovative and forward-thinking. Lack of a Web presence means a company is "behind the times." Most e-customers believe that in the near future, Web presence will influence their choices of vendors—and that vendors with no Web presence will most likely lose market share to vendors who offer online solutions and relationships.

THE IMPACT OF WEB STRATEGY ON VENDOR SELECTION

MODERATOR: Why does it matter that a vendor has a Web presence?

E-CUSTOMER: A company with a Web site gives me more confidence that the firm will be around next year.

E-CUSTOMER: It's a good indication as to how a company thinks, and I make some judgments based on that. I'd say it's an influencing factor, but not a deciding factor.

E-CUSTOMER: A Web site adds a huge degree of legitimacy to a business.

E-CUSTOMER: We have a relationship with our vendor that takes care of all of our service equipment needs. To keep costs down, they now require us to communicate and transact with them electronically via the Web.

MODERATOR: How important is it that a vendor has a Web site?

E-CUSTOMER: Not having a Web site is not a deal breaker, but a few years from now it very well may be. A Web presence reflects positively on the firm.

E-CUSTOMER: Our engineers are so spoiled by the Internet that they now say companies without a Web site don't exist.

E-CUSTOMER: A Web presence does not impact my vendor choice now. I like the personal contact I get from vendors I do business with face-to-face. In a few years, I can see potential for the Web.

MODERATOR: Is it important that your company has a Web site?

E-CUSTOMER: It's important for recruiting. We operate a very private company. We've had job applicants come in for interviews that have told us that they almost didn't come in because they couldn't find our Web site.

E-CUSTOMER: I would be a little concerned if a software manufacturer wasn't on the Web, but other than that, I don't think a Web presence influences my purchase decision.

E-CUSTOMER: A Web site is not a criterion now, but it will be a determining factor in the future.

E-CUSTOMER: In the old days, we chose our vendors based on relationships. Now it comes down to who offers the best price. I'm not sure where the Web fits into this mix.

E-CUSTOMER: It all comes down to the type of commodities I am buying. I might be able to order repetitive items online, but customized or expensive items need to be negotiated.

THE WEB AS A STRATEGIC BUSINESS VEHICLE

Most large and mid-sized businesses have Web sites these days. Large proportions of small businesses have them as well. In fact, many say that the Web is now a serious business vehicle within their organizations. Business e-customers are often attuned to the competitive challenges that the Web presents to their companies. As more companies become involved with e-commerce, the more important it is for companies to adopt the Web to be at parity with their business ecosystems. To get a better understanding of businesses as e-customers, it is useful to understand how their own strategies and organizations are aligning for e-business.

Corporate Web strategies are driven by either the IT department or the marketing department. Sometimes both departments work together to develop a joint strategy. It is not uncommon for outside consultants or production companies to be hired to conceptualize, implement, and/or manage the company's Web efforts. Many business e-customers lament that executive management needs to play a more active role in driving their corporate Web initiative.

Managers from numerous departments within the organization, such as the IT department, initiate, plan, execute, and maintain the corporate Web strategy. Additionally, division managers contribute both strategically and tactically to the company Web effort.

Business E-Wish Lists

Businesses' wish lists for improving e-commerce cluster around several common themes: better technology or site performance, better product availability, better online ordering capabilities, better online information, and better search technology. Below are comments from business e-customers on these topics.

BUSINESSES' WISH LISTS FOR BETTER
ONLINE EXPERIENCE

MODERATOR: What do you wish was better in terms of technical performance?

E-CUSTOMER: I would like to see less graphic-intensive pages. Keep the pages simple so that it doesn't take so long to download information.

E-CUSTOMER: Faster, higher capacity access. Today, it takes too long to download information. I'd like to be able to do video conferencing and that sort of business function.

E-CUSTOMER: Voice command would be great. I'm a terrible typist and I'd use the Web more if I could speak my way around the Internet.

E-CUSTOMER: Speed. In purchasing, we're the stepchild organization. We're lucky to have dial-up access. And it's real slow.

MODERATOR: What would you like to do that you aren't doing today?

E-CUSTOMER: If the Web could be used more for online bidding, my department would use it to save money and open the purchasing process up to a wider variety of vendors.

E-CUSTOMER: I would like online ordering for business forms, such as printing on demand using the Web.

E-CUSTOMER: Bidding contracts over the Internet would be a plus.

MODERATOR: What would you like to do that you aren't doing today?

E-CUSTOMER: I work in the healthcare field and I wish that a wider variety of products were available to order online.

E-CUSTOMER: The Web presents a difficult sales challenge for our complex product lines. If we were to try and sell, for example, one of our blood gas analyzers via the Web, we need to let our customers know the corresponding parts and consumables that go along with it. At the present time, this is a difficult thing for us to offer online.

MODERATOR: What do you wish was better in terms of functionality?

E-CUSTOMER: I would like to be able to generate narrower results when I search online (and not get three hundred returns to my query). Searching needs to be more efficient. Too often, online searching is counterproductive.

E-CUSTOMER: Navigating a site isn't always intuitive. If more sites had standardized, text-based search capabilities, it would make finding what I need much easier.

E-CUSTOMER: I want quick access to information—not fluff. A useful search engine or standard text-based information without heavy graphics would be great. Give me the choice.

MODERATOR: What do you wish was better in terms of information access?

E-CUSTOMER: A comparison shopping site for business-to-business products and services would be useful.

E-CUSTOMER: I wish more Web sites had newsgroups on subjects pertaining to my area of interest. For technical support questions, there is nothing better.

E-CUSTOMER: I wish there was a quick way to determine whether or not an online business venture is ISO certified. It would save me a lot of time.

Implications for Business

The business-to-business e-commerce world is vast and complex. We have only touched on some of the key issues facing companies who consider other businesses as their customers. There are some resounding suggested actions, however, that provide general direction to companies who sell to business e-customers.

For e-commerce to succeed in the business-to-business space, systems must adapt to the ways purchasing is done today, rather than attempting to totally reinvent well-established business practices. This points to:

- Seamlessly interfacing Web procurement systems with legacy enterprise purchasing systems.
- Automating procurement policies, such as purchase authority, approved brands, and credit limits into the e-commerce solution.
- Acknowledging and allowing for the importance of human contact in the sales relationship, especially in high-involvement product and service categories.

Participating in newly emerging online channels of distribution, such as trade exchanges and auctions, may be the answer for many types of businesses that need to become e-business involved. Virtually all industries comprise interdependent supply-chain players that must closely interface in the process of adding value to goods and services throughout the production process. Vertical market exchanges are emerging in a wide range of industries at an exciting clip. In fact, some industries already have competitive exchanges wooing the same buyers and sellers. As competition proliferates within specific industries, business e-customers will be forced to choose in which exchanges they will participate, as both buyers and sellers. The degree to which an exchange can simulate natural market conditions will become the primary selection criteria—i.e., whether there is adequate participation from market players to offer competitive price pressure, broad product selection, and a reliable and adequate supply of goods. In addition, exchanges will be evaluated on the compatibility of IT systems. The responsibility to build and maintain systems that can inter-operate will be the domain of everyone in the supply chain—the exchanges, the buyers, and the sellers. In order for a business ecosystem to truly benefit from e-commerce, all players must be able to participate. The ones who don't will be squeezed out. *Net net: Business e-customers know that there is more Internet in their future.*

The e-customer views the Internet as a mixed blessing. The aspects of saving time and getting better prices are positive, while the loss of the personal-touch assurance of customer service and the need to undergo a business process change make them hesitant.

Companies desiring to open up this channel and move a significant amount of their customer relationships to the Internet need to pay close attention to the aforementioned issues. Understanding customer processes and reducing the requirements to change activities, coupled with assurances of improved customer service, are paramount to success.

While e-customers realize that the economics of moving more procurement online makes growth of this activity inevitable, the adoption of widespread acceptance in b-to-b transactions will be a function of vendors making the process as painless as possible for the willing, but cautious, e-customer.

8 The E-Business Road Map with a Consumer Perspective

For most companies, integrating the understanding of customer demands into value propositions is a natural business process. New product development processes are a core competency that companies must maintain to be competitive. But often, companies don't apply the wisdom of understanding customer demands into the development and execution of their e-business strategies. Frequently, this happens because the responsibility for e-business development is organizationally separate from product development.

To help gain perspective on the challenge of comprehending the soul of the new consumer in creating an e-business strategy, in this chapter we present our E-Business Development Road Map. This road map was originally introduced in our previous book, *Dead Ahead,* as a tool to guide companies who are creating their e-business strategies for the first time. Since the original development of the road map, we have refined some of the concepts to keep in step with the evolution of the Web. In this chapter, we present the updated E-Business Development Road Map. In addition, we discuss when and how to factor the preferences of new consumers into the planning, developing, and launching process of a Web site.

Keep in mind that the premise of this book has been to examine e-business from a consumer point of view. But as we just saw in the previous chapter, there is another aspect of e-business: how to address the demands of the business-to-business market and the automation of supply chains via the Web. These are certainly related concepts and, in fact, the business strategy and technology solutions for customer-facing and supply-chain management should be integrated and leveraged. Strategy development processes should begin with understanding the customer and market requirements, as that understanding should drive internal e-business decisions in both realms. The Internet is more than a storefront, so when making decisions about strategy and technology solutions, companies need to be thinking much more broadly about the benefits that e-business can bring to the company, in all aspects of its operations.

APPLYING CONSUMER INTELLIGENCE ALONG THE WAY

Many companies that launch e-businesses—especially existing brick-and-mortar companies—assume they already know what their customers want, and treat Web sites like an afterthought instead of as a critical customer-relationship business vehicle. That is an outdated and potentially dangerous way of thinking. As the Web user population increases, it becomes more and more important to fully understand market segments and what motivates target consumers to use the Web. Companies should approach their e-business development as if they were designing a new product or service, taking all the steps to understand market requirements and customer demands. As in product development, consumer opinion should have impact at multiple phases throughout the Web site–development cycle.

Companies should approach their e-business development as if they were creating a new product or service

At key milestones along the way, direct contact with customers and prospects will provide answers critical to capturing unique opportunities and meeting market expectations. For example, what kinds of functionality do target customers or users want on Web sites? Not necessarily on any one particular Web site, but in general, how is the Web serving their overall needs? What do they wish they could do online that they can't do today? What should be easier, better, and faster on the Internet? Gaining this broader perspective is important because consumers' comments can stimulate new, creative ideas. It is also important to take a further step and analyze what customer problems of the analog world might be solved with the Web.

*Relying **entirely** on customers' insights can be limiting but disregarding them can lead to failure*

A classic comment made about the pitfalls of research in the early phases of a new product development cycle is that customers are often limited by their own knowledge of what is possible, and therefore their opinions are not valuable. There is truth and peril in that observation. Many innovative new products would never have come to market if they had relied entirely on the limited vision of the target customer. Disregarding or discounting customer feedback, however, can lead to failure.

How to Use This Chapter

If your company is in the early phases of its e-business development, use this chapter as a reality check to ensure that you are considering all the key aspects of executing your customer-centric Web strategy—and that you are factoring in the new consumers' demands along the way. If your company has already implemented its e-business strategy, this chapter can be useful as a catalyst for reminding you of when and how you should include knowledge of consumers' attitudes, behaviors, and preferences in your continuous e-business–process improvement.

The E-Business Development Road Map has six basic phases, as depicted in figure 8.1. The remainder of this chapter discusses each individual step, provides some tips about how to successfully navigate through the steps, and gives case study examples of how to use consumer research to improve chances of success.

FIGURE 8.1: THE SIX PHASES OF THE E-BUSINESS DEVELOPMENT ROAD MAP

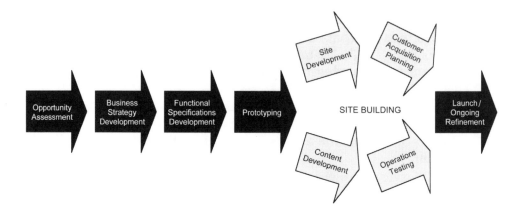

Phase One: Opportunity Assessment

MYTHS

- Customers are willing to wait until we get our e-business act together.
- Our direct competitors aren't doing anything compelling in e-business so we don't need to worry.
- We know our customers better than they know themselves. We don't need to ask them what they want from e-business.

REALITIES

- Customers are impatient and they have other options. Moving quickly is key to your survival.
- Direct competitors are not the only concern. Customers are being trained in new processes by other companies in the business ecosystem.
- It is dangerous to assume you know customers as e-customers. New consumers' expectations are different.

Many companies have determined that they must seriously embrace the Web as a strategic business vehicle, but are often basing that decision on intuition, perceived market pressures, or anecdotal customer demands. All three of these drivers are part of the decision process, but fully assessing the situation and potential opportunity is a critical step that must be approached with a systematic methodology, not just intuition and "one-off" data points.

As shown in figure 8.2, the Opportunity Assessment phase should include research in four key areas: the competitive landscape, target customer research, analysis of sales and distribution channels, and the best practices in related industries. The analysis process of these areas should move quickly. Fully understanding the implications of your time-to-market with a viable e-business presence is critical to your success—and potentially to your survival.

FIGURE 8.2: OPPORTUNITY ASSESSMENT

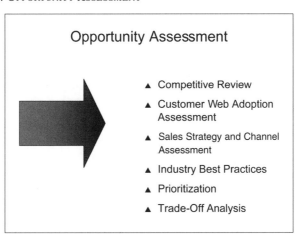

KEY ISSUES TO CONSIDER IN OPPORTUNITY ASSESSMENT

One of the most important aspects of Opportunity Assessment is understanding how rapidly your market is adopting e-business as a serious commerce vehicle. We have all witnessed the pressures that the upstart dot coms have put on existing businesses, particularly in sectors such as books, music, travel, electronics, and toy retailing. Web site–brand loyalty has been already established to some extent for the first-in brands such as Amazon.com,

Dell.com, and Yahoo.com. In fact, as we discussed in chapter 2, our research shows that over 50 percent of Web shoppers indicate that they have established an allegiance to their chosen Web sites for particular types of products or services. For later market entrants, moving zealous customers from one brand to another is an expensive, if not impossible, challenge.

But the threat of first-in timing is not just being felt in these highly visible consumer markets. And the threat isn't just coming from direct competitors, or from newborn dot coms. The most widespread and deeply felt changes will be in brick-and-mortar companies stimulated by the industry market leaders. Industry market leaders can afford the substantial investments, strategy definition, and organizational changes required to truly embrace e-business, as well as have the clout to redefine customer business processes and migrate customer relationships to the Web. Companies capable of this level of change will be raising the bar for other companies operating within their industries.

A recent cross-industry survey, which represented companies from computer, peripheral, retail, health care, automotive, transportation, electronic equipment, and other markets, indicated that one-third of those polled expect e-business channels to account for 20 percent or more of their revenue this year.[1] Some companies report having already moved as much as 75 percent of their business to the Web, resulting in improved efficiencies and cost savings. Even if you don't see it directly in your market, the probability is high that the Internet is already in your business ecosystem. Chances are that your customers are being trained to prefer Web-based business processes to traditional ways of doing business by someone in your business ecosystem.

We call this the "e-business squeeze play." Here are the basic steps in the playbook. A market leader shifts a significant number of customer relationships to the Web. By doing so, the leader takes substantial costs out of doing business. As a result, the leader has healthier profit margins, which in turn enable that company to drop prices or invest more in development—either of which puts competition in a defensive position. Realizing the significance of adopting e-business in the business ecosystem, we believe that one of the key discoveries in the Opportunity Assessment phase of the e-business road map is to learn what other companies in your business ecosystem are doing with the Web. Have they influenced your common set of customers to adopt the Web as a business vehicle?

A key discovery is to learn what other companies in your business ecosystem are doing with the Web

OPPORTUNITY ASSESSMENT: DATA REQUIRED

The fundamental external data that must be factored into the opportunity assessment are listed below. The data gathered should be compiled in a formal report that will be reviewed as a part of the recommendations from the Opportunity Assessment team. It will also be useful to teams in subsequent phases of the project.

- To what degree have your customers and prospects adopted the Web, i.e., do they have access to the Web, do they use it, what for? Which sites do they like and use regularly? It is useful to know their preferences even for areas that are not directly related to your relationship with them, as it can provide some helpful tips when developing your strategy.
- Specifically, which parts of the consumption cycle do your customers want you to address with a Web presence: shopping, buying, delivery, service and support? All of the above?
- What is your distribution pipeline doing on the Web? Do your customers currently have Web access to your products via your channels? Is that working well? Is there room for improvement?
- What do your channel partners want you to do regarding the Web?
- What are competitors offering your target prospects and customers via a Web strategy, and how well are those site experiences meeting the needs of the customer?
- Which business process improvements and cost savings can be achieved via the Web?

The risk of <u>not</u> going forward may be greater than the risks of going forward

OPPORTUNITY ASSESSMENT: DECISION POINTS

Decisions in the Opportunity Assessment phase of the road map focus on how far you go with your e-business strategy. How far do your customers want you to go? How far are your competitors pushing you to go? What are the risks of action versus inaction? The risk of *not* going forward may be greater than the risks of going forward.

The opportunity assessment should identify the "must have" elements of a Web strategy in your marketplace. Based on the comprehensive review of the current market practices and customer demands, the analysis should outline opportunities your company has to differentiate itself with a Web presence. It also suggests what the business objectives of the site should be—given the market conditions, as well as the strategic imperative, the level of priority, and the timing implications for maintaining company competitiveness.

OPPORTUNITY ASSESSMENT: OUTPUT

The output of the Opportunity Assessment phase is a formal document that should cover these basic components:

- Competitive review
- Customer assessment: level of Web access, preference, use in other categories
- Distribution channel assessment
- Level of urgency/priority
- Trade-off analysis: go versus no-go
- Recommendations on best path strategy, timeline, next-step team structure
- Recommended budget (at this stage in the road map this is a very rough, ballpark estimate)

Case Study: Customer Research in Opportunity Assessment Phase

- CHALLENGE: A company that provides services for targeting and distributing coupons to consumers via the U.S. mail wished to understand the potential opportunities to deliver online promotional offers. The company realized that consumers' preferences are changing rapidly and that offering an online alternative to their current value proposition is key to their future success—perhaps even their survival. They needed to explore, however, how the Internet has changed consumers' use of coupons and other promotional incentives, and what types of value propositions might be demanded in an e-business–driven marketplace.

- RESEARCH PROJECT DESCRIPTION: In a series of focus groups conducted across the country, the company explored potential new promotional services and offerings that could be marketed to consumers, both within their existing brand and newly developed brands. The research tested multiple concepts regarding delivery vehicles, attractiveness of offers, and reactions to potential partnerships. With the research data, the company identified the most promising new value propositions, profiled which market segments were the best fit for the proposed offerings, estimated revenue potential, and evaluated internal competencies to deliver.

- RESULTS: Based on the research findings, recommendations were created for the brick-and-mortar business to create a new e-business division, retaining the existing brand name for the new entity. The new division was to be tasked with creating and/or partnering to make available Web-based promotional and coupon offers to consumers and delivering those services via partner sites, as well as their own branded coupon portal.

Phase Two: Business Strategy Development

MYTHS	REALITIES
• Targeting specific groups of customers will limit our opportunities.	• Focusing on target customer segments enables companies to develop value propositions that uniquely address needs.
• Providing only limited offerings online is a good way to start.	

- E-business initiatives can be done with little incremental investments.

- Customers don't have patience for limited offerings, they want access to everything.
- Setting up for e-business is expensive. Face it.

The end goal of the Business Strategy Development phase is to create a comprehensive business plan complete with objectives, required actions, and organizational structures. Getting to that end goal—producing an astute, actionable business plan—requires the evaluation of both external and internal data, as shown in figure 8.3.

FIGURE 8.3: BUSINESS STRATEGY DEVELOPMENT

KEY ISSUES TO CONSIDER IN BUSINESS STRATEGY DEVELOPMENT

There are many customer-related issues to consider in the Business Strategy phase. The resolution of customer-related issues will impact how the e-business effort will be organized.

We firmly believe that e-businesses must be set up as customer-centric organizations to ensure competitiveness in this consumer-empowered market. To work through what this means in your context, it may be useful to hypothetically design your Web organization as if you were a start-up. If you were not encumbered by the structures and politics of your current organization, how would you set up the customer-centric structure most likely to succeed? To assist you in

It may be useful to hypothetically design your Web organization as if you were a start-up

this thinking, we have assembled a prototype organizational chart based on the structures of some leading Web-commerce companies, shown in figure 8.4. Here we can get some insight into what types of job roles are performed and how they are organized to keep their focus on customers.

FIGURE 8.4: PROTOTYPICAL ORGANIZATIONAL STRUCTURE CHART OF A DOT-COM COMPANY

While e-commerce companies have some organizational differences, there are many common elements in the departments and roles of their organizations. Below is a brief description of some of the most typical direct reports, the major functional areas that impact customer relationships, and how each group should use consumer data to be successful.

EXECUTIVE LEADERSHIP: The CEO of a dot com is not only the Chief Executive Officer, but he or she is also the Chief *E-Business* Officer. Company leaders must understand the company's entire business strategy—its marketing, sales, fulfillment, service, IT, financial, and e-business strategies, as well as the trends in the e-business marketplace. One of the key executive actions is to vigilantly monitor customers' and prospects' e-business preferences and know how to strategically translate those into Web site–functional specifications. In addition, CEOs should hold their direct reports responsible for being customer-involved in all aspects of their work.

CUSTOMER MARKETING: Customer acquisition is driven by this marketing department which is typically responsible for all outbound marketing tasks such as advertising, database and direct marketing, creative services, market analysis, affinity and rewards programs, public relations, and partner relations. This group is not only skilled at program execution, they are also the watchdogs for what new programs are being introduced by competitors and other market players. Customer Marketing should have research mechanisms to track customers' responses to programs and calculate ROI on marketing expenditures.

PRODUCT MANAGEMENT/MARKETING: In the e-commerce context, this department is tasked with customer retention and is responsible for producing the "experience." It includes job roles such as market researcher, producer, writer, graphic designer, analyst, and new product development. This group is responsible for conducting Web site usability testing throughout the E-Business Road Map. In addition, Product Management/Marketing is responsible for tracking customer satisfaction, often in collaboration with the Customer Service department. Many companies actually manage different aspects of the site experience as "products." For example, a travel site might manage leisure services separately from business services. Writers in this context might include vacation reporters, business news reporters, and destination reporters.

CUSTOMER SERVICE: Despite the fact that e-commerce companies handle many customer service calls online, most credible companies maintain a customer service group that handles problems via telephone as well. This group would be tasked with handling both online and telephone support. Customer Service should share in the responsibility of analyzing customer satisfaction information and creating solutions to address systemic dissatisfaction.

MEDIA SALES: Since many e-commerce sites sell advertising and sponsorships to advertisers, there's typically a group responsible for media sales. To be most effective in making ad sales, this group must be aware of the profiles of customers who visit the site and what kind of eyeballs are delivered to site advertisers. Media Sales should also be given guidelines about what types of advertising are acceptable to target consumers and be careful to sell advertising that will interest, rather than repel, them.

STRATEGIC BUSINESS DEVELOPMENT: This group is responsible for creating strategic alliances with other companies on the Web. Strategic Business Development needs to be closely linked to the target marketing strategy and have access to customer preference data so that relationships can be built to meaningfully augment the customer value proposition. In addition, this group should keep track of customer satisfaction and site traffic reports to judge how partnerships are performing for consumers.

INTERNATIONAL BUSINESS DEVELOPMENT: Because conducting Internet commerce outside the United States is still in developmental phases, the group responsible for international markets typically has its own department and executive leadership. Many times, these groups are staffed with people who are not only experts in certain geographies, but are also adept at developing strategic alliances, since many international strategies are executed through joint development with local enterprises. People in this group need to be knowledgeable about the acceptance of the Internet in target geographies; they should not assume the same strategies that are effective in the United States will work in other countries.

INFORMATION SYSTEMS (IS): This group typically includes three major functional areas: software development, systems engineering, and site operations. Even the IS department has to be customer-centric in its focus, as it is the group responsible for maintaining the customer-facing systems—customer relationship management software, databases, and other technologies critical to building online relationships. It is crucial that the IS department is involved in customer usability testing and in tracking customer satisfaction.

BUSINESS STRATEGY DEVELOPMENT: DATA REQUIRED

Much of the external data collection needed in the Business Strategy Development stage was performed in the Opportunity Assessment phase. If holes in the information were discovered in the presentation of the Opportunity Assessment, then the gaps should be filled in this next phase.

The more intensive data-collection and analysis efforts in this phase are focused on internal data. The team must have access to operating and strategic planning information, such as:

- Current and projected P&Ls
- Current and projected cost-center budgets for IT and marketing
- Cost analysis of key functional areas such as fulfillment and support
- Sales force and channel compensation models
- Current business processes and workflows
- Product profitability analysis
- Customer sales and profitability analysis

BUSINESS STRATEGY DEVELOPMENT: DECISION POINTS

There are myriad decisions in creating a rigorous Web-business plan. These decisions will concern:

- Enabling consumption functions
- Focusing business objectives
- Offering products
- Delivering the brand promise
- Building direct customer relationships
- Improving business processes

CONSUMPTION FUNCTION DECISIONS: At the most fundamental level, the key question that must be answered is: What aspects of the consumption cycle should we address with our Web site? Some companies make the mistake of thinking of the Web only as a storefront—an alternative distribution channel. While the Web is an important commerce channel for many companies, there's more to consider than just selling, such as:

- Should we allow customers to shop and find information about our products, services, company, and employment opportunities?
- Should it be at our Web site where they make the sales transactions, or someone else's, such as a channel partner or a portal—or both?
- And, if it is someone else's site, what do we need to do to make that happen?
- Should we enable customers to inquire about delivery status and track product shipments through our site?
- Should we offer customer support services via the site?

There is a plethora of drill-down questions to each of these topline issues. But the business plan must specifically address what the company will do for each of these key aspects of consumption, and for whom—which leads to another fundamental decision in the Business Strategy Development phase. The plan must pinpoint who the target visitors are: suspects, prospects, customers, partners, employees, investors, channels, etc.

BUSINESS OBJECTIVE DECISIONS: Another set of business strategy decisions is to determine the business objectives of the site. With your site, do you aim to:

- Attract and acquire new customers?
- Expand into new markets?
- Generate sales leads?
- Increase sales? Of what products? At what price?
- Build direct relationships with customers?
- Retain existing customers? Increase customer satisfaction?
- Shorten the sales cycle?
- Take costs out of the business cycle?

Each of these objectives stimulates a raft of issues that must be analyzed, and prompts multiple questions that must be resolved. For example, if you plan to attract new customers, you must flesh out:

- Who they are
- The size of the opportunity
- The value proposition and benefits you uniquely offer to your target markets
- Why the Web has made them a potential target
- How you reach them through the Web, and the associated costs of doing so

Some companies hope to increase sales through their Web presence, but don't have a clear picture of what is realistic to expect. A critical reality to keep in mind is that achieving increased sales and customer retention is directly related to how you plan to drive traffic to the site, the quality of the site experience, and the consumption functions enabled on the site. It is somewhat of a chicken-and-egg problem. If the company underfunds the site and its promotion, Web sales will suffer. But in the planning phase, it is difficult to know how much is the right amount to spend to reach target business objectives. That's one of the reasons why prototyping the site and testing the response to the prototype is critical to solidifying success metrics.

PRODUCT LINE DECISIONS: Other decisions relate to the products you intend to sell on your Web site and the pricing strategy for those items. In the business plan, you must stipulate the products and services that will be made available on the Web and commit to overcoming the strategic conflicts that ensue.

BRAND PROMISE DECISIONS: Another aspect of developing the value proposition strategy is addressing the brand promise you make to customers by asking the following questions:

- What actions might we take to ensure that both our traditional and online brand strategies are complementary? Is it possible to create a single strategy that spans both traditional and new media?
- How do we create an online value proposition that consistently fulfills and delivers our brand promise?
- How can we build trusting relationships with our customers, and increase brand loyalty?
- Are we committed to making the required investments to build or extend our brand on the Web?

CUSTOMER RELATIONSHIP DECI-SIONS: Many companies see the Web as the first chance they have had to develop direct relationships with their customers. The Web pro-vides an exciting opportunity to know who your customers are and

If the company under-funds the site and its promotion, Web sales will suffer

build a rapport with them. Companies that have relied on distribution channels to move products to market have never had much contact with their end-customers. Companies should assess and comprehend, however, the full implications of this strategy on their distribution channel relationships.

A primary reason to build direct relationships with customers via the Web is to be able to track and improve customer satisfaction. One of the disadvantages to selling strictly through distribution, instead of direct, is the lack of customer feedback on how well you are serving end-customers' needs. Used properly, the Web is a vehicle that not only allows you to build a direct rapport with your customers, but also allows you to keep pace with how you are doing in meeting their expectations.

BUSINESS PROCESS DECISIONS: One of the key objec-tives of e-business is taking costs out of business processes. Creating objectives that focus on saving money requires an astute analysis of the operational data listed above, apply-ing the "best practices" knowledge gained in the Oppor-tunity Assessment phase, and understanding how things are done in your company today.

BUSINESS STRATEGY DEVELOPMENT: OUTPUT

The output of this phase is the E-Business Plan. Like any business plan, it has core elements, including:

- Situation overview: a recap of findings from Oppor-tunity Analysis
- Business objectives
- Target audiences/markets

- Definition of the *whole experience:* key consumption functions addressed by the site
- Profitability/cost impact analysis
- Resource requirements: organization, leadership, time, budget
- Timeline

Case Study: Customer Research in Business Strategy Development Phase

- CHALLENGE: A venture capital–backed start-up possessed significant competencies in veterinary medicine and had been offering nationwide fee-based consultation services to other veterinarians via telephone and facsimile communications for several years. The company wished to launch a Web site to continue its existing business of professional-to-professional services, as well as offer another branded site to pet-owning consumers. The company determined that the market opportunities were substantial and that the company principals possessed the required competencies to deliver a defensible value proposition—both to veterinarians and to consumers. At this juncture, it needed to comprehend the best e-business strategy and business model to capture the two market opportunities.
- RESEARCH PROJECT DESCRIPTION: The company fielded a hybrid research methodology, comprising two sets of focus groups and telephone surveys—one set aimed at veterinarians, the other at consumers. The purpose was to test concepts about Web site content, fee structures, and commerce opportunities. The information derived served as the foundation for a business plan and subsequent functional specifications.
- RESULTS: The company discovered that two site brands were required to meet the needs of both markets. Among veterinarians, there was great concern about providing too much pet-care advice to consumers, for fear of misuse of information and possi-

ble maltreatment of pets. In addition, a clearer understanding of veterinarians' use of PCs and the Internet was derived, pointing to service opportunities not originally conceived at the beginning of the venture. From the consumers' perspective, it was determined that the pet-care content was highly valued and that the best initial e-commerce opportunities were for hard-to-access products, such as routine pharmaceutical refills. Consumer demand for commodity pet products, such as food, was rated low. Based on the research and market landscape assessment, the company created a two-prong business strategy.

Phase Three: Functional Specifications Development

MYTHS
- Our customers' preferences for e-business will be the same as in our traditional business.
- Our e-business team doesn't need to be concerned about the rest of the company.
- The entire world has high-speed Internet access.
- Support outside of the United States can be added later.

REALITIES
- Because the Web is empowering customers in new ways, their preferences for using the Web may be different than you expect.
- A successful e-business within an existing company needs to be designed to successfully interface the existing Web front-end functions with back-end business processes.
- Internet access and performance is not equal across the globe. Site architectures must be designed to enhance performance to the last mile.
- International support must be established from the beginning.

The business plan from the Business Strategy Development phase gives the framework for the site strategy. It also provides substantial intelligence about what the market requires, what the company hopes to gain, and what fundamental aspects of consumption will be addressed by the site strategy. In the third phase, Functional Specifications Development, the focus is to flesh out how your company will create a Web site experience that will capture the market opportunity. In this phase, you determine the functional goals and requirements of the Web site, shown in figure 8.5. Decisions made in this step culminate in a Site Requirements Document, which becomes the guideline for the team responsible for creating the prototype site.

FIGURE 8.5: FUNCTIONAL SPECIFICATIONS DEVELOPMENT

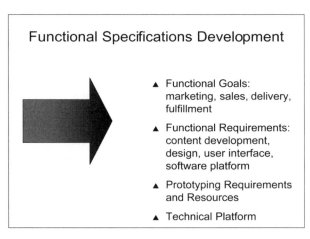

FUNCTIONAL SPECIFICATIONS: DATA REQUIRED

In this stage of the road map, it is time to learn more thoroughly about what the customer wants from the site experience, as well as to use the information about company business processes. You have already decided whether you will sell, track, and support products with your Web site in the previous phase. How you perform those functions is defined in this stage.

To get a better understanding of what customers want requires some direct contact research. Whether you gather that data in focus groups, personal interviews, or surveys, the fundamental things you need to know are:

• What do they want to do on your site?
• What are their alternative ways of performing those activities today?

- How do they learn about Web sites they frequent?
- What type of content do they prefer to see when they are shopping? What are they most likely to read?
- What do they want to buy from you?
- What are their preferences on how to buy? Do they use credit cards? If they are a business, what are their purchasing procedures that must be accommodated?
- What are their concerns about security?
- What are their attitudes about privacy and providing personal information?
- Do they want to be able to track product shipments?
- How do they prefer to be supported? Who provides them with customer service today? How well does it work? Where can it be improved? What are their response-time requirements for support?

You also need to know more about your company's business processes, beyond what you assessed to set business objectives. Here you need to understand the internal workflow and business processes that are currently in use so that you can comprehend how the Web will impact them. It involves many people's jobs throughout the organization to make the Web a component of a successful business. Therefore, the functional strategy needs to address all elements of the company. These include:

- For product and service information, how is content developed today, who is involved, and which systems are used for writing, designing, and publishing? How often does the content need to change?
- What are the graphics and design competencies internally?
- In sales, how are transactions handled? Do customers provide credit cards, do they use purchase orders, and are they sent invoices? What role does the salesperson or channel play? How will that change if the site is performing sales related tasks?
- What are the competencies in the IT department for handling a sophisticated Web presence? Which tech-

nology platforms are currently in use? Which software products does the group know how to use?
- What can be leveraged from the existing Web site?

FUNCTIONAL SPECIFICATIONS: DECISION POINTS

Decisions must be made in three key areas: the definition of the experience, the design of business processes, and the resources to be used going forward.

DEFINITION OF THE EXPERIENCE: To define the site experience means deciding what the visitors will be able to do on your site and the image they will have of your company based on that experience. From a functional perspective, that translates into decisions such as:

- How will enabled consumption functions actually work—i.e., how will customers buy, what forms of payment will you accept, and what steps are involved in the transaction process?
- What will be the organizing principle of the site: customer-segment, product, or functional area?
- Will you use personalization and profile information to tune the experience?
- What will make the site dynamic? What will be the key hook to compel visitors to continue coming back?

DESIGN OF BUSINESS PROCESSES: Every key aspect of the consumption cycle has a corollary process that has to be developed in order to make the site a reality and to integrate the Web into normal business processes. Some of these include:

- Forwarding and handling of leads generated
- Developing and updating content
- Conducting transactions and methods of payment
- Tracking products
- Supporting customers

RESOURCES FOR DEVELOPMENT: Other key decisions will be to select people for the development team and to define required technical resources. This involves assessing your company's own internal competencies and deciding whether you have the needed talent or whether you have to hire an outside vendor. There are several categories of competencies you must consider:

- Content development
- Graphic design and user interface
- Software development
- Finance and administration operations
- Outbound marketing
- Business development: striking deals with partners, portals, etc.
- Fulfillment/logistics

Before the site can be prototyped, the project must be technically defined and the appropriate technology solutions must be selected to create the site. The defined functionality will drive the technical requirement decisions. If the functionality specifications call for content to be contributed by people across the organization and for that content to be updated frequently, a distributed content publishing system is needed. If the content is to be dynamically generated based on the site visitor's preferences and past behavior, then profiling and dynamic content generation and management solutions will be needed. If your customers want to use credit cards for purchases, then encryption technology will be needed to ensure secure transactions. If customers will be able to buy multiple products in one session on your site, you will need shopping cart technology.

The technical development team needs to take numerous steps in its data gathering. The team should assess the technology used in-house in terms of hardware, operating systems, database software, financials, and so on. They should spend time talking with other companies to learn what they are successfully using, as well as asking advice from IT and Web consultants to determine the right answer. And, they should assess the skills available in-house, as well as the availability of talent on the open market, to determine who knows how to use the selected solutions.

Before the site can be prototyped, the project must be technically defined

Another key aspect of the functional specifications phase is the decision to make versus to buy the required resources to develop and launch the site. Many companies are choosing to outsource the Web site development, hosting, and management. If that is your situation, then creating a Request for Proposal (RFP) is required to solicit bids from prospective outsourcing vendors—technology vendors and/or consultants.

If you require assistance in several areas, such as graphic design and technical development, you will probably need different RFPs because often one service vendor does not have the full range of competencies needed to be a one-stop shop.

The cost of vendor services and technology solutions can range into the millions of dollars. Selecting the right vendors can make all the difference between outrageous success and utter failure. And the budget implications in terms of maintenance and growth are significant.

FUNCTIONAL SPECIFICATIONS: OUTPUT

The decisions made in this phase culminate in a Site Requirements Document, which becomes the guideline for the teams responsible for creating the prototype site. The document lays out detailed requirements for the site, in terms of software, hardware required, development phases, benchmarks, and budgets. It serves as the key guideline for the Prototyping phase of the project and contains:

- Web site objectives
- Functional goals and requirements
- Navigation
- Graphic design specifications
- Content updating
- Prototyping team: internal and external resources
- Technical requirements:
  - Hardware and software platform: including operating system, Web server, commerce server, application server, user-profiling and dynamic HTML page-generation software, database software, content-publishing software, and document-management software.

- Registration system
- Customer database design
- Back-office systems integration
- Security and firewall
- Legacy content conversion
- Target browsers
- Entitlements, i.e., rules that dictate which visitors get access to certain content
- Dynamic page generation
- Systems administration
- Search technology
- Reporting mechanisms
- Special networking requirements, such as virtual private networks

In selecting the technology platform, the kinds of questions you should ask vendors include:

- Does your current site development team know the selected software solution? If not, what will it take for them to learn and become proficient with it?
- Are there trained professionals available who know the chosen software, not just for today but in the years to come?
- Is the software solution provider a stable company? Will they be in business three years from now when you're still in need of support on the product?
- Are the components involved compatible with legacy systems? Will your internal IT department have to integrate the solution to inter-operate?
- Does the software run on an industry-standard hardware platform?
- What is the amount of site traffic that this solution can handle? What happens if the traffic doubles, triples, quadruples?
- Will you be dependent on a service provider to help maintain and expand the site? If so, what are the long-term budget implications and risks?

Case Study: Customer Research in Functional Specifications Phase

- CHALLENGE: A leading PC software company wanted to begin selling its software online, and provide online customer support to its customers. The company needed to determine its customers' functional preferences in several areas. Did they wish to purchase software directly from the company, as well as from channel partners? How did they wish to receive the software: via downloads or via CDs shipped to them? What were the transaction concerns of their target consumers? What were the preferred methods of getting customer support content, such as frequently asked questions, online documentation, bug reports, quick-turnaround e-mail, or telephone support?

- CONSUMER RESEARCH PROJECT: To answer these questions, the company fielded a telephone survey among its registered customers. By collecting and analyzing their preferences on the topics listed above, the company was able to create an online value proposition that met its target customers' requirements, both in terms of commerce and service.

- RESULTS: The company discovered that customers wanted the option to either purchase directly from the publishers or through online software reseller sites. In addition, consumers wanted to have both online and telephone customer service options. The company mapped out a Web site that allowed consumers to get help online and to easily find a toll-free telephone number on the site. Once the site was launched, the company was successful in shifting much of its telephone support traffic to the Web, thus increasing consumer satisfaction and decreasing customer service costs. In addition, by enabling customers to buy software directly from them rather than exclusively through dealers, it had developed—for the first time—a direct relationship with its customers.

Phase Four: Prototyping

MYTHS	REALITIES
• We don't have time to prototype	• You don't have time NOT to prototype
• We can determine internally if the new site concept will resonate with consumers.	• You cannot be objective about your site concept.
• We can just hire an outside firm to do e-business for us.	• You should conduct concept tests with target customers to truly assess acceptability.
	• Outside firms still require focused direction.

Prototyping the site is a critical phase in the road map, but one that some companies may mistakenly consider unnecessary. In this phase, a partially functioning site is developed so that the decisions made to date, such as site concept, technology platform, and vendors, can be validated, as shown in figure 8.6. Prototyping allows you to try out concepts to see how well they fit customers' requirements before spending too much money. It allows you to test both the technology solutions and the development teams to ensure that the selected technology is adequately scaleable and that the development teams are appropriately skilled. And it gives you the required data to refine your functional and technical specifications as well as your budget for the fully blown site. Skipping the Prototype phase can lead to unfocused efforts, uncontrolled spending, and off-the-mark site experiences.

The key endpoint of the Prototyping phase is user concept testing. Companies should always test responses to the site among target customers in a controlled setting to ensure the site approach works the way it was intended before moving on.

Skipping the Prototype phase can lead to unfocused efforts, uncontrolled spending, and off-the-mark site experiences

PROTOTYPE DEVELOPMENT: DATA REQUIRED

The Site Requirements Document will provide very specific direction about what the site should enable from a features and functions perspective and will also outline the technology required for prototyping.

FIGURE 8.6: PROTOTYPING

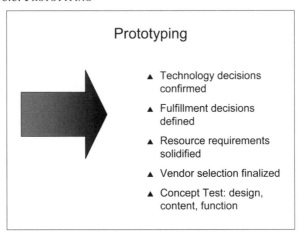

PROTOTYPE DEVELOPMENT: DECISION POINTS

While many decisions have been made in the specifications documents, myriad decisions are made on a daily basis in the prototyping phase. These are decisions about details of the experience: navigational schemes, personalization implementation, adapting the brand identity in an electronic form, the personality of the site, and page designs.

When the prototype is ready, it should be subjected to live concept testing from target users in a controlled setting, such as one-on-one interviews or focus groups. In these settings, users are often allowed to move through the site, navigate and react to the experience concept. Careful analysis of customer and prospect reactions can provide specific direction in the areas that need to be refined prior to the next phase—site building. Findings from the prototype concept testing should be presented to the members of every team.

PROTOTYPE DEVELOPMENT: OUTPUT

Prototyping yields a number of significant output components, all of which are documented in the Site Development Plan, including:

- A design that is ready for a full build, complete with page designs and navigational schema, and approved by the executive management team
- Confirmation of underlying technology decisions, such as customer-relationship management software, content-publishing platforms, e-commerce solutions, customer database, profiling, and personalization
- Commitment of content specifications for all aspects of the experience—product data, sales policies, and customer support information
- Definition of fulfillment procedures
- Selection of development partners or internal team
- Internal ownership and formalized management
- A defined and approved budget

At this juncture, it is critical that organizational buy-in and executive approval has been gained. There will be many bumps in the road along the way. It is wise to eliminate as many of those problems as possible before moving into the intense Site Development phase.

Case Study: Customer Research in the Prototype Development Phase

- CHALLENGE: A new company was launched to provide consumer review information on a wide variety of products. It needed to test its site concept with typical target customers. While there were other sites in the market that had similar objectives, the new company had some innovative ideas on content presentation and functionality. It wanted to determine if the new content and functionality effectively differentiated the company from its competitors. In other words, were the innovations sufficient to attract and retain customers?
- CONSUMER RESEARCH PROJECT: The company fielded a Site Concept Test, demonstrating its new Web site prototype to target customers in one-on-one personal interviews. The site functionality, design, and content were compared to the two leading competitors. People, who were unaware of the research sponsor

identity, were queried about the value of the new ideas relative to existing alternatives. This information was essential in making developmental priorities, look-and-feel, and content creation decisions.

- RESULTS: Priority decisions were made objectively by team members based on research findings. The company created a development schedule for site building, confident that it was focusing on the most important demands of target consumers.

Phase Five: Site Building

MYTHS	REALITIES
• We can build this site in a month	• Depending on the complexities of the strategy, it will take three to twelve months to launch
• We can hire it out. We don't need any internal resources for this job.	• Vendors will be successful only with strong guidance from internal management
• It won't be hard to stay on a timeline	• Timelines need to be managed
• We can re-purpose marketing collateral for content	• Web content requires focused development efforts
• Use the Web primarily to reach Web users	• All marketing vehicles should be used to reach Web users
• If we build it, they will come	• Driving traffic to the sites gets more challenging and expensive every day

Once the prototype concept is tested with customers and the commitments have been made in all the areas listed above, the site building begins in earnest, as shown in figure 8.7.

At this point, four aspects of site building work in parallel—each with their own dedicated teams, including:

- Technical Site Development: programming of the site software and designing all of the pages using the approved graphic and navigational standards

- Content Development: creating and acquiring the content necessary to populate the site pages
- Customer Acquisition Planning: designing the methods by which you will attract traffic to the site
- Operations Testing: the final phases of site building

FIGURE 8.7: SITE BUILDING

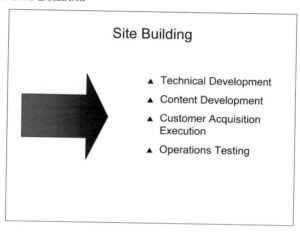

SITE BUILDING: DATA REQUIRED

All of the work and documentation performed to date should be assembled into one resource for all members of the site building teams, and should include:

- Opportunity Assessment
- Business Plan
- Site Requirements Document
- Technical Specifications Document
- Usability Research Findings
- Site Development Plan

SITE BUILDING: DECISION POINTS

While the four parallel efforts of site building are in motion, a wide range of decisions need to be made. Teams need to be managed to ensure that timelines and spending are kept in check. We recommend having regularly scheduled project update meetings where leaders from each of the four development teams report on progress, issues, and completion status. Let's look more closely at the types of decisions that are made for each of the parallel site building efforts.

TECHNICAL SITE DEVELOPMENT: Throughout the site development processes, decisions will be made that will ultimately shape the customers' experiences. It is important that the technical team be well-briefed on customer feedback and that the executive team be closely involved with the progress of each of the teams.

While all of the site building teams have a critical role, the most difficult to manage is the technical development aspect. This is because the tasks are very complex and difficult, and it is new territory for many people involved. It helps for the executive to understand the core activities that the team will be performing. The basic steps the technical development team needs to take involve coding the underlying data structures that allow the various parts of the consumption cycle to function. These include registration databases, e-commerce software, content database software, fulfillment, shipment tracking, and customer services. Many iterations and tests will be required during this phase.

Specific milestones, complete with dates, need to be established for technical development. Some suggested milestones include:

- Frequent test data loads
- Simulations of transactions and customer data pulls
- Check-offs with product marketing and customer marketing to assure data can be modified and extracted
- Check-offs with customer service for integration in current processes
- Close and frequent contact with graphic/UI (User-Interface) and content development teams

CONTENT DEVELOPMENT: Your site content, in conjunction with your site development, will be critical in establishing your customers' experience of your e-business presence. The site development plan provides the framework for content on the site. During the Site Building phase, you must look to all potential sources of content—marketing, product development, partnerships and alliances, public relations, sales, fulfillment, and customer service—to determine where and how you will derive the content. You should evaluate the practical elements of obtaining it, such as:

- Will the content be produced in-house or will it be outsourced?
- What are the costs associated with obtaining and/or preparing the content for the Web?
- How often will content be updated?
- Who will have responsibility for updating and refining content?
- Will all of your site visitors have access to all of your content, or is some—or all—of your content audience-specific?

Once these questions have been answered, you need to create working timelines in which the content is obtained and added to the technical platform of the site. We recommend that the content development team create an editorial calendar that schedules ongoing content development deadlines, assigns responsibilities, and establishes review cycles. It is typical that content is fine-tuned throughout the Operational Testing phase, so it is critical that your processes for updating content be established around the same time as the original content is identified.

CUSTOMER ACQUISITION PLANNING: This is the aspect of site building in which the customer acquisition strategies are granularly planned and implemented. Here you address building confidence among target customers in your brand and attracting them to your site. The topline marketing objectives and strategies developed for the E-Business Plan in the Business Strategy Development phase serve as a guide for detailed marketing execution. Much has been said throughout this book about customer acquisition strategies, so we won't repeat advice given in other chapters. Be aware, however, that because of the lead times in ramping marketing programs, it is important to begin planning for the marketing of the site while it is in the

It is important to begin planning for marketing of the site while it is in the early stages of development

early stages of development. That way, when it is ready to launch, you do not lose any time preparing to market it.

Important customer acquisition decisions are:

- What are the vehicles we should use to build consumer confidence and drive traffic to the site: online, print, and broadcast advertising, public relations, direct mail?
- How far in advance of the launch should we begin each marketing activity?
- How much should we spend to drive traffic to our site?
- What are our competitors spending?
- What types of special promotional offers do we need to make to encourage first-time trial of our site?
- How can we leverage our existing marketing efforts and expenditures to attract customers to our site?

The marketing team should develop a Web site–launch strategy and plan based on customer data and competitive analysis, that includes these elements:

- Marketing objectives
- Strategies: customer acquisition; customer loyalty/ retention; internal communications; partners/alliances communications
- Strategic alliances/portal deals
- Marketing communications mix: public relations; advertising; promotional offers; other programs
- Budget
- Success metrics

OPERATIONS TESTING: The final phases of site building—that is, before the site is considered operational and ready for public launch—are alpha and beta testing. The alpha test involves full functionality testing on a limited data load. In addition, alpha tests should include a round of usability testing from an outside party. At this juncture, your team will be too personally invested to perform non-biased user testing internally. Don't assume that just because a Web site is

User feedback is a requirement for successful site development going forward

intended to be easy to use, that it actually is. Usability testing is often necessary to provide a company with critical data about all elements of the experience, such as reactions to specific content, navigation, and design elements. User feedback actually becomes a requirement for successful site development going forward. Some usability test labs are set up to record how long users stay in certain areas of the site, the sequence of activities performed, what they click on first, and what they ignore. These insights are extremely valuable in creating an experience that users find productive and fulfilling.

In the Operations Testing phase, other actions occur, including:

- Refinement of functionality and design such as user interface and navigation
- Full content loading
- Schedule for beta or soft launch

Once alpha testing is conducted and refinements are made, the site is ready for beta or soft launch. Beta launches involve allowing people from outside of the development teams to use the site and give feedback on glitches, bugs, and other areas of needed refinement. Typically, this is the first opportunity to test simulated heavy traffic and determine if the site will scale properly. The schedule should allow adequate time to fix problems discovered in beta testing.

Case Study: Customer Research Example in Site Building Phase

- CHALLENGE: An e-commerce travel site faced the challenge of enabling consumers to conduct sophisticated product-pricing research and book tickets in an online environment. Although the company had conducted research throughout the development process to validate concepts, content, and graphic images, it needed to test several different approaches to searching for airfares and booking reservations. It was imperative for the site to enable consumers to successfully complete the shopping process so that it could improve upon industry-accepted look-to-book ratios.

- CONSUMER RESEARCH PROJECT: The company tested several user-interface designs for different points in the shopping sequence to determine if target customers could intuitively comprehend the complex stages of checking airfares and booking flights, and to decide which approach was best at ultimately capturing the consumer transaction. Because collecting personal travel preference information was key to offering a satisfactory experience, the site also needed to test consumers' reactions to profile questionnaires and registration processes.
- RESULTS: Through one-on-one testing of its alpha site in a Web site–usability lab, the company identified the best design approach. It also discovered numerous pages that needed improvement so that the site experience would be easy enough for a wide range of experienced and inexperienced travelers to navigate. In addition, it determined what value the site must deliver in order to motivate consumers to divulge personal information in the registration process.

Phase Six: Launch and Ongoing Refinement

MYTHS

- Once we are "live" we are done.
- Now that the Web site is up, everyone can go back to their normal jobs.
- Since we conducted customer research at the beginning, we don't have to talk to customers anymore.
- If our customers don't complain, we can assume they are satisfied.
- Customers are creatures of habit. We don't need to do anything special to keep them coming back.

REALITIES

- In e-business, you are never finished. Web sites require significant ongoing attention.
- While some people may have been on special assignment for the project and have to return to other duties, the Web site will require dedicated resources to keep it alive.
- Customers' wants and needs change over time, so research is an ongoing process.
- Tracking customer satisfaction is critical to customer retention.
- Customer retention is increasingly challenging and expensive, and must be planned.

The formal launch of the site is a significant milestone. But even after launch, the task is not complete, as shown in figure 8.8. Managing the site as a strategic customer relationship vehicle is critical. At this point, you realize that the refinement

Managing the site as a strategic customer relationship vehicle is critical

is an ongoing process and that you are never really finished. It is in this phase that many companies learn what continuous improvement really means.

FIGURE 8.8: LAUNCH AND ONGOING REFINEMENT

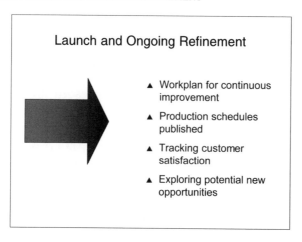

You will require a solid, ongoing Web site management team to keep the site compelling, vibrant, and effective. Technology is changing so rapidly and customer preferences are evolving so quickly, that driving change becomes a required core competency.

LAUNCH AND ONGOING REFINEMENT: DATA REQUIRED

It will be important to track site traffic and to have robust reporting mechanisms to measure how consumers are responding to the site. Standard tracking reports should be created for management review. There are many software products that enable Web site tracking.

One of the reasons that tracking is key is to ensure that you have adequate systems scalability to handle the site traffic. Too many sites have underestimated the actual traffic and have not been able to serve all of their visitors, resulting in the loss of business. Management should focus on tracking Web site traffic and capacity with the same vigilance as with tracking sales and manufacturing output.

The data required for ongoing refinement includes a periodic assessment of customer satisfaction and how well your site fits customers' requirements. It also includes an understanding of the competitive landscape and internal audits for business process effectiveness. There are several basic methods used to monitor customer satisfaction of a Web site: "contact us" feedback mechanisms—which allow customers to proactively click on a "feedback" icon and send a message to the site owners—and direct customer contact via surveys or focus groups.

User feedback from a "contact us" mechanism is useful, but unsolicited comments submitted by a small percentage of visitors do not always represent a cross-section of typical site visitors. Feedback is often limited to extreme viewpoints—both critical and constructive—and tends to represent extremes of the population, such as your loyal customer zealots or else ax grinders. It is very important for a company to listen to its users and respond to online comments, but these feedback mechanisms should not be the only way a company monitors the effectiveness of its online efforts.

Proactive online surveys are mechanisms through which site visitors answer a series of questions in some detail regarding what they liked and didn't like about a site. Surveys can provide site owners with much richer depth-of-content than responses gathered from standard feedback forms. And, surveys allow companies to choose the topics on which they want to focus the research.

The task of site monitoring is never truly completed because customer expectations change as they become more Web savvy

As with unsolicited feedback, the problem with online surveys is also self-selection sample bias—those who are willing to fill out questionnaires do not evenly represent the entire customer population, although they are not usually as extreme as the unsolicited feedback providers. Web surveys must take sample selection bias into account, because the results may give a skewed picture of the actual results. Direct contact through phone surveys and focus groups can provide rich additional information and is advisable at some affordable frequency. Whatever the mechanism, the task of site monitoring is never truly completed because customer expectations change as they become more Web savvy.

Another research consideration is how to learn from consumers who aren't your customers. Why weren't they attracted to the site by your marketing efforts? If they visited the site, why didn't they buy? If they bought once and never returned, what happened? These are all scenarios that your customer tracking studies should comprehend.

Understanding satisfaction is key to customer retention. As discussed in chapter 3, the Web world is highly competitive and customer loyalties can be short-lived. Methodically studying customer behavior and offering programs to build customer loyalty should be a permanent part of your ongoing e-business strategy. And it should be an ongoing budget item as well.

LAUNCH AND ONGOING REFINEMENT: DECISION POINTS

Once the site is implemented, you will be faced with many decisions regarding how to: make the site more effective; make it more meaningful in building your market position; build better relationships with your customers; attract more visitors; and leverage the site to take costs out of the business cycle.

There are a plethora of ongoing decisions that must be made, many of them relating to the upkeep of Web business processes, such as:

- Content updates
- Ongoing site functionality development
- Regular user-interface testing
- Quarterly customer check-ins
- Competitive analysis
- Customer satisfaction tracking

We advise that you have at least monthly reviews of the site metrics—such as traffic patterns, look-to-book ratios, and number of page views—where decisions are made about site performance, new functionality to deploy, and customer feedback. Web site metrics should be reported in the company's normal business tracking formats.

LAUNCH AND ONGOING REFINEMENT: OUTPUT

As the site is implemented, many ideas will emerge on ways to refine and improve it, post-implementation. To manage the effort, you should require the Web site management team to develop a strategic operating plan on the same business cycles as you require for other departments and P&Ls in your company. The E-Business Plan should include standard components such as objectives, planned improvements, required budgets, timelines, as well as an ongoing work plan for site upgrades, functionality improvements, and planned extensions. The Web team should work with published production schedules so that progress can be tracked and priorities established.

Case Study: Customer Research Example in Launch and Ongoing Refinement Phase

- CHALLENGE: A well-established, leading e-business was concerned about ongoing customer retention. Given the required expenditures to acquire customers, it was very motivated to build loyalty among its precious customer base. In addition, the company decided to extend its value proposition, offering a wider range of products than in its earlier days. Therefore, the company needed to comprehend numerous consumer issues: the current level of satisfaction with existing offerings among existing customers; reactions to potential new offerings among existing customers; and attitudes among e-consumers who weren't current customers, including lost customers.
- CONSUMER RESEARCH PROJECT: The company set up a layered research methodology; some aspects were longitudinal and some were more short-term. To ensure ongoing customer satisfaction, the company

had two processes: it e-mailed a satisfaction survey to customers after the shipment of every order; and it diligently reviewed and responded to comments submitted via its feedback button on its site. To gather opinions about potential new offerings among customers, the company conducted exploratory focus groups in target cities nationwide, and then followed up with an e-mail survey among a larger sample of customers. This e-mail group of customers was offered a $25 gift certificate to be used on the company's Web site. To understand non-customers, the company used an online research company that maintains databases of Web users and pre-qualifies customers based on their use of branded Web sites. The company requested a sample to be pulled on non-customers and fielded a brief study querying them about what competitive sites they patronized and why. To get to lost customers, the company monitored its customer database for purchase frequency information. For any customer who hadn't purchased from the site within a year, the company sent a "we miss you" e-mail with a few brief questions aimed at understanding why the customer no longer shopped at the site, and offered an incentive to come back. In addition, the company pulled a sample from non-responders and followed up with a telephone survey (when the telephone number was available) to discuss more deeply why the customer defected from the company's site.

- RESULTS: This rigorous, layered methodology yielded essential information for the ongoing effectiveness of the e-business. It provided the company with information on how the site experience needed to be improved. It also guided business expansion strategy and validated opportunities. The company discovered problems that had been extreme enough to cause customer defection. And, it communicated to all categories of customers that the company was, and continues to be, very interested in consumer preferences—thus potentially improving market penetration, generating positive word of mouth, and increasing customer expenditures.

Parting Shots about Research

We have observed that companies can be somewhat polarized in their consumer research practices. Some companies study their markets and their customers too much. Instead of helping to solve problems, sometimes research seems to invoke decision paralysis. These kinds of companies can hide behind research as a way of avoiding making difficult, risky decisions. In these situations, research is a business inhibitor rather than an enabler.

Some companies don't study at all. They believe research is too costly and that they know their markets best, or that there's nothing to be gained from research. Sometimes they are right. Other times they are not. It's a big gamble.

The best approach, of course, is to create balance. If you are looking to integrate the Web into your business, spend some resources on researching your customers. Never assume you know what your customers will say—you will be surprised by what they reveal to third-parties about your company, your products, and your services. It pays to find out. Base your Web development strategies partly on what you learn through research and partly on what you believe, especially in testing new concepts or ideas. Keep in mind that customers, influencers, and prospects will always be constrained by their own experience and imagination.

There are some interesting new research methodologies that have evolved with the Internet. Specifically, several e-businesses have been founded to provide companies with Web-based research. While each of these new companies has a slightly different angle on the market, all are designed to allow companies to quickly and cost-effectively field market research questions to selected profiles of Web users. These sites can potentially be useful to companies targeting new consumers and who want to get quick reactions to new ideas. To be certain that you are getting reliable data, we advise that you learn about how these research companies recruit consumers for participation before committing to the research. It is important to be sure that the samples will represent a normal and balanced cross-section of your target market.

The most productive and engaging Web sites are those that have made the effort to get to know their

Never assume you know what your customers will say

visitors, using research to identify common user attitudes or commissioning formative usability tests to discover which areas of their sites are most effective. Armed with this critical data, companies can better understand why people come to their site, what actions they take when they are there, and where they are in the consumption cycle. They can comprehend the soul of the new consumer. This knowledge can then be used to develop proactive strategies designed to optimize the customer experience and ultimately lead to long-term, satisfied customers.

9

The Next Frontier

ow that we have dissected, analyzed, and
hypothesized about the souls of today's new
consumers, the natural progression is to
think about the next wave of e-business
development. How will today's new consumers evolve
and change in their future online behavior? Who will the next
new consumers be? How will they be different than the e-customers we know today? What will it take to convert non-users
to Web users—to win their souls?

An important dimension of the next Web wave is the
migration of consumers to the Web outside of the United
States. While the United States has been the most aggressive in
Web adoption and development of dot-com businesses to date,
the opportunities outside our borders are becoming increasingly important. What are the obstacles to Web adoption outside
of the United States? How are Web users in other geographic
markets different than American new consumers? Are their
attitudes, behaviors, and preferences different from ours?

In this chapter we look at the landscape of the next frontier and speculate on what it will take to reach the next level of
e-business growth. In this context we are considering the next
frontier as the near-term future—the next few years. First, we
discuss how today's new consumers will evolve. What will
cause them to get more Web-involved and to buy more online?
Secondly, as the remainder of the United States early majority
and, subsequently, the late majority adopts the Web, what will

characterize those new consumers? What has to be different to drive them to the Web? What are their fears, their concerns, and their curiosities? Thirdly, we discuss consumers' reactions to new Web access devices and advanced services. And lastly, diverging from our United States–centric viewpoint in this book, we take a brief look at Web consumer behavior in markets outside the United States, noting where the differences and similarities are found among the world's new consumers.

Breaking through the Barriers with Today's New Consumers

When considering what must happen to induce more online buying behavior among today's Web users, it is useful to think about new consumers in two categories: Web Shoppers—those that shop on the Web, but don't actually buy online; and Web Buyers—those that actively buy online.

WEB SHOPPERS

New consumers who shop, but don't currently buy, online harbor some significant concerns about Web-based transactions, especially related to privacy and security. These consumers avidly believe in the price comparison, product sourcing, and educational benefits of the Web for shopping, but they are reticent to go the next step: provide their credit card numbers to make purchases. They are also worried about how the information collected about them as part of the buying process will be used. Their fears are fueled by frequent stories in the media about the objectionable business practices of some Web sites, and by rumors of credit card scandals.

Web Shoppers are happy to use the Web to compare prices and locate retailers, but are reticent to go to the next step: using credit cards online

Being relatively conservative, these people rely on word-of-mouth recommendations from friends and credible third-party sources for places to e-shop. Transforming this bunch of shoppers into online buyers is entirely reliant on creating positive word of mouth among influencers and building these consumers' confidence in both the safety and privacy of the transactions—a process that will take time. Boosting their willingness to purchase online will require intensive credibility-building efforts by individual e-businesses, as well as consistent ethical performance by the industry at large. The old adage that one bad apple can spoil the barrel is quite appropriate to the situation among these Web Shoppers. Continual stories of credit card fraud or privacy violations can cause these shoppers to postpone actual buying indefinitely.

In addition to security and privacy issues, the Web Shopper is concerned about online purchasing of products that may ultimately need to be returned. Again, lack of confidence is the problem to address in these situations. Consumers are fearful that products will not meet expectations in terms of quality, fit, and other tangible aspects, because they cannot physically examine the product before purchase. Therefore, while they are happy to use the Web to compare prices and locate retailers that carry the desired products, they resort to going to the traditional storefronts to purchase the products. This is a barrier shared with the other set of today's new consumers discussed in the next section, Web Buyers.

THE NEXT STEP FOR WEB BUYERS

New consumers who actively buy online, a group we call Web Buyers, demonstrate different characteristics from Web Shoppers. A study conducted by Stanford University estimates that 36 percent of Web users actually buy online.[1] These people have overcome their concerns about security and privacy and have actually made online purchase transactions, even though they are still watchful over the business practices of their chosen Web brands. Active online buyers are more constrained by their time and money than by any other factors—a reality that limits any aspect of consumption. As we learned in chapter 5, many of the new consumers we polled did not see any *truly* obstructive barriers to making more online purchases in the coming year, but they did identify issues that must be overcome to get

Active online buyers are more constrained by their time and money than any other factors

to the next level of e-commerce volume. For example, these consumers continue to voice hesitation about buying high-involvement products that require a tactile experience before purchasing. And they complain about slow network connections and sluggish Web site performance.

The challenge of breaking through the high-involvement commerce barrier and poor network performance are related issues. To improve upon the quality and performance of current e-merchandising experiences will require e-businesses to deploy new technologies that enrich the experience and ultimately provide consumers with better visual and audio information as part of the buying process. High-involvement products that require close visual inspection include items such as decorative products, furniture, jewelry, some types of clothing, cosmetics, and art. But today's Web site–design and current bandwidth capacities are too limited to provide sufficiently rich merchandising experiences for selling these and other types of products. Depending on the product type, this problem can be overcome through the use of sophisticated technologies to dramatically upgrade the quality of the Web site experience. Increased bandwidth in more consumers' homes will enable larger files to be transmitted faster, which will allow Web sites to provide better visual merchandising experiences to site visitors.

In some cases, rather than solely focusing on improving the Web site experience, the solution to selling high-involvement products online will be to offer multi-channel alternatives. In these situations, consumers will be able to employ a combination of channels—online, catalog, and store-front—to consummate transactions.

Winners of the next e-commerce frontier will be companies that have discovered solutions for breaking through the high-involvement purchase barrier

Whether addressed through the deployment of better technology or through hybrid distribution strategies, we believe that the winners of the next e-commerce frontier will be companies that have discovered solutions for breaking through the high-involvement purchase barrier.

The Next Wave of New Consumers

At this point in Internet time in the United States, we are in the midst of the early majority phase of the innovation adoption cycle, and soon we will cross into the late majority phase. Based on our research, we believe that consumers who have not yet adopted the Web are very different from today's new consumers. They are more risk-adverse, conservative, and less confident in their use of technology. They have been subjected to the same market enthusiasm, the same volume of advertising, and the same level of dot-com frenzy that new consumers have witnessed—but they still haven't budged. And so we ask ourselves, who are these reluctant consumers and why don't they embrace the Web?

In our research of non-Web users, we learned that many of these consumers are not total technology neophytes. In fact, close to 30 percent report that they use a computer at work and some of those use the Internet for work-only purposes. More than 60 percent of the non-Web users we polled have actually seen Web pages or surfed the Web at least once using someone else's computer and ISP account.

PLANS TO USE THE INTERNET

When asked about future plans to use the Internet for personal purposes, more than 50 percent indicate they do plan on using in the future, as shown in figure 9.1. Among those who plan to use the Internet, the anticipated timeframes of when they will start using it are evenly split among less than six months, six to twelve months, and more than twelve months.

Consumers who intend to use the Internet sometime in the future differ in several ways from those who say they do not plan to use the Internet. Web intenders seem to be more open to the use of technology in other aspects of their lives. For example, consumers who intend to use the Internet have a higher adoption rate of electronic devices such as cell phones, pagers, and game machines than their counterparts. Similarly, they use advanced features of their telephone services more frequently, reporting significantly higher usage of features such as call waiting, caller ID, three-way calling, and call forwarding. There are notable differences in demographic profiles between Web intenders and non-intenders as well. Consumers who intend to use the Web are more frequently younger (less than fifty years of age) and more educated (college degree or above). Income and gender, however, are more evenly distributed between the two groups.

FIGURE 9.1: PLANS TO USE THE INTERNET FOR PERSONAL
PURPOSES BY NON-USERS OF THE WEB

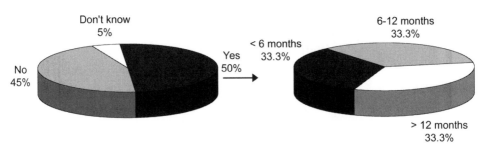

People who plan to use the Web are also more familiar with it. More than 75 percent of the Web intenders we polled have seen Web sites before, whereas less than 44 percent of people who don't intend to use the Web had such experiences. An intriguing question is this: Are Web intenders more curious than the others and, therefore, pursued experimentation with the Web, or did experiencing the Web influence a non-user to plan to become a Web user someday? The answers to these questions remain to be seen.

One of the interesting aspects of this study is how people who don't use the Web describe themselves as shoppers, as shown in figure 9.2. The shopper types shown here are defined in chapter 2. As shown by the chart, non-Web consumers tend to be primarily price-sensitive or convenience shoppers, both of which are also strong segments among Web Shoppers and Buyers. There are notable differences between people who intend versus those who do not intend to use the Web in this area as well. Web intenders indicated a stronger propensity toward being either comparison or focused shoppers than did their counterparts.

FIGURE 9.2: TYPES OF SHOPPERS AMONG NON-USERS

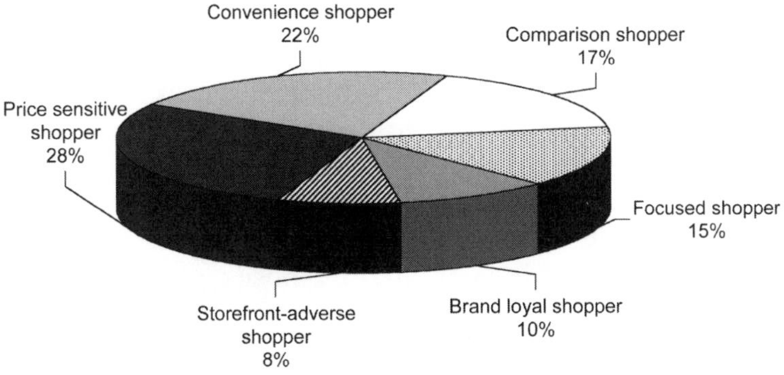

Source: Pulse of the Customer

So, we can see that some non-Web users plan to become Web users fairly soon. Others will take longer to convert. As a group, non-users are not completely technologically naïve, yet they are not as involved with other technology-related products and services as are their new consumer counterparts. They are not significantly different, however, in terms of the types of shoppers they claim to be and therefore hold promise to be attracted to the Web for many of the same benefits that appeal to today's new consumers.

Converting the Late Majority: What Will It Take?

By definition, the late majority comprises people who adopt an innovation after a majority of people has tried it.

Many non-users resent the furor that the Internet has created among their friends and in the media

These people want to be sure it works, that it is proven. They want fail-proof solutions that represent minimal risks. What will it take for the late majority to adopt the Web? The simple answer is: time. Time to resolve usage problems. Time for prices to drop. Time for anxieties to be quelled. Also, time for the frenzy to die down. Many non-users resent the furor that the Internet has created among their friends and in the media. Some of these users are resisting the Web in reaction to the perceived hype.

When asked about the primary reasons why they don't use the Web at home, non-users' most common answers are straightforward: they don't have access. Some don't have access because it is too expensive, but others don't have access for myriad reasons that can be summed up by saying that, for whatever reason, it isn't a priority in their lives. Figure 9.3 shows the reasons non-users give for not using the Internet for personal purposes.

FIGURE 9.3: REASONS WHY NON-USERS DON'T USE THE WEB AT HOME

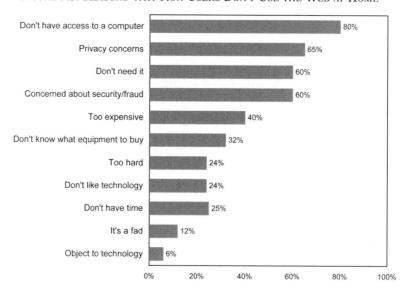

Note: Multiple responses possible.

Source: Pulse of the Customer

Many of the reasons offered indicate some very real concerns that non–Web users have about the Internet. Some worry about maintaining their privacy and credit card security. Others don't feel that they have a need for the Internet—that it adds no value to their daily routines. Others just haven't taken the time to figure it all out: deciding what to buy, how to set it up, and how to use it. It's all so daunting that they procrastinate taking the plunge.

NON-USERS' SECURITY AND PRIVACY CONCERNS ABOUT THE INTERNET

MODERATOR: Why are you concerned about security?

CONSUMER: Even if my financial liability is limited, it's still a hassle to deal with credit card fraud and to get my record cleared.

CONSUMER: Because even if you have proof, the credit bureaus still don't take a fraudulent charge off your record. You can't get a mortgage or anything for seven years.

CONSUMER: I just want my transaction to be anonymous. If I surf on a site, I don't really want somebody knowing about it.

While non-users have actively or passively decided to not use the Internet—at least not yet—they are highly aware of the dot-com wave. Some seem to enjoy vicariously experiencing the Internet through their friends. Others seem to resent being left out of the trend. Highly visible advertising campaigns seem to be contributing to some non-users' resentment and sense of alienation.

NON-USERS' SOCIAL CONCERNS ABOUT THE INTERNET

MODERATOR: Do your friends use the Internet? Is it a topic of conversation socially?

CONSUMER: With some of my friends, all they ever talk about is the Internet. It's annoying.

CONSUMER: It seems to be taking over a lot of my friends' lives.

CONSUMER: I get tired of calling my friends and always getting a busy signal because they are online.

MODERATOR: How do you feel about the Internet buzz?

CONSUMER: I really feel left out because I don't even know what my friends are talking about.

CONSUMER: The Internet can be good and bad for people. It helps them socialize somewhat. But on the other hand, they can't develop any kind of social skills if they aren't talking to real people. I don't really know how healthy chat rooms are either. I'm suspicious that they just attract a lot of freaks.

CONSUMER: I think the Web is aimed at younger, rich people because of this whole obsession with saving time in this country. But they are saving time to do what? To just sit on the Web all day?

CONSUMER: People are getting farther and farther away from knowing how things work, how to do anything.

MODERATOR: Have you noticed dot-com advertising? What do you think about it?

CONSUMER: There's a lot of pressure. On TV, the Internet is really being pushed. The projection is that everybody is using it and you need to be savvy to this thing. But, I don't want it.

CONSUMER: I find myself turning off the radio. Stop it already. It's like they're so consumed with it. It's almost like you hate it or you love it.

CONSUMER: I think it's sad, the amount of ads that you see in the newspapers that don't even have a phone number. They've only got a URL.

CONSUMER: I think it is crazy. Think of all the business they are missing when the ad doesn't even have a phone number you can call.

CONSUMER: I'm totally fed up, hyped-out with all this dot-com stuff. It used to be we'd watch the Super Bowl and it was about beer. But now everything is dot com. I want to see the beer commercials!

WHAT SEEMS INTRIGUING

Despite their reluctance to use the Web, there are things about the Web that are intriguing to today's non-users. People seem most interested in the Web as an information access and communications device, rather than a shopping vehicle. This is not surprising for several reasons. It is a noted pattern that when consumers first get Web access, they tend to shy away from online buying due to their lack of confidence and their concerns about security and privacy. Today's non–Web users are even more sensitive about these issues and are expected to be very slow to adopt the Web as a commerce vehicle. As a method for access information, however, the Web is perceived as a rich, perhaps even overwhelming, source of knowledge. And, many non-users find the Web potentially attractive due to being able to cost-effectively communicate with friends and family around the world. Of the non–Web users we polled, close to 30 percent said the main reason they would use the Internet is because of the vast information they would have access to if they used it. Another 13 percent felt the main benefit would be the educational value, and 11 percent said it would

Despite reticence to shop online, some non-users lust after the good deals that they have heard their friends rave about

help them communicate more cost-efficiently and effectively with friends and family.

Despite reticence to shop online, some non-users lust after the good deals that they have heard their friends rave about. Whether the desire for good deals will be compelling enough to move non-users to the Web will be a function of which late majority segment they belong to, a topic of subsequent sections in this chapter. Figure 9.4 depicts the reasons why non–Web consumers would consider using the Internet. In this context, people were able to pick all the reasons that applied. Again we see the propensity for non-users to consider the Web as most attractive when used as an informational vehicle rather than as a commerce or convenience vehicle.

FIGURE 9.4: REASONS WHY NON-USERS MIGHT USE THE WEB

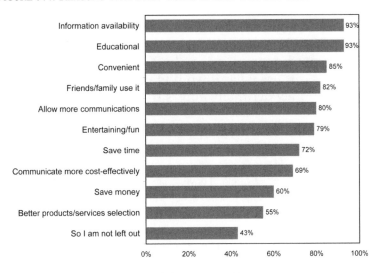

Note: Multiple responses possible.

Source: Pulse of the Customer

WHAT SEEMS INTRIGUING

MODERATOR: If you had access to the Web, what would you use it for?

CONSUMER: I would love to go on AOL and talk to somebody in another country.

CONSUMER: I have a lot of friends that live abroad, so it would certainly save money to communicate with e-mail rather than to make phone calls.

CONSUMER: You can learn about whatever interests you; there's so much. It is an easier way to find information than searching in a library.

CONSUMER: I would use it to locate hard to find products. My brother uses the net and he can get anything he wants just by searching. I'd like to find things I couldn't possibly imagine.

MODERATOR: Can you imagine buying something online?

CONSUMER: I would never buy something online.

CONSUMER: They push too hard to get me to buy, buy, buy. Maybe I just would like to know more about a topic instead of buying something.

CONSUMER: I never say never!

CONSUMER: I've heard you can get some really good deals. I have a friend who claims she saves 50 percent by shopping online instead of going to a store.

CONSUMER: My brother got a real good deal on airline tickets because he bought them online. With something like that, how can you go wrong when you know the date and the time of the flight? I'm tempted to try that.

CONSUMER: I'd use it to locate hard to find books or to read newspapers that I can't get here at home.

Even though the expense of buying the required computer and services to get Web access didn't rate very high as a main reason for not using the Internet at home, when consumers discuss what it would take to get them to adopt the Web, money definitely enters the discussion.

WHAT IT WOULD TAKE TO CONVERT

MODERATOR: What would it take to get you to use the Internet?

CONSUMER: If I could lease a laptop computer with everything built-in, I'd do it. That way I wouldn't have to lay out so much cash.

CONSUMER: I just need time to learn about it and figure out what to buy.

CONSUMER: If it were really cheap, I'd do it.

CONSUMER: I don't think anything could really interest me enough to use my free time at night on the Internet after working all day.

CONSUMER: I'm about to buy a computer so I can get on the Internet, but I'm afraid I'll get addicted.

Late Majority Segmentation

We have found that among the non–Web users, there are multiple segments that hang together based on the reason for their Web adoption reluctance. In our analysis of qualitative research of non–Web users, we have identified five different segments of consumers that are clustered based on their attitudes toward the Internet, as shown in figure 9.5.

- ACCESS ASPIRANTS: These consumers have experimented with the Web and are seriously considering taking the leap. We estimate that roughly 35 percent of current non–Web users are in this segment.
- BUDGET CONSCIOUS: These consumers are interested in the Web but find the cost of PC hardware and services to be prohibitive at this time. An estimated 10 percent of non–Web users fall into this segment.
- ANGST AVOIDERS: These consumers believe taking the leap is too much trouble and is considered anxiety-producing. Of current non–Web users, approximately 10 percent comprise this segment.
- PARANOIACS: Privacy and security concerns prevent these consumers from using the Internet. We believe about 20 percent of today's non–Web users fall into this segment.
- TECHNOLOGY REJECTERS: These consumers object to the use of technology and they prefer the old way of doing things. Roughly 25 percent of today's non–Web users fall into this group.

Based on responses about plans to adopt the Web for personal purposes, we believe that the sequence of segment adoption will roll out as depicted below. Access Aspirants will be the next wave of new consumers, followed in quick succession by the Budget Conscious and Angst Avoiders. Paranoiacs will eventually adopt the Web, but it is questionable whether Technology Rejecters will ever become Web users.

FIGURE 9.5: NEXT WAVE SEGMENTATION

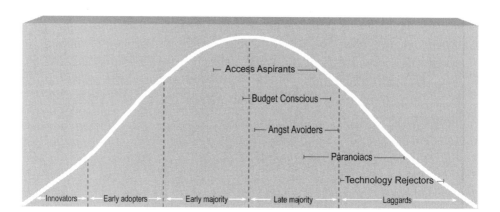

ACCESS ASPIRANTS

Some consumers have experimented with the Web but haven't made the leap to purchase an access device and Internet service—at least not yet. These people use machines at work, at friends' houses and public places, but they haven't yet decided if they really need more than occasional access. Among these consumers, money is not the issue. It is more about the time required to make a purchase decision. And often these consumers are concerned about how quickly technology changes.

Everyone in this group plans to use the Internet in the future, but not immediately. More than 70 percent expect to begin their use in six months or more. The primary reasons these consumers are attracted to the Web are information availability, the belief that they would save money, and because it is educational. These consumers are more likely than the non–Web user norm to be convenience and focused shoppers and are less likely to be price sensitive.

Access Aspirants have experimented with the Web but haven't made the leap to purchase an access device and service—at least not yet

ACCESS ASPIRANTS

MODERATOR: Why don't you use the Web at home today?

CONSUMER: I don't have a computer at home. I go over to friends' houses and go onto the Internet with them.

CONSUMER: Sometimes at work I browse around a little and have found some very informative things. I was quite surprised. Before that, I used to get irritated when friends would talk about the Internet because I wasn't familiar with it. So I was dismissive about it.

CONSUMER: I might use it to get some information like restaurants in a city I am going to visit. But I wouldn't use the Internet to buy clothes. To take an hour to stroll down the street, walk into a store, and browse is relaxing. It keeps me sane.

CONSUMER: I can see it would be useful to be able to locate a hard-to-find item, like an obscure book.

CONSUMER: It's going to get to the point where you have to have it or you'll be left behind.

BUDGET CONSCIOUS CONSUMERS

Some consumers have not adopted the Web for one simple reason: they can't afford it financially. Many of these people wish they had access, and often use their friends' machines. In fact, close to 60 percent of the consumers we polled in this group plan to use the Web for personal reasons, sometime in the midterm future (more than six months). Their primary reasons for using the Web are that it is educational and that it will make it easier and more cost-effective to communicate with family and friends. As to be expected, these consumers are very price-sensitive and like to comparison shop. The availability of low-price access devices and Internet access services will be significant motivators in converting this group into new consumers.

Budget Conscious consumers have not adopted the Web for one simple reason: they can't afford it

BUDGET CONSCIOUS

MODERATOR: Why don't you use the Web at home today?

CONSUMER: I think it would be nice to be rich and to shop on the computer, but I can't afford a computer right now.

CONSUMER: I would use the Internet if I didn't have to invest in a computer. I don't really want to invest in a computer because I don't know if I want to go with a PC or a Mac. I don't want to invest in something that becomes obsolete. I'm also watching to see if prices are going to come down.

CONSUMER: I haven't bought a computer for home yet because the technology is just changing so quickly. Every time I think this is the one I want to get, somebody will say "No, wait; get this one instead."

CONSUMER: If I could get something sort of cheap and easily accessible, I think I would use the Internet.

CONSUMER: I don't want to spend a lot of money on something and then six months later have it become obsolete.

ANGST AVOIDERS

Some consumers have not adopted the Web because it seems too hard, it would create too much anxiety, and, so far, it just doesn't seem worth the trouble. The time required to make a decision, the general uncertainty about what to buy, and the lack of confidence in knowing how to use the Web all contribute to a level of anxiety that gets in the way. More than 55 percent of consumers polled in this group plan to use the Internet in the future. They would use the Web for a variety of reasons, with no singular reason standing out from others. These consumers also represent a mixture of shopping types, being price sensitive, comparison, and convenience shoppers at the same time. Devices and services that make the Web adoption decision a no-brainer will be important in swaying this group to become new consumers. If access devices are sufficiently low-cost and plug-and-play, the anxiety of buying the wrong product will dissipate.

Angst Avoiders have not adopted the Web because it seems too hard

THE NEXT FRONTIER ■ 273

ANGST AVOIDERS

MODERATOR: Why don't you use the Web at home today?

CONSUMER: Any benefit I might gain by ordering online is not worth the risk of getting something that I have to return. I'll just go to the store.

CONSUMER: There are so many things about the Internet that I'm not aware of that I would probably use it if I knew more. I need to take a class or something.

CONSUMER: I tried an auction site the other day and it was confusing. I'm still not sure what I did wrong. I looked for a telephone number and couldn't find one. I sent an e-mail and got a generic response. I just needed to talk to someone, but couldn't make that happen.

CONSUMER: I'm not a technologically adept person. I find it frustrating. When I try to get to a Web site and can't, I don't know what I'm doing wrong. I really don't know how to solve the problem.

PARANOIACS

Some consumers are very fearful of security risks and the potential invasion of privacy, and therefore are not willing to use the Web. These consumers are quite mindful of the security breaches that have happened on the Internet and can clearly articulate their hesitancies about using it for personal reasons. Interestingly, this group has the highest usage of computers and the Internet at work, as compared to other segments of non–Web shoppers.

While we group consumers who are worried about security and privacy into one cluster, there are some notable differences in their attitudes. People who indicate that they are concerned about security and credit card theft are more open to the Internet. In fact, close to 50 percent say they plan to use the Internet for personal reasons sometime in the future. People who are concerned about privacy are less optimistic about eventually using

Paranoiacs are very fearful of security risks and the potential invasion of privacy, and therefore are not willing to use the Web

the Internet; only 20 percent of these consumers plan to use it. Evidently, while credit card–fraud issues are perceived to be solvable with technology and tough business practices, privacy concerns are much deeper and long-term in nature.

PARANOIACS

MODERATOR: Why don't you use the Web at home today?

CONSUMER: I hear all of this talk about how much personal information is known and easily accessible from the Internet about its users. If they get our social security numbers, it will be awful.

CONSUMER: I don't feel comfortable giving a credit card number.

CONSUMER: I don't like the Internet because there's too many people, too many things that have access to my private life.

CONSUMER: Big brother is not only watching, he's listening.

CONSUMER: Whether we like it or not, I think the Internet is a revolution that is going on right now and it is swallowing up everything. We have no control over it. Absolutely none. I really resent that.

CONSUMER: I don't want it to take away my privacy. I really care about that.

TECHNOLOGY REJECTERS

There is a group of consumers who reject the use of the Web for one key reason: they prefer to perform certain life activities in the way to which they are accustomed and see no need for technology. Consumers in this category think of themselves as renaissance people who believe that our society is deteriorating rather than progressing due to technology. Often these consumers reject other forms of innovation as well, such as cellular phones, cable TV, and advanced telephone services. This group is less likely to have seen a Web page than others. And less than 24 percent plan to use the Internet for personal purposes sometime in the future. As

Technology Rejecters prefer to perform life activities in the ways to which they are accustomed—without the Internet

shoppers, Technology Rejecters are more brand loyal, have less of a tendency to comparison shop, and dislike retail stores more than other shopper segments. We believe that these people will be among the last of the laggards to adopt the Web and will only become adopters when it will be absolutely necessary to survive in our culture—a time that is still years away if ever.

TECHNOLOGY REJECTERS

MODERATOR: Why don't you use the Web at home today?

CONSUMER: I've never used the Web, never even used a computer. I'm still having trouble with my television!

CONSUMER: The Internet is taking over everything. I just wish people would be more into talking to each other and having eye contact.

CONSUMER: Communicating through e-mail is not like having a conversation. It's too impersonal.

CONSUMER: Even if it was free, I wouldn't want it.

CONSUMER: So what if you save time using the Internet? You just fill that time with something else. You just keep going and going, doing more and more. It's too much.

CONSUMER: Seems like it could get so out of control that everyone will be isolated.

CONSUMER: Even if you do save money, shopping on the Internet takes all the personalization out of everything.

Alternative Access Devices

Many new types of alternative Web access devices are coming to market that will appeal to today's new consumers, and to the next wave as well. Form factors range from cellular phones, to PDAs, to dedicated Web and e-mail access devices, to TV set-top boxes. While some of these products have been on the market for several years, continuous innovation has resulted in improved, easier-to-use, and lower-price technologies. Now that we know that building these devices is feasible, key questions arise: What problems are these devices actually going to solve, and who will want to buy them? Now that we have built the devices, will they come?

We conducted some focused research in an effort to answer these questions and discovered some interesting findings among current Web users and non-users. As one would expect, the reception of alternative devices varies widely depending on consumers' current use of the Web.

Among new consumers—people who actively use the Web to shop and, in some cases, buy, as well as do other activities—the preferred primary Web access device is their PC. This is an expected response: these consumers have already invested in their PCs, they are comfortable with their machines, and they see no reason to change. When presented with the concept of low-priced (under $300) Web and e-mail access devices, new consumers are intrigued, but not interested in buying—at least the majority is not. Their objections are interesting, however. Most say they would not have a use for an alternative Web or e-mail access device because such devices don't handle file attachments and they don't have productivity tools such as word processing. We expected business Internet users to express this opinion, since the PC and the Internet are heavily used as work productivity tools. But home users of the Web, who normally are perceived to be using the Internet for other reasons, seem to be actively using standard productivity tools and routinely e-mailing attachment files for personal reasons as well.

Some experienced Web users see value in alternative access devices. In particular, new consumers who have multiple Web users in the household can imagine using these low-priced widgets as a second device, although it requires an additional phone line for simultaneous access, an expense most consumers say they are not willing to bear. Others found the specialized functionality of certain devices interesting, such as integrated telephone directories or integrated TV programming.

Among non–Web users—people who are not yet new consumers—interest levels in alternative Web access devices was higher. Of the non–Web consumers we polled, approximately 40 percent indicated that they would be interested or very interested in a $300 access device with a $10 per month service charge. And among consumers who are planning to use the Web sometime in the future, more than 60 percent were interested in these devices—especially the access aspirants and budget-conscious groups. Among these consumers, the low-price point and easy-to-use form factor solved many of the problems that have prevented their Web adoption. A price of $300 seems acceptable to a wide range of demographic profiles. And the devices that are simple to plug in and connect are appealing to people who are fearful of technology and lack confidence in making it work.

Another interesting future technology we have discussed with current Web users and non-users is integrated messaging and universal mailbox services. These services are described as offering one mailbox for all types of messages: voice-, e-mail, and fax. Consumers can access all of their messages in one mailbox via voice- or e-mail. Irrespective of their Web usage, our research shows that consumers have mixed reactions to this concept, stemming from their current dependence on messaging technology in managing their personal and professional lives. People who are frequently away from their offices and homes see the benefits of being able to check messages using this type of mail service, as it efficiently collects all message types for easy access. This is seen as easier than checking multiple message sources. These types of consumers tend to be very dependent on both e-mail and voice mail—a condition which presents a double-edged sword. Some consumers comment that they get so much junk mail these days, due to Web sites' spam activities, that accessing their e-mail via a phone call would be intolerably tedious. Even if the system only reads the subject line of every e-mail received, the daily volume would be unacceptable to access via a voice-activated message system. These are consumers who routinely delete spam without reading past the first two words of the subject line, an activity that takes less time than listening to a computerized voice read the subject line over the telephone.

So, now that these devices are built and available, some consumers indicate they will indeed buy them, particularly people who are not yet Web users and who are looking for a low-cost, hassle-free way of becoming part of the Internet generation.

ALTERNATIVE DEVICES

MODERATOR: What do you think about low-price Web and e-mail access devices? Would you consider buying one?

NON–WEB CONSUMER: Low-price Web and e-mail devices are attractive to me because of the price and they look easy to use. Plus, they don't take up a lot of room.

NON–WEB CONSUMER: It looks easy to use, like I could just plug it in.

NON–WEB CONSUMER: I might buy one just so that I can communicate with my friends.

WEB CONSUMER: I can see having one for my kids so they don't tie up my computer.

WEB CONSUMER: I might put one in my bedroom so I could conveniently get my e-mail instead of going to my office.

WEB CONSUMER: I don't see the value. I already have a PC and plus you can't do attachments with that machine. What good is it?

Global Consumers: Similarities and Differences

In this book, our focus has been solely on American consumers. Our primary research has been conducted within the boundaries of the United States, largely because American consumers have been the earliest adopters of the Internet. That is rapidly changing, and we are beginning to study markets outside of the States. But we have not been alone in our United States focus. Most American e-businesses have taken a very United States–centric view of the Web and have created value propositions that are realistically only deliverable to people in the United States. There are plenty of good reasons for this. E-business was easier to invent for the United States market, and the most ready opportunity was in the States. American start-ups were being funded by American venture capital. American consumers have had affordable access to reasonable Web performance, as well as to PCs, for quite some time. The language, currency, and method of payment are homogeneous. And the tax laws were designed to stimulate e-commerce development.

Much of the next frontier on the Web will be outside United States borders, as more new consumers come online around the world

Certainly new opportunities continue to abound for American e-businesses. But we believe that much of the next frontier on the Web will be outside United States borders, as more new consumers come online around the world.

To supplement our own United States research, we have been tracking primary research conducted by other organizations outside the States to understand new consumer behavior in other markets and to compare behavioral patterns found in our work. Clearly there are similarities as well as differences in global Web consumer behavior. Every geographic market is in a different stage of Internet penetration. There are gating factors that greatly impact the rate at which consumers adopt the Web, including:

- Telecommunications infrastructure
- Economic conditions
- Penetration and usage of personal computers
- Access to the Internet at work, which is generally a precursor to personal usage
- Transaction/payment systems and the acceptance of credit cards

The status of each of these market-condition factors dramatically affects the stage of Web diffusion in every culture. It is interesting to note, however, that the more similar the market conditions, the more similar the consumer behavior becomes across geographies.

GEOGRAPHIC SIMILARITIES IN ONLINE PURCHASES AND MOTIVATIONS

While the barriers each country faces in adopting the Web are unquestionably significant in enabling consumer access, we have noted in our comparative analysis that once consumers get access, their interests and activities begin to be similar across cultures. Here are examples to illustrate our point:

- The demographic profile of Internet users in the United Kingdom are similar to that of North American users several years ago, due to the United Kingdom's widespread adoption of the Internet lagging behind the United States by several years. United Kingdom Internet users, however, are embracing e-commerce more rapidly than North American users did several years ago, largely because the market is now more mature and learning curves are faster.[2] This is an excellent illustration of our Web effect theory: Once consumers get access to the Internet, they rapidly develop a preference and it soon becomes a requirement for daily-life activities.

- In Sweden, studies show that the consumers who are more likely to make online purchases are those that have been online the longest. Of the Swedish Web shoppers, 75 percent began using the Web in 1997 or earlier. This is very similar to patterns noted in American consumers—the more experienced they are on the Web, the more likely they are to purchase online. High-dollar purchases (more than $120) tend to be more frequent, and are often for travel and computer products.[3]

- In South Korea, nearly half of Korean Internet users have purchased items online. The patterns of usage are very similar to the United States. By product, PCs and computer peripherals are found to be the best-selling items, followed by books, music, video CDs, tapes, and electronic appliances—all standardized items for which buyers don't need to physically check the quality or size before purchasing. The primary reasons given for Internet shopping are to save time and convenience.[4]

- In Japan, the methods for locating products purchased online are quite similar to those in the United States. Leading the list of how products are found online are search engines, e-mail or news mailing lists, online shopping malls, newspaper or magazine articles, and ads, friends, and banner ads.[5]

- In Asia and the Pacific—the broader region including Australia, China, India, Indonesia, Japan, Korea, Malaysia, New Zealand, the Philippines, Singapore, Taiwan, and Thailand—94 percent of online sales comes from Japan, Korea, and Australia, the most highly developed markets in the region. Product categories that show the greatest sales are very similar to best-sellers in the United States—computer hardware and software, financial brokerage, travel, and consumer electronics. The potential for e-commerce is seen by market trackers to be enormous, although the markets for computer products, financial services, and travel are considered by some to be overcrowded.[6]

- Consumers in Arab countries show similar patterns to other geographies in terms of products purchased and reasons for online shopping. Software was the most popular item for Internet shoppers (48 percent), followed by books (28 percent), computers and peripherals (26 percent), and audio CDs (11 percent). The majority of participants in the study said one of the main reasons they shop online is the availability of consumer products not found in local markets. Ease of making a purchase and the convenience of comparing products and prices were other key reasons for online shopping. Most purchases were made by credit cards and most were confident with secure Web sites.[7]

- A key reason why new international consumers use the Web for e-commerce is access to products outside of their countries. In Australia, Web buyers reported that 68 percent of their purchases were made from overseas sources.[8] Similarly, in Japan, access to foreign products is a key reason Internet users shop online.[9] And in Arab countries, 82 percent of online purchases made by consumers were from non-domestic vendors.

- We also see some similar attitudes in the business-to-business market, between the United States and Asian countries. In a supply chain–usage survey of five hundred companies in Singapore, China, Taiwan, Korea, and Japan, major barriers to using the Internet for procurement included security concerns and the inability to nego-

Once consumers get access, their interests and activities begin to be similar across cultures

tiate prices online. Despite considerable differences among the countries studied, it was noted that the person-to-person functions in the procurement process are not likely to disappear anytime soon—a situation we noted in chapter 7 among American procurement professionals. The study suggests that in these Asian countries, efforts to expand Internet-based procurement might be most productive if focused on ways in which e-commerce can supplement and facilitate, rather than replace, person-to-person interactions.[10]

GEOGRAPHIC DIFFERENCES

As discussed above, there are significant differences across geographies in terms of Internet infrastructure readiness, cost of access, and acceptable business practices. To illustrate the differences among geographies in terms of access expense, a study of European Internet use and access costs by Booz, Allen and Hamilton contrasted the average cost of forty hours a month using the predominant ISP in several markets. Given these parameters, it found that the costs are $85 in Spain, $76 in Germany, $62 in France, and $49 in Britain, as compared to $37 in the United States.[11]

Even if all access were equally good and affordable, there would still be differences in world cultures that impact new consumers' Web behavior. Most of the differences noted in our secondary research relates to the acceptance of credit cards as a consumer payment method. Here are some examples:

- In Sweden, the key barrier to more online commerce is that a suitable payment system is not yet in place. And for certain classes of items, it is not economical to pay for freight and transport costs for goods that are low in price.[12]
- In South Korea, most new consumers (94 percent) feel uneasy about possible leakage of their personal information in the process of making online payments with their credit cards. To deal with these concerns, a new electronic payment system enabling

consumers to purchase online using bank account numbers instead of credit cards is being developed through an alliance with the nation's six major banks.[13]

- Companies wishing to penetrate the Japanese online market should be mindful of cultural and social factors that impact what Japanese Internet users will buy, how they wish to pay for online goods and services, and what will motivate return visits. For example, 70 percent say that anxiety about personal-information security is a drawback to doing e-commerce. It is expected to continue hindering the growth of retail e-commerce in Japan.[14] This issue has created potential opportunities for companies that offer multi-channel alternatives, where shoppers place orders online and physically go to the retail storefront to make payments and pick up products.

- In Argentina, where most of the e-commerce activities today are in the business-to-business sector, 70 percent of consumers surveyed have never made an online purchase and are reluctant to give out credit card details online. As a side note, the majority of those surveyed also have a good knowledge of English but expressed dissatisfaction with the lack of Spanish language content and local sites.[15]

THINKING GLOBAL IN THE WEB WORLD

One characteristic that is pervasive across geographies is the consumer need to feel confident in their e-commerce activities. As we discussed in chapter 3, building consumer confidence is essential to engendering consumer loyalty. To develop confidence among consumers outside the United States, companies must focus on the basics: offer better Web experiences, make it easy to buy in the currency of choice, and properly set consumers' expectations. There are three key ingredients to success for capturing the opportunities outside of the United States: companies must *think globally, act locally, and be relevant*. There are many complexi-

Companies must think globally, act locally, and be relevant

ties to fulfilling this vision, particularly from a content- and technical-infrastructure perspective. Thinking globally and acting locally in the Web context requires a company to "design in" international commerce rather than "bolt on" after the fact. Being relevant is a mindset—a goal that impacts all actions from the technical to aesthetic.

To be truly effective and live up to the potential of the Internet as a global business vehicle, a Web site must meet the business and cultural requirements of all the geographic regions in which a company does business. Many companies already do business outside of United States borders and realize the implications of this challenge. Others may have started out being focused on only a single country, but by the very nature of establishing a presence on the Web, may be encountering an opportunity to branch out geographically.

Regardless of how a company arrives at being a global business, there are some dynamic challenges to address— issues like government regulation and taxation of e-commerce. Privacy and security of data collected online are also growing concerns. Offering an acceptable method of payment is a pragmatic and critical step as well. Laws governing these business practices are different in every country. Delving into these issues goes beyond the confines of this book. And because these areas are actively being refined, what is proper today may need to be revised six months from now, and six months from then.

ACTING LOCALLY: THE KEY TO BUILDING CONFIDENCE

Many companies believe that they need only to provide some basic translated marketing materials to draw the international visitor into the site. But as the Web penetrates worldwide consumer markets, it is becoming increasingly important that sites allow for multilingual online commerce capabilities and customer service interaction to build consumer confidence. As we saw in the secondary research cited above, international new consumers like buying online because of access to non-domestic products, so the

Localizing content is a fundamental step in making a Web site a relevant experience for customers

commerce opportunities look good for multi-national e-businesses who do it right.

Localizing content is a fundamental step in making a Web site a relevant experience for customers, wherever they are. Localization involves converting a site from the language, functional, cultural, and presentation require-ments of one market into those of another. Specific actions required include: determining a product selection and a related pricing structure to make available to the local mar-ket; creating or converting content relevant to the local market to the local language; integrating business and cul-tural practices in those markets; and resolving back-end process issues, such as the use of customer information in databases and the identification of required online applica-tions and forms. Even if the content remains essentially the same, local tastes, preferences, and conventions may influ-ence how products or services are positioned.

RELEVANCE AND LOCAL TECHNICAL READINESS

The technical readiness factors unique to each market sector and geography are important to understand in cre-ating a relevant Web experience. A critical but often over-looked aspect of delivering positive, relevant Web site experiences is designing for local access parameters like bandwidth, phone connection charges, and quality of the "last mile" connection. For instance, sites with lots of ani-mated graphics may work well in some countries, but not in others where entertainment value is a low priority and long page-loading times are prohibitively expensive. Companies should plan for these kinds of limitations, so that investments in the site architecture and applications can be leveraged across markets.

Implications for Business

These first few years of e-business have been excit-ing, chaotic, exhilarating—and wealth-producing—for people who were able to catch and ride the Internet wave. For new consumers, it has been a heady time of newfound empowerment, discovery, and experimentation. It has also been a time that few pundits were able to predict five years in advance. Most people will admit that the magnitude of the Web wave caught us all by surprise. Will the next five years offer as much drama, as much opportunity, as much room for impact? In some ways it may be hard to top what we've already experienced thus far in the go-go world of e-business, but we believe the next frontier holds much promise to pervasively improve the quality of our lives as consumers. Businesses that hope to be part of the next frontier need to listen carefully to their markets, because the soul of the new consumer will continue to evolve rapidly.

What do we predict will occur in this next phase of evolution? We believe that new shopper segments will continue to emerge and that new consumers will be shape-shifters, changing their demands and expectations in response to new online and hybrid-channel value propositions. For several more years, new waves of early and late majority consumers will get Web access. Attracting these new consumers and converting them into e-commerce customers will require persistent ingenuity.

Building new customer confidence will be both more and less challenging as time goes by. It will be less challenging because as more consumers successfully buy more online, the resulting positive word of mouth will buoy less confident consumers. The concept of e-commerce will become commonly accepted. But building consumer confidence in new Web brands or restoring confidence in tarnished brands will become more challenging as consumers are familiar and comfortable with their preferred sites. It will be increasingly difficult for new Web brands to entice customers, especially those segments that are convenience motivated or brand loyal shoppers.

Winning the comparison and price-sensitive shoppers presents another challenge: positioning based on being the low-price leader or the best deal is a precarious strategy. There's always another company that is willing to sell at lower prices or offer a better deal. It will be interesting to see when the e-business market finally self-corrects—when all the venture capital and funds from IPOs are depleted and companies are forced to be operationally sound and profitable enterprises. What will happen to low-price, best-deal Web brands that haven't been able to build a loyal following among a fickle set of consumers? And what happens to the comparison and price-sensitive shopper then? If history is a good predictor, as it usually is, there will be a consolidation in the industry. The surviving e-businesses will stake out and protect predictable positions, each differentiated based on a mix of service, price, innovation, and breadth of offerings. When that will happen and how well the new consumer will adapt are interesting questions. If good deals evaporate online, will consumers keep shopping online, or will they revert to their previous methods of purchasing? This won't play out as a binary issue. In other words, some may backslide to old behaviors and others will be hooked by the convenience of the Web—as long as it remains convenient.

In the meantime, what happens to consumers' sense of entitlement to freebies designed to stimulate online buying behavior? What will happen if Web sites stop offering special incentive programs? This has got to be one of the scariest decisions that e-business executives have to make—if, when, and how to pull back on expensive loss-leader promotional offers. Knowing the right timing on this decision will require close analysis of consumers' attitudes and competitive market conditions. And, knowing the inflection point of when to shift customer acquisition spending to customer retention spending is also a key e-business challenge. We predict that on the Web, it may well be more expensive to retain customers than to acquire them—an inversion of traditional marketing-strategy common sense.

How will privacy concerns get resolved? We are hopeful that this doesn't become a government-regulated issue. The Internet evolves at such a rapid pace, particularly as compared to government bureaucracy, it seems inevitable that the two will always be out-of-sync, resulting in an impotent solution. But will it be enough for companies to voluntarily comply with ethical privacy practices? And can the e-business industry even agree to what "ethical" privacy practices are? In some ways, the outlook for this type of agreement and its successful execution seem equally dim. If nothing happens to effectively control Web sites' intrusive business practices, what will consumers do? They will modify their behavior to force the industry to their own comfort levels. Some consumers are blasé about privacy; those people will continue to browse, shop, and buy online. Other consumers will modify their behavior, disable cookies, and only browse and shop—but not buy—online. Whether new consumers buy or not, they will passively resist junk e-mail by deleting it on sight, or continually change their secondary e-mail addresses. And they will become more adamant about only doing business with sites that don't abuse their space.

We also predict that Web site performance and the richness of the online shopping experience will improve dramatically with technology improvements. This will help in the merchandising of high-involvement products that are currently struggling to get e-commerce traction. In addition, new hybrid clicks-and-mortar enterprises will continue cropping up to resolve consumers' issues with end-to-end online consumption (shopping, buying, delivering, and servicing.)

The Web will continue to be adopted by more consumers around the world. For companies to succeed, thinking globally, acting locally, and being relevant will be required. To hit the target with the right timing, companies must pay close attention to the status of the Web Effect in their markets—access quickly leads to demands. Success in the next frontier will require obsessively listening to customers, vigilantly monitoring the competition, continuously honing the value proposition, and thriving on change. One last key ingredient for success—realizing the importance of the *soul* of the new consumer.

Appendix: Research Methodologies

*T*he *Soul of the New Consumer: The Attitudes, Behaviors, and Preferences of E-Customers* is based on more than three years of research among Internet users and customers. As a consulting and research services firm, Cognitiative, Inc. has had contact and conversations with thousands of new consumers and e-business customers through our Pulse of the Customer℠ research series and through our proprietary client work. We have used a breadth of data-collection methods in gathering content for this book, including focus groups, telephone surveys, and e-mail panel surveys. All primary research noted in this book, unless otherwise sourced, was conducted by Cognitiative, Inc.

The primary author, Laurie Windham, is a graduate school–trained and experienced practitioner in research methods, including the scientific method, as well as quantitative and qualitative analysis techniques. She has been conducting market research and analysis for twenty years, specializing in the study of consumer behavior in a wide range of technology markets, including PCs, home electronics, and communications services. All focus groups cited in this book were conducted by Ms. Windham. In addition, all of Cognitiative's research methodologies were designed and executed under her guidance. Other research professionals at Cognitiative have assisted in data collection and survey administration as well. Ken Orton was instrumental in analyzing research data and comprehending implications to e-businesses.

The methodologies employed for each chapter are described below. There are, however, several general characteristics about our research process and philosophy that apply to all of the research presented in this book. The research we have conducted is qualitative and directional in nature. We use research to ferret out the psychodynamics of the relationships between buyers and sellers on the Web, which, by their very nature, are qualitative. We are confident of the representative value of our research and firmly believe that we have accurately captured the attitudes, behavior, and preferences of new consumers. Our three-year research process has consistently validated the reliability of our findings, year after year. We believe that the best way to develop a deep understanding of new consumers is through rigorous qualitative exploration rather than broad, closed-ended survey questionnaires. Therefore, we do not endeavor to present our data as statistically representative of the new consumer population with confidence intervals and calculated margins of error. We draw our confidence from the substantial critical mass of our in-depth qualitative and quantitative data, as well as from our years of experience in studying consumer behavior.

To ensure that we are capturing truly representative, qualitative findings, we have been diligent in monitoring the results of other organizations' broad, statistical studies of Web consumers and cross-comparing our findings. In this way, we have continually reinforced our confidence in the validity of our research findings. In the common metrics shared between these various studies and our ongoing work, we have found virtually identical patterns in consumers' Web behaviors and opinions. Those studies are referenced and footnoted throughout this book.

The reader will note the use of two research reporting methods: dialog boxes and charts. The dialog boxes contain actual transcribed conversations from focus groups and telephone interviews conducted by Cognitiative. These quotes were selected from hundreds of hours of transcripts to provide the reader with a deeper insight into consumers' opinions on selected topics. The graphic charts depict data gathered in broader sample surveys, ranging from one hundred to one thousand sample sizes, depending on the topic. Below is a description of the numerous studies used to develop each chapter.

Chapters One through Five

Chapters 1 through 5 draw on Cognitiative's Q4 1999 and Q1 2000 Pulse of the Customer research series that included e-mail panel and focus group methods. Respondents were screened to have recently made online purchases, and to have purchased products during the 1999 holiday season. A total of approximately one thousand Web consumers responded to e-mail panel questionnaires in these two periods. Questionnaires comprised open-ended questions to which respondents expressed in their own words their attitudes and preferences about their Web experiences. Their answers were analyzed and tabulated by Cognitiative research analysis staff. While the process of tabulating responses to open-ended questions is very laborious, we believe that this is the best way to get a deep understanding of consumer attitudes from a wide cross-section of consumers. The questionnaires also featured several closed-ended questions to enable comparative tabulations of less subjective questions. Chapter 4 also features content derived from in-depth focus groups conducted in mid-1999 regarding attitudes toward privacy, personalization, and promotional e-mail.

Chapter Six

Research conducted in support of chapter 6 was fielded via focus groups and an e-mail panel in Q3 1999. Groups were conducted in Phoenix, Dallas, and San Francisco among consumers who were screened based on their buying behavior. The total sample of close to one hundred people was screened with three primary criteria: they were active online, catalog, and retail store shoppers. The methodology was designed to enable contrasting channel behaviors and preferences.

Chapter Seven

Research supporting chapter 7 was conducted in multiple Pulse of the Customer studies, as well as through proprietary research we conducted for our clients. We thank those clients who graciously allowed us to use some of the data we gathered on their behalf. All of the data presented about business customers was gathered in 1999 and early 2000, through a combination of telephone surveys, focus groups, and e-mail panels.

Chapter Eight

Research presented in chapter 8 takes the form of e-business case studies. All of these examples are based on our work with clients, whose names we withhold to protect their privacy. This chapter also references the methodology of the E-Business Development Road Map, which was originally introduced in our first book, *Dead Ahead: The Web Dilemma and the New Rules of Business.*

Chapter Nine

Chapter 9 draws on several research studies. Research presented regarding attitudes of non–Web users was gathered in both a nationwide telephone survey of two hundred respondents and focus groups in San Francisco and New York, all conducted in Q1 2000. Data presented about Web users was derived from a series of focus groups conducted in San Francisco, Dallas, and New York.

Our Three-Year Foundation of Research

In addition to the specific studies mentioned above, *The Soul of the New Consumer* is based on our three-year study of the migration of new consumers and businesses to the Web as a vehicle for managing their daily lives. In our research, we have focused on the evolution of e-customers' expectations as they discover the empowering virtues of the Web. It has been a fast-paced and fantastic voyage thus far. We remain committed to the continuation of our studies and continue to make our Pulse of the Customer findings available to clients and subscribers. For more information, please visit *www.cognitiative.com.*

Endnotes

CHAPTER 1

1. *Merriam-Webster's Collegiate® Dictionary,* 10th ed., s.v. "consumer."
2. R.L. Shayon, *Television and Our Children* (New York: Longman, 1953).
3. R.S. Wurman, *Understanding* (Rhode Island: Ted Conferences, Inc., 2000).
4. Ellen Wartella and Byron Reeves, *Historical Trends in Research on Children and the Media: 1900–1960* (CYFC, 1995).
5. R. Kraut and V. Lundmark, "Internet Paradox: A Social Technology That Reduces Social Involvement and Psychological Well Being?" *American Psychologist* (1999).
6. Stanford Institute for the Qualitative Study of Society, Stanford University, as referenced by Kathleen O'Toole, "Study Takes Early Look at Social Consequences of Net Use," *Stanford Online Report* (*www.stanford.edu,* 2000).
7. R.S. Wurman, *Understanding.*
8. *www.Sears.com.*
9. *www.Mastercard.com.*
10. R.S. Wurman, *Understanding.*
11. R.D. Putnam, "Bowling Alone: America's Declining Social Capital," *Journal of Democracy* 6, no. 1 (1995): pp. 65–78.
12. Don Van Natta, Jr., "Courting Web-Head Cash," *New York Times,* 13 February 2000.
13. Philip Kotler, *Marketing Management* (New Jersey: Prentice Hall, 1994).
14. Ibid.
15. R.S. Wurman, *Understanding.*

16. Kathleen O'Toole, "Study Takes Early Look at Social Consequences of Net Use," *Stanford Online Report.*

17. Katie Hafner, "A Credibility Gap in the Digital Divide," *New York Times,* 5 March 2000.

18. Milton Friedman, *There's No Such Thing as a Free Lunch* (Illinois: Open Court, 1975).

19. Recording Industry Association of America (RIAA), "Recording Industry Sues Napster for Copyright Infringement," *http://www.riaa.com/piracy/press/120799.htm* (Washington, DC: December 7, 1999).

20. Amy Harmon, "Potent Software Escalates Music Industry's Jitters," *New York Times,* 7 March 2000.

21. Mick Jagger and Keith Richards, "You Can't Always Get What You Want," (Abkco Music and Recordings, 1986).

CHAPTER 2

1. F. Herzberg, "One More Time: How Do You Motivate Employees?" *Harvard Business Review* 46: pp. 53–62.

2. Michael J. Weiss, *The Clustered World: How We Live, What We Buy, and What It All Means about Who We Are* (Pennsylvania: Little Brown & Company, 2000).

3. Don Peppers, Martha Rogers, and Bob Dorf, *The One-to-One Field Book: The Complete Toolkit for Implementing a One-to-One Marketing Program* (New York: Bantam Doubleday Dell Publishing Group, Inc., 1999).

4. Stanford Institute for the Qualitative Study of Society, Stanford University, as referenced by Kathleen O'Toole, "Study Takes Early Look at Social Consequences of Net Use," *Stanford Online Report.*

CHAPTER 3

1. *www.Business.com/pr_991130.html.*

2. Robert Frank, "How Music.com Found Itself a Hot Address," *Wall Street Journal,* 3 March 2000, sec. B.

3. Amazon.com's 1-Click settings include your shipping address, shipping method, and payment information. They are created when you use a credit card to make an order with Amazon.com that is not a gift or an out-of-print title.

4. Andrew Grove, *Only the Paranoid Survive* (Boston: Bantam Books, 1999).

CHAPTER 4
1. *Merriam-Webster's Collegiate® Dictionary,* 10th ed., s.v. "privacy."
2. Richard Kellett, Privacy presentation produced by the Office of Government Wide Policy, 2000, quoted in John C. Dvorak, "The Privacy Pinch," *Forbes* (February 7, 2000): p. 138.
3. Simson Garfinkle, *Database Nation: The Death of Privacy in the 21st Century* (O'Reilly & Associates, 2000).
4. John C. Dvorak, "The Privacy Pinch," *Forbes* (February 7, 2000): p. 138.
5. Michael Moss, "A Web CEO's Elusive Goal: Privacy," *Wall Street Journal,* 7 February 2000, B1.
6. Ibid.
7. Andrea Petersen, "A Privacy Firestorm at Double-Click," *Wall Street Journal,* 23 February 2000, sec. B.
8. Louis Harris & Associates, study for IBM, as referenced by Michael Moss, "A Web CEO's Elusive Goal: Privacy," *Wall Street Journal.*
9. Ibid.
10. Heather Green, Norm Alster, Amy Borus, and Catherine Yang, "Privacy: An Outrage on the Web," *Business Week* (February 14, 2000): p. 38.
11. "Privacy: Special Report," *www.PCComputing.com,* (March 2000): p. 99.
12. Louis Harris & Associates, study for IBM, as referenced by Michael Moss, "A Web CEO's Elusive Goal: Privacy," *Wall Street Journal.*
13. Ibid.

CHAPTER 5
1. Kelly Zito. "Dot-Com Companies Score during Super Bowl with TV Ads," *San Francisco Chronicle,* 1 February 2000.
2. Philip Kotler, *Marketing Management* (New Jersey: Prentice Hall, 1994), p. 191.

CHAPTER 6
1. Stanford Institute for the Quantitative Study of Society, Stanford University, as referenced by Kathleen O'Toole, "Study Takes Early Look at Social Consequences of Net Use," *Stanford Online Report.*

2. Calmetta Coleman, "Making Malls (Gasp!) Convenient," *Wall Street Journal*, 8 February 2000, B1.
3. *Merriam-Webster's Collegiate® Dictionary*, 10th ed., s.v. "news."
4. Pew Research Center for the People and the Press (January 1999), as referenced in R.S. Wurman, *Understanding*.
5. Geoffrey Sauer and B. Helen Liu, "The Impact of Television on Literacy: Good or Bad?" *www.english-server.hss.cmu.edu.*
6. Stanford Institute for the Quantitative Study of Society, Stanford University.
7. Ibid.
8. Ibid.
9. Sandeep Junnarkar, "Web Banks Look to Branch Out," *www.CNET.com* (February 16, 2000).

CHAPTER 8

1. Jennifer L. Baljko, "E-Biz Revenue on the Rise," *Electronic Buyer's News*, 30 August 1999, p. 50.

CHAPTER 9

1. Stanford Institute for the Qualitative Study of Society, Stanford University, as referenced by Kathleen O'Toole, "Study Takes Early Look at Social Consequences of Net Use," *Stanford Online Report*.
2. CommerceNet and Nielsen Media Research, "E-Commerce Survey Shows 27% of British Adults Now Use the Internet on a Regular Basis," *www.commerce.net/news/press/102799.html* (October 27, 1999).
3. SIFO IT-Monitorn, "Sweden Is E-Commerce Leader in the Nordic Countries," *Computer Sweden*, no. 40.
4. Michael Kim, "Nearly 50 Percent of Korean Users Shop Online," *Korea Information Culture Center (www.asia.internet.com/cyberatlas/01816-Korea.html).*
5. DSA Analytics, "The Internet User and Online Commerce in Japan," Release 1999.2.
6. Boston Consulting Group, "E-Tail of the Tiger: Retail E-Commerce in Asia Pacific," as referenced in "Battle Lines Drawn as Asia-Pacific Retailers Join Competition for Rapidly-Expanding Online Market," *www.bcg.com/asia_online/press_release.asp* (February 28, 2000).

7. Fawaz Jarrah, "Internet Shoppers in Arab World Spend US$95 Million," *www.ditnet.co.ae/itnews/newsmay99/newsmay77.html* (June 13, 1999).
8. Australian Bureau of Statistics, May 1999.
9. DSA Analytics, "The Internet User and Online Commerce in Japan."
10. CommerceNet, "CommerceNet Asia Issues Results of First Major Internet Study of Asian Supply Source," *www.commerce.net/news/press/110399.html* (November 3, 1999).
11. Alan Cowell, "Europe Plays Internet Catch-Up: A Bewildering Choice of Portals, Most of Them Pricey," *New York Times,* 11 March 2000, B1–2.
12. SIFO IT-Monitorn, "Sweden Is E-Commerce Leader in the Nordic Countries," *Computer Sweden.*
13. Michael Kim, "Nearly 50 Percent of Korean Users Shop Online," *Korea Information Culture Center.*
14. DSA Analytics, "The Internet User and Online Commerce in Japan, an Executive Summary," Release 1999.2, as referenced in *www.dsaasiagroup.com/Executive%20Summary.htm.*
15. NUA Internet Surveys, "Reuters: Net Remains Privilege of Argentinean Elite," (August 11, 1999).

Index

information technology. *see* IT
innovations
  customer retention programs
    and, 100
  diffusion of, 14–15, 15 *f1.2*
Institute for the Quantitative
  Study of Society, 4
integration, 35
international business development, 225
Internet. *see also* online; Web sites
  acceptance of, 3
  adoption of, 257, 261–263, 262
    f9.1, 263, 268–269, 279, 288
  alternative devices for, 275–278
  attraction to, 266–268, 267 *f9.4*
  benefit consumers from, 36–42
  change from, 21–29
  communication and, 174–176
  cost of, 268–269
  distrusting of, 14
  early majority phase of, 15, 261
  empowerment from, 2
  familiarity of, 262 *f9.1*, 262–263
  increased relationships through,
    4, 13
  late majority phase of, 263–275
  multi-source of information
    from, 21–23
  news immediacy and, 171–172
  non-users of, 261–263, 262 *f9.1*,
    263 *f9.2*, 264, 264 *f9.3*,
    265–267, 269–275, 276–277
  other businesses impacted by,
    151, 153 *f6.1*, 153–154
  outside U.S. for, 257, 278–285
  precursors to acceptance of,
    6–14
  social isolation from, 4, 13
  speed of connection on, 16, 18,
    54, 54 *f2.7*, 150, 164
  television vs., 173
inventory, 149, 167
investing, 176–177
invoices, 200
isolation. *see* social isolation
ISP, 18
IT (information technology),
  185–186, 186 *f7.4*, 189–190,
  201–203, 208

Japan, 280, 283

late majority, 15, 263–268
  segmentation and, 269–275
launch and ongoing refinement,
  249 *f8.8*
  case study for, 252–253
  data required for, 248–249
  decision points for, 251–252
  myths and realities for, 248
  output for, 252
  site monitoring and, 250–251
lawsuits, 103
leadership
  executive, 223–224
legitimacy, 75
leisure, 171
lifestyles
  sixty-two clusters of, 58
loyalty
  actions impacting on, 55
  benefit-oriented segments for,
    60–70
  brand, 63–64, 217–218
  business e-commerce and, 193
  components for Web brand, 43
    f2.3, 43–44
  enticing, 53–55, 54 *f2.7*
  extension to other categories
    and, 51–52
  familiarity and, 39
  first-in and, 217–218
  lack of, 78
  maintaining, 35–36, 98, 100
  meeting expectations for, 42–43,
    43 *f2.2*
  one-to-one approach for, 58–59,
    69
  retail brand vs. method for, 178
  shopper motif and, 60–70
  targeting for, 68–69
  Web site, 50–51, 51 *f2.6*

magazines, 83, 83 *f3.3*, 85, 194 *f7.8*
mailbox services
  universal, 277
malls, 163
mall sites, 51, 53
marketing
  business e-commerce and,
    193–194, 194 *f7.8*

Books from Allworth Press

Dead Ahead: The Web Dilemma and the New Rules of Business by Laurie Windham with Jon Samsel (hardcover, 6¼ × 9¼, 256 pages, $24.95)

Money Secrets of the Rich and Famous by Michael Reynard (hardcover, 6¼ × 9¼, 256 pages, $24.95)

Your Living Trust and Estate Plan: How to Maximize Your Family's Assets and Protect Your Loved Ones, Second Edition by Harvey J. Platt (softcover, 6 × 9, 304 pages, $14.95)

The Retirement Handbook: How to Maximize Your Assets and Protect Your Quality of Life by Carl W. Battle (softcover, 6 × 9, 256 pages, $18.95)

The Trademark Guide: A Friendly Guide for Protecting and Profiting from Trademarks by Lee Wilson (softcover, 6 × 9, 192 pages, $18.95)

The Copyright Guide: A Friendly Guide for Protecting and Profiting from Copyrights by Lee Wilson (softcover, 6 × 9, 192 pages, $18.95)

The Patent Guide: A Friendly Guide to Protecting and Profiting from Patents by Carl W. Battle (softcover, 6 × 9, 224 pages, $18.95)

The Law (In Plain English)® for Small Businesses, Third Edition by Leonard DuBoff (softcover, 6 × 9, 256 pages, $19.95)

The Internet Publicity Guide: How to Maximize Your Marketing and Promotion in Cyberspace by V. A. Shiva (softcover, 6 × 9, 224 pages, $18.95)

The Internet Research Guide, Revised Edition by Timothy K. Maloy (softcover, 6 × 9, 208 pages, $18.95)

The Secret Life of Money: How Money Can Be Food for the Soul by Tad Crawford (softcover, 5½ × 8½ , 304 pages, $14.95)

Old Money: The Mythology of Wealth in America, Expanded Edition by Nelson W. Aldrich. Jr. (softcover, 6 × 9, 340 pages, $16.95)

Writing for Interactive Media: The Complete Guide by Jon Samsel and Darryl Wimberley (hardcover, 6 × 9, 320 pages, $19.95)

Please write to request our free catalog. To order by credit card, call 1-800-491-2808 or send a check or money order to Allworth Press, 10 East 23rd Street, Suite 510, New York, NY 10010. Include $5 for shipping and handling for the first book ordered and $1 for each additional book. Ten dollars plus $1 for each additional book if ordering from Canada. New York State residents must add sales tax.

To see our complete catalog on the World Wide Web, or to order online, you can find us at *www.allworth.com*.